102 022 034 1

KT-574-562

Sheffield Hallam University
Learning and Information Services
Withdrawn From Stock

The Individualized Society

ONE WEEK
LOAN

This book is due for return on or before the last date shown below.

The Individualized Society

Zygmunt Bauman

Polity

Copyright © Zygmunt Bauman 2001

The right of Zygmunt Bauman to be identified as author of this work has been asserted in accordance with the Copyright, Designs and Patents Act 1988.

First published in 2001 by Polity Press in association with Blackwell Publishers Ltd

Editorial office:
Polity Press
65 Bridge Street
Cambridge CB2 1UR, UK

Marketing and production:
Blackwell Publishers Ltd
108 Cowley Road
Oxford OX4 1JF, UK

Published in the USA by
Blackwell Publishers Inc.
350 Main Street
Malden, MA 02148, USA

All rights reserved. Except for the quotation of short passages for the purposes of criticism and review, no part of this publication may be reproduced, stored in a retrieval system, or transmitted, in any form or by any means, electronic, mechanical, photocopying, recording or otherwise, without the prior permission of the publisher.

Except in the United States of America, this book is sold subject to the condition that it shall not, by way of trade or otherwise, be lent, re-sold, hired out, or otherwise circulated without the publisher's prior consent in any form of binding or cover other than that in which it is published and without a similar condition including this condition being imposed on the subsequent purchaser.

ISBN 0–7456–2506–1
ISBN 0–7456–2507–X (pbk)

A catalogue record for this book is available from the British Library.

Library of Congress Cataloging-in-Publication Data

Bauman, Zygmunt.
  The individualized society / Zygmunt Bauman.
    p. cm.
  ISBN 0–7456–2506–1 (alk. paper) — ISBN 0–7456–2507–X (pbk.: alk. paper)
  1. Individualism.   2. Postmodernism–Social aspects.   I. Title.
HM1276 .B38 2001
302.5′4—dc21   00-024882

Typeset in 11 on 13 pt Sabon
by Kolam Information Services Pvt Ltd, Pondicherry
Printed in Great Britain by TJ International, Padstow, Cornwall

This book is printed on acid-free paper.

SHEFFIELD HALLAM UNIVERSITY
WL
302.54
BA
COLLEGIATE LEARNING CENTRE

Contents

The Way We Act

Acknowledgements

I am in debt to John Thompson, on whose initiative these papers and lectures have been collected in one volume, whose help with the selection was to me invaluable, and who also suggested the title for the collection. And I am immensely grateful to Ann Bone for the skill, dedication and patience with which she has put the result in a shape fit for publication.

Lives told and stories lived: an overture

'Men are so necessarily mad' – Blaise Pascal quipped – 'that not to be mad would amount to another form of madness.' From madness there is no escape but another madness, Ernest Becker insists, commenting on Pascal's verdict, and explains: humans are 'out of nature and hopelessly in it'; individually and collectively, we all rise above the finitude of our bodily life and yet we know – we cannot but know, though we do everything we can (and more) to forget it – that the flight of life would inevitably (and literally) run into the ground. And there is no good solution to the dilemma, because it is precisely the fact of having risen above nature that opens our finitude to scrutiny and makes it visible, unforgettable and painful. We do all we can to make our natural limits a most closely guarded secret; but were we ever to succeed in that effort we would have little reason to stretch ourselves 'beyond' and 'above' the limits we wished to transcend. It is the sheer impossibility of forgetting our natural condition that prompts us, and allows us, to rise above it. Since we are not allowed to forget our nature, we can (and must) go on challenging it.

Everything that man does in his symbolic world is an attempt to deny and overcome his grotesque fate. He literally drives himself into a blind obliviousness with social games, psychological tricks, personal preoccupations so far removed from the reality of his situation that they are forms of madness – agreed madness, shared madness, disguised and dignified madness, but madness all the same.[1]

'Agreed', 'shared', 'dignified' – dignified by the act of sharing and by the outspoken or tacit agreement to respect what is shared. What we call 'society' is a huge contraption which does just that; 'society' is another name for agreeing and sharing, but also the power which makes what has been agreed and is shared dignified. Society is that power because, like nature itself, it was here long before any of us arrived and will stay here after every one of us has long gone. 'Living in society' – agreeing, sharing and respecting what we share – is the sole recipe for living *happily* (if not forever after). Custom, habit and routine take the poison of absurdity out of the sting of the finality of life. Society, Becker says, is 'a living myth of the significance of human life, a defiant creation of meaning'.[2] 'Mad' are only the unshared meanings. Madness is no madness when shared.

All societies are factories of meanings. They are more than that, in fact: nothing less than the nurseries of *meaningful life*. Their service is indispensable. Aristotle observed that a solitary being outside a *polis* can be only an angel or a beast; no wonder, we may say, since the first is immortal and the second unaware of its mortality. Submission to society, as Durkheim points out, is a 'liberating experience', the very condition of liberation 'from blind, unthinking physical forces'. Could not one say, asks Durkheim rhetorically, that 'it is only by a fortunate circumstance, because societies are infinitely more long-lived than individuals, that they permit us to taste satisfactions which are not merely ephemeral?'[3] The first of the quoted sentences is, as it were, pleonastic: what the submission to society offers is not so much liberation from 'unthinking physical forces' as a liberation from thinking about them. Freedom comes in the form of exorcizing the spectre of mortality. And it is this tautology which renders the exorcism effective and makes certain types of satisfactions taste like the defeat of ruthlessly blind 'physical forces'. When shared with those born earlier and those likely to live longer, satisfactions 'are not merely ephemeral'; more exactly, they are cleansed (ephemerally) from the stigma of ephemerality. Inside a mortal life one can taste immortality, even if only metaphorically or metonymically – by shaping one's life in the likeness of forms which are agreed to be endowed with undying value, or by coming into touch and rubbing shoulders with things which by common agreement are destined for eternity. One way or another, something of the durability of nature may rub off on the transience of the individual life.

In the same way in which knowledge of good and evil begets the potent and staunch need for moral guidance, knowledge of mortality triggers the desire for transcendence, which takes one of two forms: either the urge to force the admittedly transient life to leave traces more lasting than are those who left them, or the wish to taste this side of the edge of transient life experiences 'stronger than death'. Society feeds on that desire in both its forms. There is an energy in that desire waiting to be channelled and directed. Society 'capitalizes' on that energy, draws its life-juices from that desire, in so far as it manages to do just what is wanted: to supply credible objects of satisfaction, alluring and trustworthy enough to prompt efforts which 'make sense' and 'give sense' to life; efforts which are sufficiently energy and labour consuming to fill the time span of life, and sufficiently varied to be realistically coveted and pursued by all ranks and stations however profuse or meagre their talents and resources.

This may be, as Becker suggests, madness, but one can also argue that it may rather be a rational response to the condition which human beings cannot change, while yet they have to cope with its effects. Whatever it is, society 'manipulates it', much as it manipulates that other knowledge, of good and evil – but its freedom of manoeuvre in this case is greater, and its responsibility more grave, since humans ate from the Tree of Good and Evil, but only heard of the Tree of Life and have no memory of tasting its fruit.

Where there is use, there is always a chance of abuse. And the line dividing use from abuse among the vehicles of transcendence on offer was and remains a most hotly (perhaps *the* most hotly) contested of the borders which human societies have drawn; it is also likely to remain so for a long time to come, since the fruits of the life-tree are not available on any duly licensed market stall. The object of all economies is the management of *scarce* resources, but the fate of the *economy of death transcendence* is to manage – supply and distribute – *substitutes* for notoriously *absent* resources: the *surrogates* which have to deputize for the 'real stuff' and render life liveable without it. Their main application is to prevent (or, short of preventing, to put off) discoveries similar to Leonardo da Vinci's sad conclusion: 'While I thought that I was learning how to live, I have been learning how to die' – a wisdom which may sometimes prompt a blossoming of genius, but more often than not would result in a paralysis of will. It is for this reason that the life meanings on offer and in circulation cannot be sorted out as 'correct' and 'incorrect', true or fraudulent. They bring satisfactions which differ in emotional fullness, profundity and duration, but they all stop short of the genuine need-satisfaction.

Two consequences follow. One is the astounding inventiveness of cultures whose 'main business' is to supply ever new, as yet untried and undiscredited variants of transcendence strategies and resuscitate ever anew the trust in the ongoing search despite the way the explorers stumble from one disappointment to another frustration. The trade in life meanings is the most competitive of markets, but with the 'marginal utility' of the commodities on offer unlikely ever to shrink, the demand prompting competitive supply is unlikely to dry up. Second is the awesome opportunity to capitalize on the untapped and forever unexhausted volumes of energy generated by the continuous and never fully quenched thirst for life meaning. That energy, if properly seized and channelled, can be turned to many sorts of uses: thanks to its ubiquitousness and versatility, that energy constitutes fully and truly the culture's 'metacapital' – the stuff of which many and different bodies of 'cultural capital' can be and are moulded. Any kind of social order could be represented as a network of channels through which the search for life meanings is conducted and the life-meaning formulae conveyed. The energy of transcendence is what keeps the formidable activity called 'social order' going; it makes it both necessary and feasible.

It has been suggested before that separating 'right' and 'wrong' life meanings and formulae is a task that is not merely daunting but, if undertaken, is bound to fail. This does not mean, though, that all life meanings on offer are of equal value; from the fact that none is exactly on target, it does not follow that they all miss the targets by the same margin. Every culture lives by the invention and propagation of life meanings, and every order lives by manipulating the urge for transcendence; but once capitalized, the energy generated by the urge can be used and misused in many different ways, though the profits from each allocation benefit clients unequally. We may say that the gist of 'social order' is the redistribution, the differential allocation of culturally produced resources and strategies of transcendence, and that the job of all social orders is to regulate their accessibility, turning it into the principal 'stratifying factor' and the paramount measure of socially conditioned inequality. Social hierarchy with all its privileges and deprivations is built out of the differential value measures of life formulae available to various categories of human beings.

It is in the field of such socially regulated redistributions of the capitalized 'energy of transcendence' that the issue of the truth and falsity of life meanings can be sensibly posited and a credible answer can be sought. The energy may be *misused*, and it is – when the possibilities of meaningful life are reduced, concealed or belied and the energy is directed away from their discovery. Social manipulation of the urge for transcendence is unavoidable if the individual life is to be lived and life in common is to continue – but it tends to include a *surplus manipulation* which diverts rather than brings closer the chances which life entails.

Surplus manipulation is at its most vicious when it turns the blame for the imperfections of the culturally produced life formulae and the socially produced inequality of their distribution on the self-same men and women for whose use the formulae are produced and resources needed to deploy them are supplied. It is then one of those cases when (to use Ulrich Beck's expression) institutions 'for *overcoming* problems' are transformed into 'institutions for *causing* problems';[4] you are, on the one hand, made responsible for yourself, but on the other hand are 'dependent on conditions which completely elude your grasp'[5] (and in most cases also your knowledge); under such conditions, 'how one lives becomes the *biographical solution of systemic contradictions.*'[6] Turning the blame away from the institutions and onto the inadequacy of the self helps either to defuse the resulting potentially disruptive anger, or to recast it into the passions of self-censure and self-disparagement or even rechannel it into violence and torture aimed against one's own body.

Hammering home the 'no more salvation by society' commandment and turning it into a precept of commonsensical wisdom, a phenomenon easy to spot on the surface of contemporary life, pushes things down to a 'second bottom': the denial of collective, public vehicles of transcendence and the abandonment of the individual to the lonely struggle with a task which most individuals lack the resources to perform alone. Rising political apathy and the colonization of public space with the intimacies of private life, Richard Sennett's 'fall of the public man', the rapid fading of the old art of fastening social bonds and making them last, the schizophrenic fear/desire of separation and being left alone (the perpetual vacillation between 'I need more space' and Ally McBeal's 'I am so tired of on my own'), the white-hot passions which accompany the desperate search for communities and the fissiparousness of the ones that are found, the undying demand for new and improved punitive regimes with which to torment one's scapegoated body, coupled paradoxically with the cult of the body as, simultaneously, 'the last line of trenches' to be tooth-and-nail defended, and a source of an endless series of pleasurable and ever more pleasurable sensations to absorb and process the excitements on offer, the continuously growing popularity of chemically, electronically or socially produced drugs hoped at different moments to sharpen sensations of life and to tone them down or silence them – all may have common roots firmly anchored in that 'second bottom'.

On both levels, the tendency is the same: the *conditions* under which human individuals construct their individual existence and which decide the range and the *consequences* of their choices retreat (or are removed) beyond the limits of their conscious influence, while references to them are blotted out or deported to the misty and rarely explored background of the stories which the individuals tell of their lives in their efforts to invent or discover their logic and recast them into convertible tokens of interpersonal communication. The conditions and the narratives alike undergo a process of relentless *individualization*, though the substance of the process is different in each case: 'conditions', whatever else they may be, are things that happened to one, came uninvited and would not leave if one wished them to go, while 'life narratives' stand for the stories people spin out of their own doings and neglects. If projected into discourse, the difference is between something one takes for granted and something about which one asks the questions 'why' and 'how'. These are, as it were, *semantic* distinctions between *terms*. The point of the utmost sociological relevance, though, is how the terms are deployed in the shaping up of the story – that is, where the boundary between one's doings and the conditions under which one acted (and, by definition, could not have acted otherwise) is drawn in the course of the narrative.

Marx said, famously, that people make history but not under conditions of their choice. We may update that thesis as the times of 'life politics' demand, and say that people make their lives but not under conditions of their choice. In the original as well as in its updated version, however, the thesis may be thought to imply that the realm of the conditions beyond choice and the field of action hospitable to purpose, calculation and decision are separate and stay so; that though their interaction presents a problem, the boundary which sets them apart is unproblematic – objective, and so not negotiable.

The assumption of the 'givenness' of the boundary is, however, itself a major, perhaps the decisive factor which makes the 'conditions' what they are: a no-choice matter. 'Conditions' limit people's choices by exempting themselves from the ends-and-means game of life actions on the ground of their declared and accepted immunity from human choices. As W. I. Thomas put it – something that people assume to be true tends to become true as a consequence (more precisely, as a cumulative consequence of their actions). When people say 'there is no alternative to X', X moves from the territory of action to that of the action's 'conditions'. When people say 'there is nothing to be done', there is nothing indeed that they can do. The process of individualization which affects the 'conditions' and the life narratives alike needs two legs to progress: the powers setting the range of choices and separating realistic choices from pipe-dreams must be firmly set in the universe of 'conditions', while life stories must confine themselves to toing and froing among the options on offer.

Lives lived and lives told are for that reason closely interconnected and interdependent. One can say, paradoxically, that the stories told of lives interfere with the lives lived before the lives have been lived to be told...As Stuart Hall put it using another vocabulary, 'while not wanting to expand the territorial claim of the discursive infinitely, how things are represented and the "machineries" and regimes of representation in a culture do play a *constitutive*, and not merely a reflexive, after-the-event, role.'[7] Life stories are ostensibly guided by the modest ambition to instil ('in retrospect', 'with the benefit of hindsight') an 'inner logic' and meaning into the lives they retell. In fact, the code they knowingly or unknowingly observe shapes the lives they tell about as much as it shapes their narratives and the choice of villains and heroes. One lives one's life as a story yet to be told, but the way the story hoping to be told is to be woven decides the technique by which the yarn of life is spun.

The boundary between 'background' and 'action' ('structure' and 'agency', πασχειν and ποιειν) is, arguably, the most hotly contested of the boundaries which give shape to the *Lebenswelt* map and so, obliquely, to the trajectories of life courses. At this boundary the most frenzied of ideological battles are fought; along this boundary armed vehicles and mobile cannons belonging to embattled ideologies are anchored to the ground to form the 'imaginary', the 'doxa', the 'good sense' – the 'no trespassing line' fortified against assaults by thought and mined against wandering imagination. Despite the most earnest of efforts, this is a notoriously mobile boundary; and a curious boundary too, in so far as the act of questioning it tends to be the most effective form of contest. 'Things are *not* as they seem to be', 'things are not what you insist they are', 'the devil is not as black as it is painted' are the war cries which the defenders of this particular boundary have every reason to fear the most, as so many spokesmen for divine verdicts, laws of history, state reason and Reason's commandments have learned the hard way.

Elaborating on the research-and-theory strategy of Cultural Studies, the formidable British contribution to the cognitive frame of contemporary social science, Lawrence Grossberg suggested that the concept of 'articulation' grasped best the strategic logic of the battles conducted on the boundary under discussion ('the process of forging connections between practices and effects, as well as of enabling practices to have different, often unpredicted effects'):

> Articulation is the construction of one set of relations out of another; it often involves delinking or disarticulating connections in order to link or rearticulate others. Articulation is a continuous struggle to reposition practices within a shifting field of forces, to redefine the possibilities of life by redefining the field of relations – the context – within which a practice is located.[8]

Articulation is an activity in which we all, willy-nilly, are continually engaged; no experience would be made into a story without it. At no time, though, does articulation carry stakes as huge as when it comes to the telling of the 'whole life' story. What is at stake then is the acquittal (or not, as the case may be) of the awesome responsibility placed on one's shoulders – and on one's private shoulders alone – by irresistible 'individualization'. In our 'society of individuals' all the messes into which one can get are assumed to be self-made and all the hot water into which one can fall is proclaimed to have been boiled by the hapless failures who have fallen into it. For the good and the bad that fill one's life a person has only himself or herself to thank or to blame. And the way the 'whole-life story' is told raises this assumption to the rank of an axiom.

All articulations open up certain possibilities and close down some others. The distinctive feature of the stories told in our times is that they articulate individual lives in a way that excludes or suppresses (prevents from articulation) the possibility of tracking down the links connecting individual fate to the ways and means by which society as a whole operates; more to the point, it precludes the questioning of such ways and means by relegating them to the unexamined background of individual life pursuits and casting them as 'brute facts' which the story-tellers can neither challenge nor negotiate, whether singly, severally or collectively. With the supra-individual factors shaping the course of an individual life out of sight and out of thought, the added value of 'joining forces' and 'standing arm in arm' is difficult to spot, and the impulse to engage (let alone engage critically) with the way the human condition, or the shared human predicament, is shaped is weak or non-existent.

Much has been made recently of the so-called 'reflexivity' of contemporary life; indeed, we all – the 'individuals by decree' that we are, the 'life politicians' rather than members of a 'polity' – tend to be compulsive story-tellers and find few if any topics for our stories more interesting than ourselves – our emotions, sensations and intimate *Erlebnisse*. The point is, though, that the game of life we all play, with our self-reflexions and story-telling as its most prominent parts, is conducted in such a way that the rules of the game, the contents of the pack of cards and the fashion in which the cards are shuffled and dealt seldom come under scrutiny and even less frequently become a matter of reflection, let alone of serious discussion.

The placid consent to go on playing the game in which the dice may be loaded (though there is no way to find out for sure), and the renunciation of all interest in whether (and how) the odds are being piled against the players, seem to many thoughtful minds so bizarre and contrary to reason that all sorts of sinister forces and unnatural circumstances have been enrolled one after another to account for its happening on such a large scale. The bizarre behaviour would seem less odd and easier to comprehend were the actors *forced* to surrender – by routine coercion or threat of violence. But the actors in question are 'individuals by decree', free choosers; besides, as we all know, one can take a horse to water, but one cannot make it drink. Alternative explanations have therefore been sought, and ostensibly found in 'mass culture'; with the 'media' specializing in brainwashing and substituting cheap entertainment for serious reflection and the 'consumer market' specializing in deception and seduction being cast as the main villains. Sometimes the 'masses' were pitied as hapless victims of the market/media conspiracy, sometimes they were blamed for being all-too-willing accomplices of the plot – but always a sort of collective brain damage was implied; clearly, falling into the trap did not 'stand to reason'.

A bit more flattering for human beings are explanations which admit reason on to the stage: yes, humans use their wits, skills and considerable know-how to get by, but the knowledge on offer is fraudulent and misleading and offers little chance to spy out the genuine causes of their troubles. Not that humans lack reason and good sense; it is, rather, that the realities they must cope with in the course of their lives are burdened with the original sin of falsifying true human potential and cutting off the possibility of emancipation. Humans are neither irrational nor duped, but however diligently they examine their life experience they will hardly come across a strategy which could help them to change the rules of the game in their favour. This is, in a nutshell, what the explanation through 'ideological hegemony' suggests. According to this explanation, ideology is not so much an articulated creed, a set of verbal statements to be learned and believed; it is, rather, incorporated in the way people live – 'soaked in' by the way people act and relate. Once the hegemony has been achieved, hints and clues pointing in the wrong direction (wrong from the point of view of the actors' interests) are densely scattered all over the world within which the actors put their lives together; there is no more possibility of avoiding them or of unmasking their fraudulence so long as it is just their own life experiences that the actors must rely on in setting their 'life projects' and planning their actions. No brainwashing is required – the immersion in daily life shaped by the preset and prescribed rules will be quite enough to keep the actors on the set course.

The idea of 'ideology' is inseparable from that of power and domination. It is an undetachable part of the concept that any ideology is in somebody's interest; it is the rulers (the ruling class, the elites) who make their domination secure through ideological hegemony. But to achieve that effect they need an 'apparatus' which, sometimes openly but mostly surreptitiously, will conduct cultural crusades leading to the hegemony of the kind of culture which promises to defuse rebellion and keep the dominated obedient. Ideology without a 'cultural crusade', waged or planned, would be akin to a wind that does not blow or a river that does not flow.

But crusades and other wars, indeed all struggles, including the most ferocious among them, are (as Georg Simmel pointed out) forms of sociation. Struggle presumes encounter, a 'combat', and so it means mutual engagement and interaction between warring sides. 'Cultural crusades', proselytizing, converting presume such engagement. This makes one wonder if the use of 'ideological hegemony' as an explanation for the popularity of inadequate articulations has not lost its credibility by now, whether or not it had it under different but now bygone circumstances.

Times of direct engagement between the 'dominant' and the 'dominated', embodied in panoptical institutions of daily surveillance and indoctrination, seem to have been replaced (or to be in the course of being replaced) by neater, slimmer, more flexible and economical means. It is the falling apart of heavy structures and hard and fast rules, exposing men and women to the endemic insecurity of their position and uncertainty of their actions, which has made the clumsy and costly ways of 'direct control' redundant. When, as Pierre Bourdieu put it, *la précarité est partout*, panopticons with their large and unwieldy staff of surveillants and supervisors can be abandoned or dismantled. To be sure, one can do equally well without the preachers and their homilies. 'Précarité' is better off without them. 'Precariousness', that new warrant of submission, is all the greater because people have been left to their own devices, lamentably inadequate when it comes to 'getting a hold' on their present condition, a hold strong enough to encourage thoughts of changing the future. Disengagement is nowadays the most attractive and widely played game in town. Speed of movement, and particularly the speed of escape before birds have time to come home to roost, is today the most popular technique of power.

The high and mighty of our times do not wish to be embroiled in the trials and tribulations of management, surveillance and policing; above all, in the responsibilities arising from long-term commitments and 'till death us do part' engagements. They have elevated to the rank of the highest merit the attributes of mobility and flexibility, travelling light, on-the-spot readjustment and continuous reincarnation. Having at their disposal a volume of resources on a par with the volume of choice, they find the new lightness nothing but a fertile and thoroughly enjoyable condition. When translated into no-choice, obligatory canons of universal behaviour, the self-same attributes generate a lot of human misery. But they also (and by the same token) make the game immune to challenge and so insure it against all competition. *Précarité* and TINA ('there is no alternative') enter life together. And only together can they leave.

Why do we, spurred into action by discomforts and risks endemic to the way we live, all too often shift our attention and aim our effort at the objects and objectives causally unconnected with the genuine sources of those discomforts and risks? How does it happen that – rational beings as we are – the energy generated by life anxieties keeps being diverted from its 'rational' targets and is used to protect, instead of removing, the causes of trouble? In particular: what are the reasons why the stories we tell nowadays and are willing to listen to rarely, if ever, reach beyond the narrow and painstakingly fenced-off enclosure of the private and the 'subjective self'? These and related questions have in recent years become (it is my turn to publicly confess) my obsession. This collection of lectures given and essays written during the last three years are documents of that obsession.

The questions listed above are the sole common element that unites the otherwise scattered and apparently unconnected topics of this book. The search for an answer to these questions was the prime motive, and approaching the admittedly elusive answer from ever new sides was the main purpose. I do believe that close engagement with the ongoing effort to rearticulate the changing human condition under which the 'increasingly individualized individuals' find themselves as they struggle to invest sense and purpose in their lives is, under present circumstances (which I tried to sketch in *Liquid Modernity*), the paramount task of sociology.

This task does not consist (cannot consist) in 'correcting common sense' and legislating the true representation of human reality in place of the wrong ones endemic in lay knowledge. The essence of the task is not closure, but opening; not the selection of human possibilities worth pursuing, but preventing them from being foreclosed, forfeited or simply lost from view. The calling of sociology is nowadays to enlarge and to keep the width of that part of the human world which is subject to incessant discursive scrutiny and so keep it saved from ossification into the 'no-choice' condition.

Articulation of life stories is the activity through which meaning and purpose are inserted into life. In the kind of society we live in articulation is and needs to remain an individual task and individual right. This is, though, an excruciatingly difficult task and a right not easy to vindicate. To perform the task and to exercise the right in full, we all need all the assistance we can get – and sociologists can offer much help if they acquit themselves as well as they may and should in the job of recording and mapping the crucial parts of the web of interconnections and dependencies which are either kept hidden or stay invisible from the vantage point of individual experience. Sociology is itself a story – but the message of this particular story is that there are more ways of telling a story than are dreamt of in our daily story-telling; and that there are more ways of living than is suggested by each one of the stories we tell and believe in, seeming as it does to be the only one possible.

There is another common thread to the lectures and essays contained in this volume: that the crucial effect of the struggle to expand the boundaries of articulation by bringing back into view the areas banished to the background and left out by the life stories unexamined shall be the radical widening of the political agenda. In so far as the public sphere has been stealthily yet steadily colonized by private concerns trimmed, peeled and cleaned of their public connections and ready for (private) consumption but hardly for the production of (social) bonds, this effect may also be described as a *decolonization* of the public sphere. As I tried to argue in *Liquid Modernity,* the road to a truly autonomous *ecclesia* leads through a populous and vibrant *agora,* where people meet daily to continue their joint effort of translating back and forth between the languages of private concerns and public good.

September 1999

The Way We Are

1

The rise and fall of labour

According to the *OED*, the first usage of the word 'labour' in the meaning of 'physical exertion directed to the supply of the material wants of the community' was recorded in 1776. A century later it came also to signify 'the general body of labourers and operatives who take this part in production' – and shortly afterwards also the unions and other bodies which made the link between the two meanings and in the end reforged that link into a political issue. The English usage is remarkable for bringing into sharp view the close connection – indeed, the convergence and an identity of fate – between the significance assigned to work (that 'bodily and mental toil'), the self-constitution of those who work into a class, and the politics grounded in that self-constitution. In other words, the link between casting physical toil as the principal source of wealth and the well-being of society and the self-assertion of the labour movement. Together they rose, together they fell.

Most economic historians agree (see, for instance, a recent recapitulation of their findings by Paul Bairoch)[1] that so far as levels of income are concerned, there was little to distinguish between diverse civilizations at the peak of their powers: the riches of Rome in the first century, of China in the eleventh and India in the seventeenth were not much different from those of Europe at the threshold of the industrial revolution. By some estimates, the income per head in Western Europe in the eighteenth century was no more than 30 per cent higher than that of India, Africa or China at that time. Little more than one century was enough, however, to transform the ratio beyond recognition. By 1870, income per head in industrialized Europe was eleven times higher than in the poorest countries of the world. In the course of the next century or so the factor grew fivefold – and reached fifty by 1995. As the Sorbonne economist Daniel Cohen points out, 'I dare to say that the phenomenon of "inequality" between nations is of "recent origin"; it is a product of the last two centuries.'[2] And so was the the idea of labour as a source of wealth, and the politics born of and guided by that assumption.

The new global inequality, and the new self-confidence and new feeling of superiority which followed it, were as spectacular as they were unprecedented: new notions, new cognitive frames were needed to grasp them and assimilate them intellectually. Such new notions were supplied by the new science of the economy, which came to replace the physiocratic and mercantilist ideas that had accompanied Europe on its way to the modern phase of its history, up to the threshold of industrial revolution. It was, so to speak, 'no accident' that these new notions were coined in Scotland, the country both inside and outside the mainstream of the industrial upheaval, involved and detached at the same time, physically and psychologically close to the country which was to become the epicentre of the emerging industrial order, yet for a time remote from its economic and cultural impact. The tendencies at work in the 'centre' are, as a rule, most promptly spotted and most clearly articulated on 'the fringes'. Being at the outskirts of the civilizational centre means being near enough to see things clearly, yet far enough to 'objectify' them and so to mould and condense the perception into a concept. It was not a 'mere coincidence', therefore, that it was from Scotland that the news arrived: wealth comes from work, and labour is the wealth's prime, perhaps sole source.

As Karl Polanyi was to suggest many years later, updating Karl Marx's insight, the starting point of the 'great transformation' which brought the new industrial order into being was the separation of labourers from their livelihood. That momentous event was part of a more comprehensive departure: production and exchange ceased to be inscribed into a more general, indeed all-embracing way of life, and so labour (alongside land and money) could be considered a mere commodity and treated as such.[3] We may say that it was this new disconnection that set the labouring capacity free to move and so to be put to different uses (and so also *better* uses), recombined, made part of other arrangements (and so also of *better* arrangements), which allowed the 'bodily and mental exertion' to congeal into a phenomenon in its own right – a 'thing' which may be treated like all things are, that is, 'handled', moved, joined with other 'things' or set asunder.

Without that disconnection happening, there was little chance that labour could be mentally separated from the 'totality' to which it 'naturally' belonged and condensed into a self-contained object. In the preindustrial vision of wealth, 'land' was such a totality – complete with those who tilled it and harvested from it. The new industrial order and the conceptual network which allowed the advent of a distinct – industrial – society to be proclaimed were born in Britain; and Britain stood out from its European neighbours in having destroyed its peasantry, and with it the 'natural' link between land, human toil and wealth. The tillers of land had first to be made idle to be seen as containers of ready-to-use 'labour power', and for that power to be named the potential 'source of wealth' in its own right.

That new idleness of labourers appeared to contemporaries as the emancipation of labour – part and parcel of the exhilarating sensation of the emancipation of human abilities in general from vexing and stultifying constraints and natural inertia. But the emancipation of labour from its entanglements with nature did not make labour free-floating and unattached for long; and it hardly made that 'emancipated labour' self-determining, free to set and follow its own ways. The uprooted, or just no longer workable, old and self-reproducing 'traditional way of life' of which labour was a part prior to its emancipation was to be replaced by another order, this time predesigned, 'built'; no longer a contingent sediment of the blind meanderings of fate and history's blunders, but a product of rational thought and action. Once it was discovered that labour was the source of wealth, it was the task of reason to mine, drain and exploit that source efficiently as never before.

Some commentators, like Karl Marx, sharing in the new boisterous spirit of the modern age, saw the passing of the old order as primarily the outcome of deliberate dynamiting: an explosion caused by a bomb planted by capital bent on 'melting the solids

and profaning the sacreds'. Others, like de Tocqueville, more
sceptical and less enthusiastic, saw that disappearance as a case
of implosion rather than explosion: they spied out the seeds of
doom in the heart of the 'ancien régime' (always easier to reveal or
guess in retrospect) and saw the bustle of the new masters as,
essentially, kicking a corpse, and nothing much more than giving
new and bigger dimensions to the wonder cures which the old
order had tested in a desperate, yet vain, effort to ward off its
demise. There was little contention, though, as to the prospects of
the new regime and the intentions of its masters: the old and now
deceased order was to be replaced by a new one, less vulnerable
and more viable than its predecessor – new solids were to be
conceived and constructed to fill the void left by the melted ones.
Things set afloat were to be anchored again, more securely than
before. To express the same in the presently current idiom: things
that were 'disembedded' would need to be, sooner or later, 're-
embedded'.

Tearing up the old local/communal bonds, declaring war on
habitual ways and customary laws, shredding *les pouvoirs inter-
médiaires*: the overall result of all that was the intoxicating deli-
rium of the 'new beginning'. Liquefied reality seemed to be ready to
be rechannelled and poured into new moulds, to be given a shape it
would never have acquired had it been allowed to flow in riverbeds
it itself had carved. No purpose, however ambitious, seemed to be
in excess of the human ability to think, discover, invent, plan and
act. If happy society – society of the happy – was not yet exactly
round the corner, its imminent arrival was already anticipated on
the drawing boards of thinking men, while the contours they
sketched were given flesh in the offices of the acting men. And
the purpose to which men of thought and men of action alike
dedicated their activities was the construction of a new order.
The newly discovered freedom was to be deployed in the service
of the future orderly routine. Nothing was to be left to its own,
capricious and unpredictable course, to accident and contingency;
nothing at all was to be left in its present shape if that shape could
be improved, made more useful and effective.

That new order – in which all the ends presently yet temporarily
loose were to be tied again and the castaways, flotsam and jetsam
of past fatalities, now shipwrecked, marooned or drifting, were to
be grounded, resettled and fixed in their right places – was to be

massive, solid and meant to last. Big was beautiful, big was rational; 'big' stood for power, ambition and courage. The building site of the new – industrial – order was haughtily spattered with monuments to that power and ambition, cast in iron and carved in concrete; monuments which were not indestructible, but certainly made to look that way – such as gigantic factories filled to the brim with bulky machinery and crowds of machine operatives, or huge and dense networks of canals, bridges and rail tracks punctuated by railway stations emulating the temples of eternity worship of yore.

Henry Ford is famed for declaring that 'history is bunk' and that 'we don't want tradition.' 'We want', he said, 'to live in the present and the only history that is worth a tinker's damn is the history we make today.'[4] The same Henry Ford one day doubled his workers' wages, explaining that he wished his employees to buy his cars. That was, of course, a tongue-in-cheek explanation: the cars bought by Ford's workers made up a negligible fraction of total sales, while the doubling of wages weighed heavily on Ford's productive costs. The true reason for the unorthodox step was Ford's wish to arrest the irritatingly high labour mobility. He wanted to tie his employees to the Ford enterprises once and for all, to make the money invested in the training and drill pay – and pay again, for the duration of the working lives of his workers. And to achieve such an effect Ford had to immobilize his staff. He had to make them as dependent on employment in his factory as he himself depended for his wealth and power on employing them.

Ford said loudly what others only whispered; or, rather, he thought out what others in a similar predicament felt but were unable to express in so many words. The borrowing of Ford's name for the universal model of intentions and practices typical of 'heavy modernity' or 'orthodox capitalism' had good reasons. Henry Ford's model of a new, rational order set the horizon for the universal tendency of his time: and it was an ideal which all or most other entrepreneurs of that era struggled, with mixed success, to achieve. The ideal was to tie capital and labour in a union which, like that marriage made in heaven, no human power may unmake.

The 'heavy modernity' was, indeed, the time of engagement between capital and labour fortified by the mutuality of their dependency. Workers depended on being hired for their livelihood;

capital depended on hiring them for its reproduction and growth. Their meeting had a fixed address; neither of the two could easily move elsewhere – the massive factory walls enclosed both partners in a shared prison. Capital and workers were united, one may say, for richer and poorer, in health and sickness, and until death them do part. The plant was their common abode – simultaneously the battlefield for trench war and the natural home for hopes and dreams.

So that both – capital and labour – could stay alive, each needed to be kept in the modality of a commodity: the owners of capital had to be able to go on buying labour, and the owners of labour had to be alert, healthy, strong and otherwise attractive not to put off the prospective buyers. Each side had 'vested interests' in keeping the other side in the right condition. No wonder the 'recommodification' of capital and labour had become the principal function and concern of politics and the state: the unemployed were fully and truly a 'reserve army of labour', which had to be kept in a state of readiness through thick and thin, in case they were called back into active service. The welfare state, a state bent on doing just that, was for that reason genuinely 'beyond left and right': a prop without which neither capital nor labour could survive, let alone move and act.

Some people saw the welfare state as a temporary measure, which would work itself out of business once the collective insurance against misfortune made the insured bold and resourceful enough to develop their potential to the full. More sceptical observers saw it as a collectively financed and managed cleaning-and-healing operation to be run as long as the capitalist enterprise kept generating social waste it had neither the intention nor sufficient resources to recycle – that is, for a long time to come. There was a general agreement, though, that the welfare state was a device meant to tackle the anomalies, prevent departures from the norm and defuse the consequences of norm-breaking if it happened nevertheless; the norm, hardly ever put in question, was the direct, face-to-face, mutual engagement of capital and labour, and the solving of all the important and vexing social issues within the frame of such engagement.

Whoever as a young apprentice took their first job at Ford could be pretty sure to finish their life of work in the same place. The time horizons of the 'heavy modernity' era were long term. For the workers, the horizons were drawn by the prospect of lifelong employment inside a company which might not be immortal but whose lifespan stretched well beyond the life expectation of its workers. For the capitalists, the 'family fortune' meant to last beyond the lifespan of any single family member was identical with the plants they inherited, built or intended yet to add to the family heirloom.

To put it in a nutshell: the 'long term' mentality amounted to an expectation born of experience, and amply corroborated by that experience, that the respective fates of the people who buy labour and the people who sell it are closely and inseparably intertwined for a long time to come, in practical terms forever – and that, therefore, working out a bearable mode of cohabitation is just as much 'in everybody's interest' as the negotiation of the rules of neighbourly fair play would be among house-owners settled on the same estate. As Richard Sennett found out in his recent study,[5] even the impersonal time schedules hotly resented by yesterday's free craftsmen herded into early capitalist factories and so vividly described by E. P. Thompson, as well as their later 'new and improved' versions in the form of the infamous Frederick Taylor's time measurements – these acts 'of repression and domination practised by management for the sake of the giant industrial organization's growth' – 'had become an arena in which workers could assert their own demands, an arena of empowerment'. Sennett concludes: 'Routine can demean, but it can also protect; routine can decompose labour, but it can also compose a life.' As long as the staying in each other's company was assumed to last, the rules of that togetherness were the focus of intense negotiations, sometimes of confrontations and showdowns, at some other times of truce and compromise. Unions reforged the impotence of individual workers into collective bargaining power and fought to recast the disabling regulations into workers' rights and to refashion them into constraints imposed on the employers' freedom of manoeuvre.

That situation has changed now, and the crucial ingredient of the change is the new 'short term' mentality which came to replace the 'long term' one. Marriages 'till death us do part' are now a rarity: the partners no longer expect to stay long in each other's company. According to the latest calculation, a young American with a moderate level of education expects to change jobs at least eleven times during his or her working life – and that 'job-changing' expectation is certain to go on growing before the working life of the present generation is over. 'Flexibility' is the slogan of the day, and when applied to the labour market it means an end to the job 'as we know it', work on short-term contracts, rolling contracts or no contracts, positions with no inbuilt security but with the 'until further notice' clause. Reporting the results of comprehensive research into the changing meaning of work conducted in Holland, Geert van der Laan observes that work has become a 'top class' or a 'high achievement' sport, beyond the capacity and practical reach of most job seekers; and sport, as we all know, is now tending to become less a popular pastime and more a highly competitive, elitist activity with big-money stakes. 'The small part of the population that works, works very hard and efficiently, while the other part stands on the sidelines because they cannot keep up with the high pace of production'[6] – and, let us add, because the way work is conducted gives little and ever less room for their skills. Working life is saturated with uncertainty.

One may say of course that there is nothing particularly new about that situation, that working life has been full of uncertainty since time immemorial; but the present-day uncertainty is of a strikingly novel kind. The feared disasters which may play havoc with one's livelihood and its prospects are not of the sort which can be staved off or at least resisted and mollified by joining forces, making a united stand, jointly debating, agreeing and enforcing measures. The most dreadful disasters strike now at random, picking their victims with a bizarre logic or no logic at all, scattering their blows capriciously, so that there is no way to anticipate who will be doomed and who saved. The present-day uncertainty is a powerful *individualizing* force. It divides instead of uniting, and since there is no telling who might wake up in what division, the idea of 'common interests' grows ever more nebulous and in the end becomes incomprehensible. Fears, anxieties and grievances are made in such a way as to be suffered alone. They do not add up, do not cumulate into 'common cause', have no 'natural address'. This deprives the solidary stand of its past status as a rational tactic and suggests a life strategy quite different from the one which led to the establishment of the working-class defensive and militant organizations.

When the employment of labour has become short term, having been stripped of firm (let alone guaranteed) prospects and therefore made episodic, and when virtually all rules concerning the game of promotions and dismissals have been scrapped or tend to be altered well before the game is over, there is little chance for mutual loyalty and commitment to sprout up and take root. Unlike in the times of long-term mutual dependency, there is hardly any stimulus to take a serious, let alone critical, interest in the wisdom of an arrangement which is bound to be transient anyway. The place of employment feels like a camping site which one visits for but a few nights and which one may leave at any moment if the comforts on offer are not delivered or found wanting when delivered, rather than like a shared domicile where one is inclined to take trouble to work out the acceptable rules of interaction. Mark Granovetter has suggested that ours is a time of 'weak ties', while Sennett proposes that 'fleeting forms of association are more useful to people than long-term connections.'[7]

The present-day 'liquefied', 'flowing', dispersed, scattered and deregulated version of modernity does not portend divorce and a final break in communication, but it does augur a *disengagement* between capital and labour. One may say that this fateful departure replicates the passage from marriage to 'living together' with all its corollaries, among which the assumption of temporariness and the right to break the association when need or desire dries out loom larger than most. If the coming together and staying together was a matter of reciprocal dependency, the disengagement is unilateral: one side of the configuration has acquired an autonomy it never seriously adumbrated before. To an extent never achieved by the 'absentee landlords' of yore, capital has cut itself loose from its dependency on labour through a new freedom of movement undreamt of in the past. Its reproduction and growth has become by and large independent of the duration of any particular local engagement with labour.

The independence is not, of course, complete, and capital is not as yet as volatile as it would wish and strives to be. Territorial – local – factors still need to be reckoned with in most calculations, and the 'nuisance power' of local governments may still put vexing constraints on its freedom of movement. But capital has become exterritorial, light, disencumbered and disembedded to an unprecedented extent, and the level of spatial mobility it has already achieved is quite sufficient to blackmail the territory-bound political agencies into submission to its demands. The threat (even unspoken and merely guessed) of cutting local ties and moving elsewhere is something which any responsible government must treat with all seriousness, trying to shape its own actions accordingly. Politics has become today a tug-of-war between the speed with which capital can move and the 'slowing down' capacities of local powers, and it is the local institutions which feel as if they are waging an unwinnable battle. A government dedicated to the well-being of its constituency has little choice but to implore and cajole, rather than force, capital to fly in and once inside to build sky-scraping offices instead of renting hotel rooms. And this can be done or attempted to be done by 'creating better conditions for free enterprise', that is, adjusting the political game to the 'free enterprise rules'; by using all the regulating power at the government's disposal to make it clear and credible that the regulating powers won't be used to restrain capital's liberties; by refraining from everything which might create an impression that the territory politically administered by the government is inhospitable to the preferences, usages and expectations of globally thinking and globally acting capital, or less hospitable to them than the lands administered by the next-door neighbours. In practice, that means low taxes, few or no rules, and above all a 'flexible labour market'. More generally, it means a docile population, unable and unwilling to put up an organized resistance to whatever decisions capital might take. Paradoxically, governments can hope to keep capital in place only by convincing it beyond reasonable doubt that it is free to move away – at short notice or without notice.

Having shed the ballast of bulky machinery and massive factory crews, capital travels light with no more than cabin luggage – a briefcase, laptop computer and cellular telephone. That new quality of volatility has made the engagement redundant and unwise at the same time: if entered, it would cramp movement and thus become a constraint on competitiveness and limit the chances of increased productivity. Stock exchanges and boards of management around the world are prompt to reward all steps 'in the right direction' of disengagement, like 'slimming down', 'downsizing' and 'hiving off', while punishing just as promptly any news of increased employment and the company being 'bogged down' in costly long-term projects. The Houdini-like 'escaping artist's' skills of performing vanishing acts, the strategy of elision and avoidance and the readiness and ability to escape if needs be, which is the hub of the new policy of disengagement and un-commitment, is today the sign of managerial wisdom and success. As Michel Crozier pointed out a long time ago, being free of awkward bonds, cumbersome commitments and dependencies holding back movement was always an effective and favourite weapon of domination; but the supplies of that weapon and the capacities to use them are nowadays doled out less evenly than ever before in modern history. Speed of movement has become today a major, perhaps the paramount factor in social stratification and the hierarchy of domination.

The main source of profits – of the big profits in particular, and so also of tomorrow's capital – tends to be in an ever growing measure *ideas* rather than *material objects*. An idea is produced only once, and then keeps on bringing in wealth depending on the number of people engaged as buyers/clients/consumers, not on the number of people engaged in replicating the prototype. When it comes to making ideas profitable, the objects of competition are the consumers, not producers. No wonder that the present-day engagement of capital is primarily with the consumers. Only in this sphere can one sensibly speak of 'mutual dependency'. Capital is dependent, for its competitiveness, effectiveness and profitability, on consumers – and its itineraries are guided by the presence or absence of consumers or the chances of the 'production of consumers' – of generating and beefing up the demand for the ideas on offer. In planning the travels of capital and prompting its dislocations, the presence of the labour force is at best a secondary consideration. Consequently, the 'holding power' of the local labour force on capital and more generally on the conditions of employment and availability of jobs has shrunk considerably.

Robert Reich suggests that people presently engaged in economic activity can be roughly divided into four broad categories.[8] 'Symbol manipulators', people who invent ideas and ways to make them desirable and sellable, form the first category. Those engaged in the reproduction of labour (educators or various functionaries of the welfare state) belong to the second. The third category covers people employed in 'personal services' (the kinds of occupations which John O'Neill classified as 'skin trades'), requiring face-to-face encounter with the recipients of service: the sellers of products and the producers of the desire for products form the bulk of this category. And finally there is the fourth category, to which the people who for the last century and a half formed the 'social substratum' of the labour movement belong. They are, in Reich's terms, 'routine labourers', tied to the assembly line or, in more up-to-date plants, to computer networks and electronic automated devices like checkout points. They are the most expendable, disposable and exchangeable parts of the economic system. Neither particular skills, nor the art of social interaction with clients belong to their job requirements – and so they are the easiest to replace, and command, if at all, only a residual and negligible bargaining power. They know they are disposable, and so they do not see much point in developing attachment or commitment to their jobs, in entering into lasting associations with workmates. They tend to be wary of any loyalty to the workplace or of inscribing their own life purposes into its projected future.

Alain Peyrefitte, in his retrospective study of our modern/capitalist society of 'compulsive and obsessive development',[9] comes to the conclusion that the most prominent, indeed the constitutive, feature of that society was *confidence*: confidence in oneself, in others, and in institutions. All three constituents of that confidence used to be indispensable: they conditioned each other – take out one, and the other two would implode and collapse. We could describe the modern order-making bustle as an ongoing effort to lay the institutional foundations for confidence: offering a stable framework for the investment of trust, making credible the belief that the presently cherished values will go on being cherished and desired, that the rules of pursuing and attaining these values will go on being observed, stay uninfringeable and immune to the flow of time.

Peyrefitte singles out the enterprise cum employment as the most important site for the sowing and cultivation of trust. The fact that the capitalist enterprise was also the hotbed of conflicts and confrontations should not mislead us: there is no *défiance* without *confiance*, no contest without trust. If the employees fought for their rights, it was because they were confident in the 'holding power' of the frame in which, as they hoped and wished, their rights would be inscribed; they trusted the enterprise as the right place to deposit their rights for safe keeping. This is no longer the case, or at least is rapidly ceasing to be the case. No rational person would expect to spend their whole working life, or even a large chunk of it, in one company. Most rational persons would prefer to entrust their life savings to the notoriously risk-ridden,

stock-exchange-playing investment funds and insurance companies than to count on the old age pension that the company they are
working for at present could provide. As Nigel Thrift summed it
up recently, 'it is very difficult to build trust in organizations which
are, at the same time, being "delayered", "downsized" and "re-
engineered".[10]

Pierre Bourdieu makes the link between the collapse of confidence and the fading will for political engagement and collective
action:[11] the ability to make future projections, he suggests, is the
conditio sine qua non of all 'transformative' thought and all effort
to re-examine and reform the present state of affairs – but project-
ing into the future is unlikely to occur in people who lack a hold on
their present. Reich's fourth category most conspicuously lacks
such a hold. Tied as they are to the ground, barred from moving
or, if they do move, arrested at the nearest heavily guarded border-
post, they are in an *a priori* inferior position to capital, which
moves around freely. Capital is increasingly global; they, however,
stay local. For that reason they are exposed, without weapons, to
the inscrutable whims of mysterious 'investors' and 'shareholders',
and the even more bewildering 'market forces', 'terms of trade'
and 'demands of competition'. Whatever they gain today may be
taken away tomorrow without warning. They cannot win. Neither
– being the rational persons they are or struggle to be – are they
willing to risk the fight. They are unlikely to reforge their grievances into a political issue and to turn to the political powers-that-
be for redress. As Jacques Attali forecast a few years ago, 'power
will reside tomorrow in the capacity to block or facilitate movement along certain routes. The state won't exercise its powers
otherwise than through control of the network. And so the impossibility of exercising control over the network will weaken political
institutions irreversibly.'[12]

The passage from 'heavy' or 'solid' to 'light' or 'liquefied' modernity constitutes the framework in which the history of the labour
movement has been inscribed. It also goes a long way towards
making sense of that history's notorious convolutions. It would be
neither reasonable nor particularly illuminating to explain away
the dire straits in which the labour movement has found itself
throughout the 'advanced' (in the 'modernizing' sense) part of
the world by reference to the change in public mood, whether
brought about by the debilitating impact of the mass media, a

conspiracy of the advertisers, the seductive pull of consumer society or the soporific effects of spectacle-and-entertainment society. Laying the blame at the door of blundering or two-faced 'labour politicians' won't help either. The phenomena invoked in such explanations are not at all imaginary – but they won't do as explanations if not for the fact that the context of life, the social setting in which people (seldom if ever by their own choice) go about their business of life, has changed radically since the times when the workers, crowded in mass-production factories, joined ranks to enforce more humane and rewarding terms for selling their labour, and the theorists and practitioners of the labour movement sensed in that workers' solidarity the inchoate, but inborn thirst for a 'good society' which would implement universal principles of justice.

2

Local orders, global chaos

Things are orderly if they behave as you've expected them to; that is, if you may safely leave them out of account when planning your actions. This is the main attraction of order: security which comes from the ability to predict, with little or no error, what the results of your own actions will be. You may go after whatever you are going after, concentrating on what you yourself need to do and fearing no surprise: no obstacles which you could not, with a modicum of effort, anticipate and so include in your calculation. To put it in a nutshell: things are in order if you do not need to worry about the order of things; things are orderly if you do not think, or feel the need to think, of order as a problem, let alone as a task. And once you start thinking of order, this is a sure sign that something, somewhere, is out of order: that things are getting out of hand and so you must do something to bring them back into line.

Once you start thinking of order, you'll find out that what you are missing is a clear and legible distribution of probabilities. There would be order if it wasn't possible for everything to happen, at least not for everything to happen with equal probability; if some events were virtually bound to happen, some others were quite likely, still others were utterly improbable, and all the rest were completely out of the question. Where this is not the case and instead – as far as you can tell – there is a fifty-fifty chance of any event happening, you would say that there is chaos. If the possibility of predicting and so of controlling the outcomes of your actions is the main attraction of order, the apparent lack of any link between what you do and what happens to you, between 'doing' and 'suffering', is what makes chaos odious, repugnant and frightening.

The less equal are the chances of the responses to your actions, the less random are your actions' effects – the more order, you would say, there is in the world. Any attempt to 'put things in order' boils down to *manipulating the probabilities of events*. This is what any culture does, or at least is supposed to do. Pierre Boulez said of art that it transforms the improbable into the inevitable. What he said about art applies to all sectors of culture. In 'natural', culturally unprocessed conditions, egg meeting bacon would be an extremely rare event and so improbable, almost a miracle; in England, however, in the 'good old times' when things stayed in place and everyone knew his or her place among them, the meeting of egg and bacon on the breakfast plate used to be all but inevitable, and only fools would put their bets on the meeting not happening.

The manipulating of probabilities and so the conjuring up of order out of chaos is the miracle performed daily by culture. More precisely: it is the routine performance of that miracle that we call culture. We speak of a 'cultural crisis' if the routine comes to be defied and is breached too often to be seen as reliable, let alone to be taken for granted.

Culture manipulates probabilities of events through the activity of *differentiating*. We all remember Claude Lévi-Strauss's assertion that the first 'cultural act' in history was the splitting of the population of females – however uniform they might be in their reproductive potential – into women eligible for sexual intercourse and those who were not. Culture is the activity of making distinctions: of classifying, segregating, drawing boundaries – and so dividing people into categories internally united by similarity and externally separated by difference; and of differentiating the ranges of conduct assigned to the humans allocated to different categories. As Frederick Barth famously pointed out, what culture defines as difference, a difference significant enough to justify the separation of categories, is the *product* of boundary-drawing, not its *cause* or motive.

Lack of clarity about the range of conduct to be legitimately anticipated is, I suggest, the substance of that 'danger' which Mary

Douglas discovered in the mixing of categories; the danger which people of all times and places tend to associate with humans and things 'sitting across the barricade', with beings bearing traits that should not appear together were the classifications to retain their predictive, and so reassuring, value. Their vexing habit of falling between, rather than fitting into categories reveals conventionality, and so fragility, where 'objective reality', and so steadfastness, are assumed to reside. The very sight of what Mary Douglas, following Jean-Paul Sartre, dubbed 'slimy' beings, those stubborn 'in-betweens' that play havoc with the orderliness of the world and contaminate the purity of its divisions, is a keyhole glimpse into the chaos which underlies every order and threatens to engulf it. The discovery of chaos beefs up the zeal for ordering and the passions that surround the practice of order building, order repairing and order protecting. The differentiating/segregating labours of culture would have brought little gain to the feeling of security, to that understanding defined by Ludwig Wittgenstein as the 'knowledge how to go on', had they not been complemented by the suppression of 'sliminess' – that is, of all things of uncertain origin, mixed status and unclear denomination: of ambivalence.

Since no attempt to accommodate the complexity of the world in neat and comprehensive divisions is likely to succeed, ambivalence is unlikely to be defeated and stop haunting the seekers after security. The opposite, rather, is on the cards: the more intense the desire for order and the more frenzied the efforts to install it, the greater will be the volume of ambivalent leftovers and the deeper the anxiety they will generate. There is little chance that order building will ever reach its conclusion, being a self-propelling and self-intensifying concern which rebounds in a self-defeating activity.

Because of their unsavoury yet intimate connections with the state of uncertainty, the 'impurity' of classifications, the haziness of borderlines and the porousness of borders are constant sources of fear and aggression inseparable from order-making and order-guarding exertions. Not the only source of conflict, though. Another was revealed by Michel Crozier in his eye-opening study of the 'bureaucratic phenomenon': that other source is *the use of the absence of order, of chaos, as the major weapon of power in its bid for domination*. The strategy of the power struggle is to make oneself the unknown variable in the calculations of other people, while denying those others a similar role in one's own calculations. In simpler terms, this means that domination is achieved by removing the rules constraining one's own freedom of choice, while at the same time imposing as many restrictive rules as possible on the conduct of all the others. The wider my range of manoeuvre, the greater my power. The less freedom of choice I have, the weaker are my chances in the power struggle.

'Order' emerges from this analysis as an agonistic and 'essentially contested' concept. Within the same social setting the conceptions of order differ sharply. What is 'order' to people in power looks uncannily like chaos to the people they rule. In the power struggle it is always the other side one would wish to make more 'orderly', more predictable; it is always the steps taken by the other side that one would want to routinize, to strip of all elements of contingency and surprise, while leaving to oneself the right to disregard routine and move erratically. Given the power struggle, the order building must be a conflict-ridden process.

Crozier's discovery, made in the context of what one may call 'closed systems' of bureaucratic institutions, reveals its full (and at the time of his study unanticipated) import in the conditions currently described under the rubric of 'globalization'. Let me remind you that the concept of 'globalization' has been coined to replace the long-established concept of 'universalization' once it had become apparent that the emergence of global links and networks had nothing of the intentional and controlled nature implied by the old concept. 'Globalization' stands for processes seen as self-propelling, spontaneous and erratic, with no one sitting at the control desk and no one taking on planning, let alone taking charge of the overall results. We may say with little exaggeration that the term 'globalization' stands for the disorderly nature of the processes which take place above the 'principally coordinated' territory administered by the 'highest level' of institutionalized power, that is, sovereign states. In his insightful study of the 'new world disorder' Ken Jowitt noticed the demise of the 'Joshua discourse' which overtly or tacitly assumed a law-abiding and essentially determined and preordained universe, and its replacement with the 'Genesis discourse', which instead casts the world as a site of instability, change devoid of consistent direction, spontaneity and perpetual experimentation with uncertain and essentially unpredictable outcomes; in short, as the very opposite of the image of order.

'The new world disorder' dubbed 'globalization' has, however, one truly revolutionary effect: *devaluation of order as such*. Such an eventuality could be glimpsed from Crozier's analysis, or indeed anticipated in view of the notoriously self-undermining tendency of all order building – but only now can it be observed in all its many ramifications. In the globalizing world, *order becomes the index of powerlessness and subordination*. The new global power structure is operated by the oppositions between mobility and sedentariness, contingency and routine, rarity and density of constraints. It is as if the long stretch of history which began with the triumph of the settled over the nomads is now coming to its end... Globalization may be defined in many ways, but that of the 'revenge of the nomads' is as good as if not better than any other.

The strategy of power struggle recorded by Michel Crozier, just like Jeremy Bentham's panoptical model of social control, assumed the mutual engagement of the rulers and the ruled. The imposition of norms and the execution of normative regulation tied the controllers and the controlled to each other and made them inseparable. Both sides were, so to speak, tied to the ground: reproduction of the power hierarchy required constant presence and confrontation. It is this reciprocal dependency, this perpetual mutual engagement, which the new techniques of power which have come to the fore in the era of globalization have rendered redundant. The new hierarchy of power is marked at the top by the ability to move fast and at short notice, and at the bottom by the inability to slow down those moves, let alone arrest them, coupled with its own immobility. Escape and evasion, lightness and volatility have replaced weighty and ominous presence as the main techniques of domination.

No longer is that 'normative regulation' necessary to secure domination. Those aspiring to rule could give a sigh of relief: normative regulation was a cumbersome, messy and costly technique, primitive and economically irrational and ruinous by contemporary standards. Its redundancy is felt as emancipation and is experienced by the global elite as the command of reason and a sign of progress. Lack of constraints, deregulation and flexibility seem a gigantic leap forward when compared with the costly and laborious methods of disciplining drill practised in modern panopticons.

Thanks to the new techniques of disengagement, non-commit-
ment, evasion and escape now at the disposal of the elites, the rest
may be held in check, disabled and so deprived of their constraining power simply by the utter vulnerability and precariousness of
their situation, with no need to 'normatively regulate' their conduct. The employees of a Ford-type factory could exercise their
'nuisance' power and force the managers to negotiate a bearable
modus vivendi and to compromise so long as all sides gathered at
the negotiating table knew that they as much as their counterparts
had nowhere else to go and had to see the bargain through. The
owners and the shareholders depended for their income on the
good will of the workers as much as the workers depended for
their livelihood on the jobs they offered. This is no longer the case;
one side (but not the other) is painfully aware that their negotiating partners may leave the table at any moment; one more push
and the mobile partners may simply take their belongings elsewhere and there will be no one left to negotiate with. For those in
the handicapped and weaker position, the sole method of keeping
the mobile managers and volatile shareholders in place (and so
keeping their own jobs a bit longer) is to entice them to come and
stay by a convincing display of their own weakness and lack of
resistance. The uncertainty into which the new mobility of the
global elite has cast the multitude dependent on the elite's willingness to invest has a self-perpetuating and a self-enhancing
capacity. The rational strategies prompted by this kind of uncertainty deepen the insecurity instead of mitigating it, and accelerate
the disintegration of the normatively regulated order.

'Précarité est aujourd'hui partout,' concluded Pierre Bourdieu.
Partly a result of a deliberate policy of 'precarization' initiated by
supranational and increasingly exterritorial capital and meekly
carried out by the little-choice-left territorial state governments,
and partly the sediment of the new logic of power bids and self-
defence, precariousness is today the major building block of the
global power hierarchy and the main technique of social control.
As Bourdieu pointed out, claims on the future are unlikely to be
made unless the claimants have a firm hold on their present; and it
is precisely the hold on the present that most of the inhabitants of
the globalizing world most conspicuously lack.

They lack a hold on the present because the most important of
the factors which decide on their livelihood and social position,

and the prospects of both, are out of their hands; and there is pretty little or nothing that they can do, singly or severally, to bring these factors back under their control. The localities inhabited by them and other people in a similar plight are but airfields on which magnificent flying machines of the global fleet land and take off according to their own, unknown and inscrutable, flight schedules and itineraries; and it is that capricious air traffic on which they have to rely for survival. And it is not just survival that is at stake, but the way they live and the way they think about their living.

The autonomy of the local community of Ferdinand Tönnies's canonical description was based on an enhanced density of communication accompanied by an intensity of daily intercourse. When information could not travel without its carriers and the transportation of both was slow, proximity offered advantage over distance and the goods and the news originating in the close vicinity had a distinct advantage over those travelling from afar. The boundaries of local community were drawn in no uncertain terms by the volume and speed of mobility, determined in its turn by the available means of transportation. Space, to put it in a nutshell, mattered. But now it matters less; Paul Virilio, announcing 'the end of geography', has suggested that it does not matter at all: its past significance as an obstacle or even the limit to communication has now been cancelled.

The news circulated in the framework of daily face-to-face interaction does not have a greater chance of reinforcement-through-repetition than electronically transmitted and disseminated information has; on the contrary, it is in a handicapped position when it comes to gaining attention. Even if it succeeds, the odds are that it will be dwarfed, stifled and stripped of its interest and authority by the globally produced and globally circulated information which beats them hands down in terms of spectacularity, authority of numbers and power of conviction. Even the interpretation of ostensibly 'local' affairs tends to be derived mostly from the same exterritorial sources. As for locally born and promoted views – in order to level up with the electronic information, be treated seriously, trusted and grip the mind, they need first to be electronically recorded and 'seen on TV', and so surrender or forfeit their asset of the distinct community link. The chances of forming autonomous homemade 'community opinion' deploying the resources under autonomous community control are dim or nil.

Electronic transmission of information is now instantaneous and demands no more than a plug in a socket; communal exchange trying to ignore the electronic media would have to rely, as it always did, on the orthodox media of gatherings and conversations whose speed has 'natural limits' and whose costs are high and – at least in comparative terms – rising. The result is the *devaluation of place*. The physical, non-cyber space where non-virtual communication takes place is but a site for the delivery, absorption and recycling of the essentially exterritorial, cyberspace information. Charging the access to cyberspace at the local call tariff perhaps sounded the death knell of communal autonomy; it was at any rate communal autonomy's symbolic burial. The cellular telephone, offering independence even from wired networks and sockets, delivered the final blow to the claim physical proximity might have had on spiritual togetherness.

The rising 'other-directedness' of locality portends hard times for the orthodox form of the community, that form wrapped around the core of a dense web of frequent and lasting interactions, the basis of the long-term investment of trust. As Richard Sennett pointed out in his *Corrosion of Character*, '"No long term" is a principle which corrodes trust, loyalty, and mutual commitment', but nowadays 'a place springs into life with the wave of a developer's wand, flourishes, and begins to decay all within a generation. Such communities are not empty of sociability or neighbourliness, but no one in them becomes a long-term witness to another person's life'; under such conditions, 'fleeting forms of association are more useful to people than long-term connections.'[1]

The degradation of locality rubs off on the 'locals' – people who are not free to move and change places for lack of the necessary resources – the circumstance which makes all the difference between the welcome tourists-in-search-of-pleasure or business-travellers-in-search-of-business-opportunities and the resented 'economic migrants' in-search-of-livelihood. The degree of immobility is today the main measure of social deprivation and the principal dimension of unfreedom; a fact symbolically reflected in the rising popularity of prison confinement as the way to deal with undesirables.

On the other hand, speed of mobility, the ability to act effectively regardless of distance, and the freedom to move offered by the absence or facile revocability of localized commitments are nowadays the major stratifying factors on the global as much as on the local scale. The emergent hierarchy of power is akin more to the usages of nomadic than sedentary societies; sedentariness, and particularly no-choice sedentariness, is fast turning from asset into liability.

Not that long ago Michael Thompson published a study of the respective social significance of transience and durability – demonstrating the universal and permanent tendency of privileged classes to surround themselves with durable possessions and to make their possessions durable, and a similar tendency to associate social weakness and deprivation with things short-lived and transient. This correlation, which held for most, perhaps all, known societies of the past, is in the process of being reversed. It is the sign of privilege to travel light and to avoid lasting attachment to possessions; it is the sign of deprivation to be lumbered with things that have outlived their intended use and to be unable to part with them.

The entry ticket to the new global elite is the 'confidence to dwell in disorder' and the ability to 'flourish in the midst of dislocation'; the membership card is the capability of 'positioning oneself in a network of possibilities rather than paralyzing oneself in one particular job'; and the visiting card is the 'willingness to destroy what one has made' – 'to let go, if not to give'; all the features gleaned by Richard Sennett in his character study of Bill Gates in the same book, the emblem and model-figure of the new cyber-age elite. What makes such features into the principal stratifying factor – indeed, the metafactor, the factor that endows with significance and sets in motion all the other paraphernalia of social position – is that these features exert quite opposite effects on life depending on the circumstances of their bearers. The traits of character which beget exuberant and joyful spontaneity at the top turn 'self-destructive for those who work lower down in the flexible regime'.

Indeed, the new freedoms of the contemporary reincarnation of absentee landlords make the life regime of 'those lower down' more flexible by the day (and so increasingly uncertain, insecure and unsafe); if not by design, then in the unintended yet nevertheless inevitable effects. As Roger Friedland quipped, those on the top 'celebrate what others suffer'. The enchanting and willingly embraced lightness of being turns into the curse of cruel yet indomitable fate once it moves down the social ladder.

Chaos has ceased to be enemy number one of rationality, civilization, rational civilization and civilized rationality; no longer is it the epitome of the powers of darkness and unreason which modernity swore it was and did its best to annihilate. True, the governments of nation-states and their court scribes go on paying lip-service to the rule of order, but their daily practices consist in the gradual, but relentless dismantling of the last obstacles to the 'creative disorder' eagerly sought by some and placidly accepted by others as the verdict of fate. The 'rule of order' in the political parlance of our time means little more than the disposal of social waste, the flotsam and jetsam of the new 'flexibility' of livelihood and life itself. For the rest, it is more flexibility, more precariousness and more vulnerability, the very opposite of the rule of order, which are in store.

When power flows, and flows globally, political institutions share in the deprivation of all those who are 'tied to the ground'. 'Territory', now disarmed and by no stretch of the imagination self-contained, has lost much of its value, attraction and magnetic power for those who can move freely, and becomes an ever more elusive target, a dream rather than reality, for those who, themselves immobilized, would wish to slow down or arrest the moves of the exquisitely mobile masters of the vanishing art. For the mobile, the tasks of territorial management and administration look increasingly like a dirty job which ought to be avoided at all costs and ceded to those further down in the hierarchy, too weak and vulnerable to refuse the chores even if they know how idle and ineffective their efforts are bound to be. And since all commitment to a place and all engagement with its inhabitants is seen as a liability rather than an asset, few 'multinational' companies would agree today to invest in the locality unless bribed – 'compensated' and 'insured against risks' – by its elected authorities.

Time and space have been differentially allocated to the rungs of the global power ladder. Those who can afford it live solely in time. Those who cannot, live in space. For the first, space does not matter. As to the second, they struggle hard to make it matter.

3

Freedom and security: the unfinished story of a tempestuous union

Seventy years ago Sigmund Freud noted in *Das Unbehagen in der Kultur*: 'Civilized man has exchanged a portion of his possibilities of happiness for a portion of security.' Happiness, Freud pointed out, 'comes from the ... satisfaction of needs which have been dammed up to a high degree'. Happiness, therefore, means *freedom*: freedom to act on impulse, to follow one's instincts and desires. It is this kind of freedom that tends to be surrendered, or at least severely constrained, for the sake of 'a portion of security'. Security, on the other hand, means protection against three kinds of suffering which threaten human beings: suffering coming 'from our own body', 'from the external world' and 'from our relations to other men'. Security may be offered only if the wayward, obstreperous and erratic (often explosive) venting of desires is replaced with *order* – 'a kind of compulsion to repeat which, when a regulation has been laid down once and for all, decides when, where and how a thing shall be done, so that in every similar circumstance one is spared hesitation and indecision'. Indecision is not a pleasant state of the spirit and thus the imposition of order has its tangible benefits. Nevertheless – because it is compulsive and thus constrains human freedom, order cannot but be buffeted, and so continually threatened, by the rebellion of 'dammed-up needs'. The 'urge for freedom' is 'directed against particular forms and demands of civilization or against civilization altogether'[1] – that is, against trading off a portion of freedom for a portion of security, or against the very *principle* of trade-off between freedom and security. That order which we call civilization is vulnerable and precarious, and destined to stay that way.

Note that the trade-off between freedom and security is not a choice between good and evil. If anything in Freud's description comes out as unambiguously repulsive and inhuman, it is the trade-off itself. The values between which the choice is made are both desirable; in every trade-off, therefore, gains are mixed with losses. Each act is ambivalent in its motives as much as in its consequences. Freedom without security is bound to cause no less unhappiness than security without freedom. Compromise between them, though, since it inevitably entails a partial sacrifice, is not a guarantee of happiness either. Humans need both freedom and security – and the sacrifice of either is a cause of suffering. Yet sacrifice cannot be escaped, and thus the urge for happiness is bound to be frustrated. Happiness, Freud insists, 'is from its nature only possible as an episodic phenomenon... We are so made that we can derive intense enjoyment only from a contrast and very little from a state of things.'[2] But that means that the purpose which civilization set out to fulfil will never be achieved. There will be discontents in every civilization, and it is precisely these discontents endemic to the civilized life that keep the civilization dynamic, forever a-changing and prevent the freezing of any of its conceivable forms. The perfect balance between freedom and security is perhaps a logical incongruence and practical impossibility, but this by itself is a most powerful reason to seek ever better formulae for trade-off.

Between the devil and the deep blue sea

It was Freud's view that the affliction most typical of civilized life stems from the suppression of individual freedom, reluctantly complied with at an enormous psychical expense – and seldom, if ever, final. The tension between freedom and security tends to be internalized and then to confront the individual 'from inside' – in the form of the struggle between superego (that 'garrison in a conquered city'[3]) and the 'id' (the warehouse of the suppressed desires), waged on the battlefield of the 'ego'. The malady characteristic of the civilized person resides, therefore, inside the human psyche. It is there that it needs to be spotted, diagnosed and cured. True, it is the civilization which 'is largely responsible for our misery', and a person 'becomes neurotic because he cannot tolerate the amount of frustration which society imposes on him in the service of its cultural ideas'[4] – but the overwhelming power of civilization (of the constraints imposed in the name of security) over each and every individual is as unquestionable as the 'pleasure principle' which prompts the individual to embark on the voyage to happiness. Things are bound to stay that way; the ailments which haunt the 'civilized person' will go on being generated, and the sole fashion in which the resulting unhappiness can be mitigated is for the ailing person to come to terms with the pressures that cannot be wished away and will not go away of their own accord.

In his most recent book,[5] Alain Ehrenberg, that indefatigable explorer of contemporary mutations of modern individualism, reminds his readers of the alternative diagnosis of present-day psychical troubles once advanced by Janet in – unsuccessful – competition with Freud's diagnosis. In Janet's view, the characteristic ailments of modern individuals derive from a 'deficit of the ego' – an inability to cope with reality, to absorb it and to find one's way through it. Rather than imposing Freud's straightforward, unambiguous, no-beating-about-the-bush, no-questions-asked 'cultural ideas', Janet sees social reality as falling apart in the individuals' hands and escaping their comprehension; it appears incoherent, fluid, poorly marked and elusive. Janet's diagnosis, in Ehrenberg's view, has now come into its own and should belatedly receive its deserved recognition. It is not the overwhelming pressure of an ideal which they cannot live up to that torments contemporary men and women, but the *absence* of ideals: the dearth of *eindeutig* recipes for a decent life, of firmly fixed and steady orientation points, of a predictable destination for the life itinerary. Mental depression – a feeling of one's impotence, of inability to act, and particularly the inability to act *rationally*, to be adequate to the tasks of life – becomes the emblematic *malaise* of our late modern or postmodern times.

Impotence, inadequacy: these are the names of the late modern, postmodern disease – *das Unbehagen der Postmoderne*. Not the fear of non-conformity, but the impossibility of conforming. Not the horror of transgression, but the terror of boundlessness. Not demands transcending one's power to act, but straggling acts in a vain search for a steady and continuous itinerary.

The absence of obtrusive and insidious constraints and limits we tend to call freedom. Most of us, the residents of the late modern or postmodern world, are in this sense as free as our ancestors could only dream of being. And they did dream; the miraculous disappearance of norms and limits was an alluring vision when life was lived in daily fear of transgression. The nightmares of our ancestors of fifty or a hundred years ago were superhuman powers with their superhuman demands. The horror-and-hate figure was Big Brother watching every move day and night and promptly punishing anyone falling out of line, and the devils were the Joneses one had to 'keep up with'. To get rid of all that meant emancipation – the victory of freedom, and there was no sweeter dream than such a victory. Today, however, the powers-that-be have turned their eyes the other way or removed themselves from sight, the line one could fall out of is nowhere to be seen and so Big Brother, were he still wishing to reprimand or punish us, would have trouble deciding where to start; and as to the Joneses, there are so many of them, various, different, and going their own ways – and they could not care less about our struggle to find our 'true and authentic' selves.

Not through any fault on their part, our ancestors thought of freedom as a state in which one is not told what to do and not forced to do what one would rather not do; by that definition, they would probably describe the situation most of us are in today as freedom incarnate. What they did not and could not foresee was that the kind of freedom they envisaged would come with a price-tag attached, and the price would be heavy.

The price in question is insecurity (or, rather, *Unsicherheit*: a much more complex discomfort, which includes uncertainty and unsafety alongside insecurity); a heavy price, indeed, considering the number of choices a free person must confront daily. Such choices must be made without the conviction that the moves will bring anticipated results, that today's investments will bring gains tomorrow and that steering clear of options which seem bad today will not turn tomorrow into a painful loss. It is not clear whom and in what to trust, since no one seems to be in control of how things are going – no one can issue a reliable guarantee that they will indeed go in the anticipated direction. Living under conditions of insecurity is a *Risikoleben*, and it is the acting person who is bound to pay the costs of the risks taken.

Individually, we stand; individually, I fall

The title given by Norbert Elias to his last, posthumously published study, *The Society of Individuals*,[6] flawlessly grasps the gist of the problem which has haunted social theory since its inception. Breaking with the tradition established since Hobbes and reforged by John Stuart Mill, Herbert Spencer and the liberal orthodoxy into the *doxa* – the unexamined frame for all further cognition – of our century, Elias replaced the 'and' and the 'versus' with the 'of'; and by so doing he shifted the discourse from the *imaginaire* of the two forces locked in a mortal, yet unending battle of freedom and domination, into that of a 'reciprocal conception': society shaping the individuality of its members, and the individuals forming society out of their actions while pursuing strategies plausible and feasible within the socially woven web of their dependencies.

Casting members as individuals is the trademark of modern society. That casting, however, was not a one-off act like divine creation; it is an activity re-enacted daily. Modern society exists in its activity of 'individualizing', as much as the activities of the individuals consist in the day-by-day reshaping and renegotiating of the network of their mutual entanglements called 'society'. Neither of the two partners stay put for long. And so the meaning of 'individualization' keeps changing, taking ever new shapes – as the accumulated results of its past history set ever new rules and turn out ever new stakes of the game. 'Individualization' now means something very different from what it meant a hundred years ago and what it conveyed in the early times of the modern era – the times of the extolled 'emancipation' of humans from the tightly knit web of communal dependency, surveillance and enforcement.

Ulrich Beck's *Jenseits von Klasse und Stand?*, followed a few years later by his *Risk Society: Towards a New Modernity*,[7] opened a new chapter in our comprehension of the 'individualizing process'. The two works presented this process as ongoing and unfinished history, with its distinct stages – though without a *telos* or a preordained destination, but an erratic logic of sharp twists and turns instead. It can be said that just as Elias 'historicized' Sigmund Freud's theory of the 'civilized individual' by exploring the civilization as an event in (modern) history, so Beck historicized Elias's account of the birth of the individual by re-presenting that birth as an aspect of continuous and continuing, compulsive and obsessive *modernization*. Beck also stripped the picture of individualization of its time-bound, transient accoutrements, which now becloud understanding more than they clarify the picture (first and foremost, of the vision of linear development, a 'progress' plotted along the axes of emancipation, growing autonomy and freedom of self-assertion) – thereby opening to scrutiny the variety of individualization's historical tendencies and their products and allowing a better comprehension of the distinctive features of its current stage.

One may say in retrospect that class division (or gender division for that matter) was a by-product of unequal access to the resources required to render the self-assertion effective. Classes differed in the range of identities available and in the facility of choice between them. People endowed with fewer resources, and thus with less choice, had to compensate for their individual weaknesses by the 'power of numbers' – by closing ranks and engaging in collective action. As Claus Offe has pointed out, collective, class-oriented action came to those lower down on the social ladder as 'naturally' and 'matter-of-factly' as the individual pursuit of their life goals came to their employers.

Deprivations 'added up', so to speak, and congealed in 'common interests' – and were seen as amenable solely to a collective remedy: 'collectivism' was a first-choice strategy for those who were on the receiving end of individualization yet unable to self-assert as individuals deploying their own, individually owned, blatantly inadequate resources. The class orientation of the better-off was, on the other hand, partial and, in a sense, derivative; it came to the fore mostly when the unequal distribution of resources was challenged and contested. It can be said, however, that by and large the 'disembedded' individuals of the 'classic' modernity era deployed their new empowerment and the entitlements of autonomous agency in a frantic search for 're-embeddedness'.

Let there be no mistake: now, as before, individualization is a fate, not a choice: in the land of individual freedom of choice the option to escape individualization and to refuse to participate in the individualizing game is emphatically *not* on the agenda. That men and women have no one to blame for their frustrations and troubles does not mean, now any more than in the past, that they can protect themselves against frustration by using their own domestic appliances, or pull themselves out of trouble, like Baron Munchhausen, by their bootstraps.

If they fall ill, it is because they were not resolute and industrious enough in following the health regime. If they stay unemployed, it is because they failed to learn the skills of winning an interview or because they did not try hard enough to find a job or because they are, purely and simply, work-shy. If they are not sure about their career prospects and agonize about their future, it is because they are not good enough at winning friends and influencing people and have failed to learn as they should the arts of self-expression and impressing the others. This is, at any rate, what they are told – and what they have come to believe, so that they behave 'as if' this was, indeed, the truth of the matter. As Beck aptly and poignantly puts it, 'how one lives becomes a *biographical solution to systemic contradictions.*' Risks and contradictions go on being socially produced; it is just the duty and the necessity of coping with them which is being individualized.

To cut a long story short: there is a growing gap between individuality as fate and individuality as a practical capacity for self-assertion (as 'individuation', the term selected by Beck to distinguish the self-sustained and self-propelled individual from a merely 'individualized' individual, that is, a human being who has no choice but to act as if the individuation had been attained); and bridging that gap is, most crucially, *not* part of that capacity.

Can there be politics in the individualized society?

The self-assertive ability of individualized men and women falls short, as a rule, of what genuine self-constitution would require. As Leo Strauss has observed, the other face of unencumbered freedom is insignificance of choice – the two faces conditioning each other: why bother to prohibit what is anyway of little consequence? A cynical observer would say that freedom comes when it no longer matters. There is a nasty fly of impotence in the sweet ointment of the kind of freedom that has been shaped through the pressures of individualization; that impotence is felt as all the more odious and upsetting in view of the empowerment that freedom was expected to deliver and guarantee.

Perhaps, as in the past, standing shoulder to shoulder and marching in step might offer a remedy? Perhaps if individual powers, however wan and meagre, were condensed into a collective stand and action, things could be done jointly which no man or woman on their own could dream of doing? The snag is, though, that these days the most common troubles of the individuals-by-fate are *not additive*. They simply do not sum up into a 'common cause'. They are shaped from the beginning in such a way as to lack the edges or 'interfaces' allowing them to be dovetailed with other people's troubles. Troubles may be similar (and the increasingly popular chat shows go out of their way to demonstrate their similarity and to hammer home the message that their most important similarity lies in the fact that they are handled by each sufferer on his or her own), but unlike the common interest of yore they do *not* form a 'totality which is greater than the sum of its parts' and acquire no new quality, easier to handle, by being faced up to and confronted together.

The sole advantage the company of other sufferers may bring is to reassure each one that fighting the troubles *alone* is what all the others do daily – so reinvigorating the flagging resolve to go on doing just that: fighting alone. One may perhaps also learn from other people's experience how to survive the next round of 'downsizing', how to handle children who think they are adolescents and adolescents who refuse to become adults, how to get fat and other unwelcome 'foreign bodies' 'out of one's system', how to get rid of addictions that are no longer satisfying or partners who are no longer pleasurable. But the first thing one learns from the company of others is that the only service that company can render is advice on how to survive in one's own irreparable solitude, and that the life of everyone is full of risks which need to be confronted and fought alone.

And so there is another snag as well: as de Tocqueville long ago suspected, setting people free may make them *indifferent*. The individual is the citizen's worst enemy, suggested de Tocqueville. The individual tends to be lukewarm, sceptical or wary of the 'common good', of the 'good society' or 'just society'. What is the sense of *common* interests unless they let each individual satisfy her or his *own*? Whatever else individuals may do when coming together portends constraint on their freedom to pursue what they see fit for themselves, and won't help such a pursuit anyway. The only two useful things that 'public power' can be expected, and desired, to deliver is to observe 'human rights', that is, to let everyone go her or his own way, and to enable everyone to do it in peace – by guarding the safety of a person's body and possessions, locking the criminals in prisons and keeping the streets free from muggers, perverts, beggars and obnoxious and malevolent strangers.

With his usual, inimitable wit, Woody Allen unerringly grasps the fads and foibles of the late modern individuals-by-decree, browsing through imaginary advertising leaflets of 'adult summer courses' which Americans would be eager to attend: the course in Economic Theory includes the item 'Inflation and depression – how to dress for each'; the Course in Ethics entails 'the categorical imperative, and six ways to make it work for you'; and the prospectus for Astronomy has the information that 'The sun, which is made of gas, can explode at any moment, sending our entire planet system hurtling to destruction; students are advised what the average citizen can do in such a case.'

To sum up: the other side of individualization seems to be the corrosion and slow disintegration of citizenship. Joël Roman, co-editor of Esprit, points out in his recent book *La Démocratie des individus*[8] that 'vigilance is degraded to the surveillance of goods, while general interest is no more than a syndicate of egoisms, engaging collective emotions and fear of the neighbour' – and urges people to seek the 'renewed capacity for deciding together' – now salient mostly for its absence.

If the individual is the citizen's worst enemy, and if individualization spells trouble for citizenship and citizenship-based politics, it is because the concerns and preoccupations of individuals *qua* individuals fill the public space, claiming to be its only legitimate occupants – and elbow out everything else from public discourse. The 'public' is colonized by the 'private'; 'public interest' is reduced to curiosity about the private lives of public figures, tapering the art of public life down to a public display of private affairs and public confessions of private sentiments (the more intimate the better). 'Public issues' which resist such a reduction become all but incomprehensible.

The prospects of the individualized actors being 're-embedded' in the republican body of citizenship are dim. What prompts them to venture on to the public stage is not so much the search for common causes and ways to negotiate the meaning of the common good and the principles of life in common – as the desperate need of 'networking': sharing intimacies, as Richard Sennett keeps pointing out, tends to be the preferred, perhaps the only method left of 'community building'. This building technique can only spawn 'communities' which are as fragile and short-lived as scattered and wandering emotions, shifting erratically from one target to another and drifting in a forever inconclusive search for a secure haven; communities of shared worries, shared anxieties or shared hatreds – but in each case 'peg' communities: a momentary gathering around a nail on which many solitary individuals hang their solitary individual fears. As Ulrich Beck puts it in the essay 'On the mortality of industrial society', 'what emerges from the fading social norms is naked, frightened, aggressive ego in search of love and help. In the search for itself and an affectionate sociality, it easily gets lost in the jungle of the self . . . Someone who is poking around in the fog of his or her own self is no longer capable of noticing that this isolation, this "solitary-confinement of the ego" is a mass sentence.'[9]

Togetherness, individual style

Individualization is here to stay; all who think about the means to deal with its impact on the fashion in which we all conduct our lives must start from acknowledging this fact. Individualization brings to an ever growing number of men and women an unprecedented freedom to experiment – but (*timeo Danaos et dona ferentes* . . .) it also brings an unprecedented task of coping with its consequences. The yawning gap between the right of self-assertion and the capacity to control the social settings which render such self-assertion feasible or unrealistic seems to be the main contradiction of 'second modernity'; one that through trial and error, critical reflection and bold experimentation we would need to collectively learn to collectively tackle.

In *Das Zeitalter der Nebenfolgen und die Politiesierung der Industriegesellschaft*, Ulrich Beck suggests that nothing less than 'another Reformation' is needed, and that it calls for the 'radicalization of modernity'. He proposes that 'this presumes social inventions and collective courage in political experiments' – only to add right away that what is presumed are 'inclinations and qualities that are not exactly frequently encountered, perhaps no longer even capable of garnering a majority'. Yet here we are – we have no other conditions in which to act, and in these conditions, like it or not, act we will – bearing the consequences of our actions and/or our failure to act.

Drifting from one risk to another is in itself a nerve-wracking experience, generating a lot of unalloyed and unmitigated anxiety and fear and allowing no rest to vigilance; a huge fly indeed in the sweet ointment of freedom. This is not, though, the end of the damage.

Pierre Bourdieu has reminded us recently of an old and universally binding rule:

[T]he capacity for future projections is the condition of all behaviour considered to be rational ... [T]o conceive of a revolutionary project, that is to have a well thought-out intention to transform the present in reference to a projected future, a modicum of hold on the present is needed.[10]

The big trouble is that, because of the endemic *Unsicherheit*, a 'hold on the present' is one feature conspicuously missing from the condition of contemporary men and women. None of the most important levers and safeguards of their current situation come under their jurisdiction, let alone control, practised singly or severally. Many people have already been directly hit by the mysterious forces variously dubbed 'competitiveness', 'recession', 'rationalization', 'fall in market demand' or 'downsizing'; each one of us can easily name quite a few acquaintances who suddenly lost the ground they stood on ... But the blows reverberate far beyond their direct targets, and it is not just those who were overnight demoted, degraded, deprived of their dignity and/or their livelihood who have been hit. Every blow carries a message for all those who have been (for a time) spared, and prompts them to assess their own future by the severity of the likely sentence, not by the (unknown) length of its temporary suspension. The message is simple: everyone is *potentially* redundant or replaceable, and so everyone is vulnerable and any social position, however elevated and powerful it may seem now, is in the longer run precarious; even the privileges are fragile and under threat.

Blows may be targeted, but the psychological and political devastation they cause is not. The fear they generate is diffused and ambient. As Bourdieu puts it, that fear 'haunts consciousness and the subconscious'. To climb the heights, one must have one's feet firmly on the ground. But it is the ground itself which feels ever more shaky, unstable, undependable – no solid rock underneath on which to rest the feet in order to bounce. Trust, that indispensable condition of all rational planning and confident action, is floating, vainly seeking ground firm enough to cast an anchor. The state of precariousness, Bourdieu observes,

> renders all future uncertain, and so forbids all rational anticipation – and in particular disallows that minimum of hope in the future which one needs to rebel, and especially to rebel collectively, against even the least tolerable present.

It is common and fashionable nowadays to deplore the growing nihilism and cynicism of contemporary men and women, their short-sightedness, their indifference to long-term life projects, the mundaneness and selfishness of their desires, their inclination to slice life into episodes, each to be squeezed to the last drop with no concern for the consequences. All these charges have ample evidence to support them. What most moral preachers fulminating against moral decadence fail to mention, though, is that the reprehensible tendency they condemn draws its strength from being a *rational* response to the world in which one is compelled to treat the future as a *threat*, rather than as a shelter or promised land. What most critics fail to discuss as well is that this world, like any other human world, has been human-made; far from being a product of inscrutable and invincible laws of nature or sinful yet irredeemable human nature, it is, to no small extent, a product of what can only be called the *political economy of uncertainty*.[11]

The major vehicle of this particular political economy of our times is the escape of power from politics; a flight connived with by traditional institutions of political control, above all by the governments of states, and more often than not actively aided and abetted by them through the policies of deregulation and privatization. The overall result of this process is, as Manuel Castells puts it,[12] a world in which power flows, while politics stays tied to the place; power is increasingly global and exterritorial, while all established political institutions stay territorial and find it difficult, nay impossible, to rise above the local level. After two centuries of the modern effort to tame and domesticate blind and erratic forces of nature and replace them with rationally designed, predictable and manageable human order – it is now the outcomes of *human* activities that confront the actors as eccentric and capricious, wayward and impenetrable, but above all unbridled and uncontrollable 'natural' forces. Societies once struggling to make their world transparent, danger-proof and free of surprises now find their capacity to act hanging on the shifting and unpredictable moods of mysterious forces such as world finances and stock exchanges, or watch helplessly, without being able to do much about it, the continuous shrinking of labour markets, rising poverty, the unstoppable erosion of arable land, the disappearance of forests, growing volumes of carbon dioxide in the air and the overheating of the human planet. Things – and the most important things above all – are 'getting out of control'. As the human ability to cope with problems at hand grows, so do the risks and new dangers which every new move brings, or may bring, in its wake.

The overwhelming feeling of 'losing a hold on the present' is the result, which in its turn leads to a wilting of political will; to disbelief that anything sensible can be done collectively, or that solidary action can make any radical change in the state of human affairs. That condition is seen increasingly as a 'must' – a supreme necessity which can be interfered with by humans only at their own peril. We hear again and again that the sole medicine for the morbid side-effects of deregulated competitiveness is more deregulation, flexibility and a yet more resolute refusal to meddle. And in case one remains unconvinced, the clinching argument against resistance is the all-too-tangible absence of an agency powerful enough to carry out whatever decisions may be taken by joint deliberation and agreement. Even those who think they know what is to be done throw the towel into the ring when it comes to deciding who – what kind of an effective institution – is going to do it.

This is why, as Cornelius Castoriadis observed, our civilization 'stopped questioning itself'. This, Castoriadis adds, is our main trouble. When people accept their impotence to control the conditions of their life, if they surrender to what they take to be necessary and unavoidable – society ceases to be autonomous, that is, self-defining and self-managing; or, rather, people do not believe it to be autonomous, and thus lose the courage and the will to self-define and self-manage. Society then becomes *heteronomous* in consequence – other-directed, pushed rather than guided, plankton-like, drifting rather than navigating. Those on board the ship placidly accept their lot and abandon all hope of determining the itinerary of the vessel. At the end of the modern adventure with a self-governing, autonomous human world, we enter the 'epoch of universalized conformity'.[13]

Making the individualized society safe for democracy

Many historians and political philosophers, with good reason, trace the beginnings of modern democracy to the stout refusal to be taxed without the consent of the taxed. More than just the care of one's pocket was involved – a *principle* was at stake (though only obliquely, and in an inchoate form): the idea of the subject as a *citizen*, and of the citizen as a member of the body politic having a say, together with other members, in all matters concerning their rights and duties, entitlements and obligations. It is that idea which was laid at the foundation of modern democracy and of the modern vision of the republic – *res publica* – as a body politic whose members collectively deliberate how to shape the conditions of their cohabitation, cooperation and solidarity.

Such a model of modern democracy was never implemented in full. There are reasons to believe that implemented in full it can never be; that its true strength lies precisely in its permanent, and incurable, 'unfulfilment'. As Jacques Rancière suggests,[14] democracy is not an *institution*, but essentially an *anti-institutional force*, a 'rupture' in the otherwise relentless trend of the powers-that-be to arrest change, to silence and to eliminate from the political process all those who have not been 'born' into power or make a bid to the exclusive right to govern on the grounds of their unique expertise. While powers-that-be promote the rule of the few, democracy is a constant plea on behalf of all; a bid to power on the grounds of *citizenship*, that is, of a quality belonging to all in equal measure. Democracy expresses itself in a continuous and relentless critique of institutions; democracy is an anarchic, disruptive element inside the political system; essentially, a force of *dissent* and change. One can best recognize a democratic society by its constant complaints that it is *not* democratic enough.

The force exerted by democratic pressure on a political system, the success or failure of its push towards the ideal of an autonomous society, depends on the balance between freedom and security. The pressure of the democratic vision, if not in theory then in practice, fades and shrinks when the balance is slanted in favour of either of the two essential conditions of political participation and responsible citizenship: when either freedom or security are wanting. The political history of modernity may be interpreted as a relentless search for the right balance between the two conditions – for a postulated, and forever not-yet-found, 'point of reconciliation' between freedom and security, the two aspects of the human condition that are simultaneously contradictory and complementary. The search has been thus far inconclusive. Most certainly, it remains unfinished. It goes on. Its continuation is itself the *conditio sine qua non* of the modern society's struggle for autonomy.

Through most of modern history the main danger to democracy was rightly spied in the constraints imposed on human freedom by the policing powers of the institutions in charge of 'collectively assured security'. It seems that nowadays democracy is threatened primarily from the opposite side: it is the collectively guaranteed security that leaves ever more to be desired – being gradually abandoned as a valid objective of public policy and disparaged as a value worth defending. The deficit of freedom results in an incapacity to self-assert, to resist, to 'stand up and be counted'. The deficit of security results in a dissipation of the courage to imagine a plausible cause for resistance and to rally in the name of a society more hospitable to human needs and cravings. In both cases, the outcome is remarkably similar: a weakening of democratic pressures, a growing inability to act politically, a massive exit from politics and from responsible citizenship.

We now have good reasons to suspect that complete, conflict-free reconciliation and peaceful coexistence of freedom and security is an unattainable goal. But there are equally strong reasons to suppose that the main danger to *both* freedom and security lies in calling off the search for such coexistence or even in slackening the energy with which that search is conducted. As things stand at the moment, most attention needs to be focused on the security side of the sought union. Since an autonomous society is inconceivable without autonomous citizens, and since the autonomy of citizens is unthinkable anywhere but in an autonomous society – the efforts, to stand a chance of success, need to be applied simultaneously on the 'macro' and the 'micro' levels. Something must be done in order to enhance the self-governing capacity of the extant body politic, or to extend the reach of the body politic so as to bring the power back under the political control it has recently escaped. And something must be done in order to enhance the 'hold on the present' of individuals, so that they may regain their lost courage and resume the obligations of responsible citizenship.

What is to be done is a matter for the political process to decide. But it seems most likely that on the 'macro' level the search would focus on ways to lift political institutions to the level of globality on which the powers that truly count now 'flow' – and thus on an opening up for political action of a space which lies, for the moment, politically vacant. On the 'micro' level, under the present conditions of 'structural redundancy', the venture to which the search would eventually lead is what Claus Offe and his associates[15] have named 'basic income' or 'the decoupling of income entitlements from employment': making the foundations of individual livelihood independent of the vagaries of the market and insured against the risk-infested meanders of technology-led change.

The second question, yet more mind-boggling than the first, is who is to do what is to be done... The road to an agency capable of meeting the bill looks suspiciously like a vicious circle – or, to use a more fashionable metaphor, Catch-22. A political force of truly global capacity is needed to check and restrain the presently uncontrolled global powers – but it is precisely the fact that global powers stay uncontrolled that prevents the rising of effective political institutions to the global level...

On our ability to untie or cut this Gordian knot the fate of the republic, the citizenship, democracy and human autonomy will depend in the foreseeable future.

4

Modernity and clarity: the story of a failed romance

Ambivalence, ambiguity, equivocality... These words convey the feeling of mystery and enigma; they also signal trouble, whose name is uncertainty, and a dismal state of mind, called indecision or hesitation. When we say that things or situations are ambivalent, what we mean is that we cannot be sure what is going to happen, and so neither know how to behave, nor can predict what the outcome of our actions will be. Instinctively or by learned habit, we dislike and fear ambivalence, that enemy of security and self-assurance. We are inclined to believe that we would feel much safer and more comfortable if situations were unambiguous – if it were clear what to do and certain what would happen if we did it.

In the phenomenon of ambivalence the doubts of reason and the indecision of the will, the respective ailments of the two integral ingredients of the human mind, meet and merge. The world – the domain of reason – appears unclear (that is, emitting obscure, even contradictory, signals) when the will is not sure what to choose; unclarity of the world as reported by reason, and uncertainty as suffered by the will, grow together and recede together. The world is rock solid and prompts no doubts as long as habitual, routine actions will do. We perceive the world as unclear when we start to hesitate – when the routine actions fail and we can no longer rely on the guidance of habit. The indecision of will is then projected upon the world 'out there' and rebounds as a perception of unclarity. What reason, in bringing the message of the 'under-determination' or otherwise doubtful nature of the world, ulti-mately tells of is the lack of self-confidence of the human will.

The other way of saying all this is to point out an intimate connection between the perception of the world as shaky and questionable and the range of human freedom. The less I can do and the less I may want (that is, the more limited my choices are), the more straightforward are 'the facts of life'. The wider the realm of my choices grows – the imaginary world of future possibilities – the less obvious and compelling appear the signals coming from the real world here and now.

This is, however, but a first approximation. A closer look reveals that the experience of freedom is not cut out of one block (in the same way as the will itself, split between practice and imagina-tion); it is torn apart between the premonition of 'what I may do' and the sense of 'what I wish to be done'. Ability and wanting may coincide and blend seamlessly into a firm resolution to act. But all too often they do not overlap, and ambivalence is the first intuition of their lack of fit. If the volume of possibilities exceeds the capacity of the will, ambivalence surfaces in the shape of rest-lessness and anxiety; if the opposite is the case, and the states one can wish to attain are not matched by the ability to reach them, ambivalence manifests itself in dissent, withdrawal, or a desperate urge to escape.

Having melted all that was solid and profaned all that was sacred, modernity ushered in the era of permanent disharmony between the wants and the abilities. For the same reason, this was the era of ambivalence in both its manifestations. And, of course, the era of freedom. And of that specifically *modern*, sceptical kind of critique which is rooted in a gnawing suspicion that things are not as they seem to be and that the world which happens to be ours has no grounds solid enough to render it necessary and inevitable. The synchronized appearance of ambivalence, freedom and scepti-cism was not a 'mere coincidence'. One wonders whether the presence of any one element of that modern trinity without the other two is at all thinkable.

Scepticism as such was not, of course, a modern invention. When it erupted all over Europe with the erosion of the old certainties of the Christian civilization of the Middle Ages, reach-ing its peak at the threshold of the modern era, in the seventeenth century – it took the form of rereading, rehashing and overhauling the ancient arguments advanced long before by the likes of Aenesidemus or Sextus Empiricus; it was even given the name of 'Pyrrhonian crisis', to honour the Hellenic codifier of the stock-in-trade sceptical argument. And yet there was a profound and highly significant difference between the sceptical thought of antiquity and its modern reincarnation. For Sextus Empiricus, universal doubt should and would result in mental health; for Montaigne and those who followed him – it would lead to madness. The ancient Pyrrhonists, says their exquisite historian and analyst, Richard H. Popkin, 'simply achieved *ataraxia*, peace of mind and imperturbability'.[1] As for the early modern sceptics of the sixteenth and seventeenth centuries, however, used to the 'cosmic importance' of the *mores* and the *customs* they and their contemporaries lived by, 'the doubting did not lead to peace of mind, but to nightmares – that there is no reality, that we are always deceived, that God is a deceiver, that we are not possessed of any truth or certitude.'[2] Ancient scepticism was an aristocratic gesture. The voluntary sceptics of classical Greece hoped that once it became known that nothing is by itself good or bad and that there is no way one could prove that things indeed have the value one believes them to carry, the torments of desire would evaporate, together with the agony of unfulfilled hope and the horror of loss; and so they welcomed the pleasures of the tranquillity which would descend in their wake. There was nothing voluntary or aristocratic about the 'Pyrrhonian crisis'. It was the *hoi polloi* world that was being shaken to its foundation. The sceptics of the early modern era were horrified by the chaos which was ever more visible through the ever more threadbare tissue of the traditional order; they were appalled and frightened out of their wits by their discovery and swore never to rest until the rock-steady foundations of clear and unambiguous knowledge of the world were found or constructed. Leibniz, for instance, interpreted 'the suspension of judgment (*epoché*) as "doubt" and doubt as an involuntary state of ignorance which leaves us at the mercy of impulses originating in the passions. Obviously the man who is prey to a passion is perturbed; and it would seem absurd to try to achieve imperturbability through perturbations.'[3]

For the ancient sceptics, facing up to the ultimate unknowability of the world and refusing to go by the (unfounded, merely habitual) daily routines was a badge of distinction – a sign of the elevation and serenity of philosophers, lifting themselves through their own mental effort from the mundane hassle of *hoi polloi* into a Platonistic world of contemplation and reflection. But early modern philosophers saw (or had to see) their role and duty differently. They were to partake of the great modern endeavour of order building in a world smarting among the ruins of the ancien régime. That new order was to be the work of reason, the sole trustworthy weapon of its human builders, and the translation of the 'it is' of reason into the 'you ought' of human action was the vocation of the philosophers. Modern philosophers were haunted from the start by the urge to build the bridges to mundane life, not to burn them. Sceptical forebodings were therefore a bane, sceptical arguments a nuisance, unclarity of the world an irritant, hesitation a sign of ignorance clamouring to be replaced by knowledge-based certainty.

There was a *Wahlverwandtschaft* – an elective kinship of sorts between the assumed vocation of modern philosophers and the concerns of the modern powers, faced with the awesome task of a 'new beginning' – erecting an artificial order amidst the debris of the timeless, self-reproducing and self-caring, but no longer viable, 'natural' one. The link between the two tasks was offered by reason; ruled by the law of non-contradiction and the excluded middle, reason was the sworn, and hopefully invincible, enemy of ambivalence and indecision. And philosophers were, by the nature of their skills and occupations, spokesmen of reason.

The 'ideologists', the learned members of L'Institut National, established in 1795 with a brief to explore the ways and means of forming the right type of men-citizens and regulating their desires ('good and bad tendency of our will', explained the *Mémoire* of its founder, Destutt de Tracy, 'is always directly proportional to the extent and exactitude of our knowledge'; 'It is the task of the ideologist to create a conscious, rational, ideological order'), sought to develop moral and political sciences which would enjoy 'as much certitude as the mathematical sciences'.[4] One of the most illustrious members of the Institut, Condorcet, argued that human societies are represented as grand geometrical constructions, in which all is determined by 'fixed and constant causes'; 'It is possible therefore to create a social mathematics, to calculate geometrically all future moves of human societies...the way one calculates solar eclipses or return of the comets.'[5]

Enlightenment was a selective programme, and paving the way to the rule of reason required twofold measures and a two-pronged strategy. One strategy was for the owners and guardians of true knowledge. For Spinoza, for instance, as Popkin indicates,

> there is no possible sceptical problem because one knows, and knows that one knows, or one is in ignorance. The sceptic who wants to debate Spinoza will just be sent to contemplate whether he knows or understands something perfectly (which amounts to clear and certain knowledge). If the sceptic doubts whether he has such knowledge he is then dismissed as an ignoramus who does not know what is essential for the debate.[6]

Let us add that Spinoza's opposition indicated not just a philosophical division, but a social split. 'Knowing perfectly' was not an option available, or offered, to just anybody; in fact, it was attainable only by a chosen few. Mercenne, Gassendi and even Descartes pointed out repeatedly that what would raise doubts in the mind of a philosopher could still be certain for ordinary mortals. The latter can go about perfectly well armed with their daily certitudes, all the more trustworthy and unshakeable for not being reflected upon. The rational strategy in this case would call not so much for the inducement of *hoi polloi* to think critically and reflect upon the apparently unambiguous evidence of their experience, as for the shaping of the experience in such a way as to make it truly unequivocal, therefore rendering all reflection redundant. For Helvetius, for instance, since ordinary (ignorant) men and women are devoid of the critical faculty, the task of setting apart good from evil is totally in the hands of legislators, able to follow the advice of reason and give the human environment a form which promotes the good and discourages the evil. In Eric Voegelin's summary,

> The function of regeneration is transformed to the analyst in the role of the organizing legislator who will create externally the social situation which in its turn will induce the external conformism of conduct to moral standards by a play of psychological mechanism of disordered man...
> What happens, in brief, is that the analyst-legislator arrogates to himself the possession of the substance of good in society while denying it to the rest of mankind. Mankind's split into the mass of

pleasure-pain mechanisms and the One who will manipulate the mechanisms for the good of society. The nature of man, by a kind of division of labour, is distributed among masses and leaders so that only society as a whole is integral man.[7]

'One should not complain of the badness of men but of the ignorance of legislators' – as it was summed up by Helvetius himself. While Cabanis pointed out that 'medicine and morality, branches of the same science, the science of man, rest on the same basis.' The structure of the environment determines and modifies 'physical sensibility', and through it 'the ideas, sentiments, passions, virtues and vices'. 'It is through the study of constant relations between physical and moral states that one can guide humans towards happiness, make a habit of good sense and necessity of morality.'[8] Destutt de Tracy praised Pinel, one of the pioneers of both modern psychiatry and modern education, for 'proving that the art of curing demented men is not different from the art of handling the passions and directing the opinions of ordinary people; both consist in the formation of habits'; and showing by the same token that the moral education of the masses ought to rest on the close observation of savages, of peasants inhabiting remote villages, of children and animals.[9] Well, even Kant, relying in his hope for the moral reform of mankind on the rational faculties of the common man, bewailed the distrustful stance taken by the rulers regarding the 'enlighteners', pointing out that the latter 'do not address themselves in familiar terms to the *people* (who themselves take little or no notice of them and their writings), but in *respectful* terms to the State'; it was the task of the state, Kant insisted, to create conditions in which reason-guided moral judgement may thrive and rule supreme; progress could only follow the route 'from the top downwards'.[10]

The harmony between modern philosophers and modern rulers was never complete; dissonance, time and again erupting into open conflict, was as prominent as the ostensible consensus between the philosophical pursuit of unequivocal truth and the political pursuit of unambiguous order. Kant, perhaps the most perceptive among the Enlighteners and the staunchest advocate of the 'free agent' concept of man, envisaged that much, warning that 'we' (the philosophers) can *dictate* to people in advance what they *ought* to do, but cannot *predict* what they *will* do. The rulers, naturally, wanted more; for them, it was the results that counted, not the principles that led to their achievement. Hence the charge of abstraction, impracticality, living in cloud-cuckoo land which they all too often, and independently of their own political sympathies or styles, raised against the intellectual 'idle dreamers'. And yet there was a unity of purpose that in spite of all the reciprocal rancour and friction made the efforts of the modern spokesmen of legislative reason and of the political practitioners of legislation mutually resonant and complementary. This was the war declared on the twin dangers of ambiguity of thought and contingency of action. In short, the war on ambivalence.

Facing the unclear, the impenetrable, the unexpected was by no means a modern novelty. One thing was novel, though: the non-availability of the tested ancient and medieval means of avoiding rather than confronting the dire psychological and pragmatic consequences of the resulting uncertainty of human fate and prospects. Modernity rejected the ancient solution in both its radical, sceptical/cynical/stoical version of lofty resignation and its moderate Aristotelian version of the *phronesis*-based compromise; it also rejected the Christian solution of unqualified trust in God and resignation to the ultimate mystery of Providence. The first solution was unacceptable since, unlike classical antiquity, modernity had a job to do: *creating* an order which otherwise would not come about, shaping the future which otherwise would assume an unacceptable form. For this purpose it needed exact knowledge of the connections and sequences of causes and effects with a degree of precision akin to that of the architect or medicine man. The second, Christian, solution would not do either in a modern world in which perhaps not everything was in human power, but only such things as were or could be submitted to human control were proclaimed worthy of thought and concern. Modernity did not deny the ultimate mystery of existence – not in so many words, at any rate; it simply took it off the rational agenda and left it to the care of admittedly impractical people, the poets, having declared it not worth the time devoted to its solution and concentrating instead on clarifying and straightening up the confused and twisted evidence about the state of affairs within reach and within its controlling ambitions.

But the installation and maintenance of order – the *structuring* of the human condition – was now, after the collapse of the

premodern self-reproducing routine, one of those affairs clamouring for human control. The idea of 'structure' refers to the manipulation of probabilities; a setting is 'structured' if certain events are
more probable than others, if certain others are utterly unlikely,
and if the hierarchy of probabilities remains relatively constant.
Order-keeping in human affairs boils down in the end to enhan-
cing the probability of one kind of behaviour and decreasing the
likelihood of, or eliminating altogether, other kinds of behaviour.
If this effort is successful, the turn of events may become predictable, and the consequences of actions calculable; it may become
possible, in other words, to shape the future in advance.

Early modernity is famous for the profusion of utopian literature published, read and debated. Modern utopias were anything
but flights of fancy or the waste products of the imagination
running wild. They were blueprints for the human-controlled
world to come, a declaration of the intent to force that world to
come, and the serious calculation of the means necessary to do it.
They served, as well, as test-tubes in which the basic ingredients of
modern thinking were mixed and the body of modern ambitions
sedimented and given shape. A remarkable feature of modern
utopias was the attention devoted to the meticulous planning of
the environment of daily life – the plotting and designing of the
city space, in which most, if not all, the denizens of the future
worlds were expected to live. It was hoped that the clarity and
uniformity of the external setting would secure a similar clarity
and uniformity of human behaviour, leaving no room for hesitation, uncertainty or ambivalence.

The preoccupations of the writers and readers of the early
modern utopias have been recently insightfully explored and
thoroughly documented by Bronislaw Baczko.[11] Having collated
dozens of popular utopian treatises of the time, he found that
'throughout the century all they do is continually reinvent the
same city.' Utopian inventions were strikingly similar to each
other, bearing vivid testimony to the shared obsession that gave
birth to all of them: that of transparency and unequivocality of
setting, capable of healing or warding off the agony of risky
choice. 'There is nothing chaotic in these cities: everywhere a
perfect and striking order reigns...' 'It is easy to get one's bearings
in them.' 'Everything in the city is functional...' 'Perfect regularity
prevails there. The streets are wide and so straight that one has the

impression that they were laid out with a ruler.' 'Nearly all the elements of the city are interchangeable.' Cities 'resemble each other to the point that after having visited one of them, one has the feeling of having seen them all.' 'A stranger has no need to ask for information...the architecture speaks to him in a universal language.' And another important matter: the utopian blueprints conveyed the idea of an *absolute beginning*, which was to become the routine premise of modern action. No perfect order may emerge out of the inherently ambiguous, chaotic convolutions of historical accidents. Hence 'city planning is imagined and thought of as a refusal of *all* history.' The cities which the utopian pioneers of the modern spirit wished and pressed to build 'kept no vestige of their past'; they embodied a 'fierce interdiction against any trace of history'.

The most historically minded of human civilizations declared war on history; this is what, in the final account, the fight against ambivalence amounts to. The context of human life can no longer be left to accident, allowed to be an outcome of a game played by discordant and uncoordinated forces. The setting in which humans make their decisions needs to be carefully designed and clearly marked with legible, unequivocal signs. Both the dearth and the excess of meaning, both the scarcity and the abundance of possible *Auslegungen* are disorders which a rational organization of the human world cannot in the long run tolerate and can treat only as *temporary* irritants. Modernity was after a perfect, one-to-one fitting of names and things, words and meanings; a set of rules free of blank spots and cases overloaded with instructions; a taxonomy in which there was a file for each phenomenon but no more than one file for any one of them; a division of tasks in which there was an agent for every part of the action but no more than one agent for each; in short, after a world in which there is an unambiguous (algorithmic rather than merely heuristic) recipe for every situation and no situation without a recipe attached. But to create a world matching such demanding standards one needed first to clear the building site of the scattered sediments of past actions, which, as it happened, all stopped short of the ideal. Modernity was therefore the era of *creative destruction*, of perpetual dismantling and demolition; the 'absolute beginning' was another face of the instant obsolescence of all successive states, and thus never-ending attempts to get rid of yesterday's history.

In other words, the modern mind has entertained the project of replacing history with *legislation*; of substituting logically cohesive legal norms for the uncontrolled, perhaps uncontrollable, 'laws of history' (the modern mind could conceive of history only as a mirror-image of its own pragmatics: as a *law-setting agency* – though perhaps an imperfect one, buffeted by the cross-waves of passion and prejudice). The modern mind is legislative reason, and modern practice is the practice of legislation.

If we return now to the inherent antinomy of the human will,[12] it will seem plausible to suggest that the essence of modern legislative efforts (or the efforts of fighting ambivalence with unequivocal legal rules) was the intention to secure harmony between the potentially discordant 'I can' and 'I want' aspects of the will. In Freud's old yet unsurpassed articulation, 'order is a kind of compulsion to repeat which, when a regulation has been laid down once and for all, decides when, where and how a thing shall be done, so that in every similar circumstance one is spared hesitation and indecision';[13] and the way in which modern civilization aimed at such an order was to change the 'pleasure principle', 'under the influence of the external world', 'into the more modest reality principle'. 'Reality principle', in simple terms, means cutting the 'I want' to the size of 'I can'.

As if following Hegel's injunction, modernity defined freedom as known and understood necessity. Durkheim pointed to social constraints, the constant pressure of a *conscience collective* and punitive sanctions threatening idiosyncratic, norm-defying behaviour as the necessary conditions of 'true freedom'; the alternative, Durkheim insisted, was not greater freedom, but slavery – the socially uncoerced individual could only be a hapless victim of erratic instincts and desires. The secret of individual liberation lay in the coercive power of the societally established Law. To be free meant to want what one can, to wish to do what one must do, and never to desire what one cannot achieve. A properly 'socialized' individual (also described as a 'happy individual' and a 'genuinely free individual') is one who experiences no discrepancy and no clash between wants and abilities, not wanting to do what he or she cannot do but wanting to do what he or she must; only such an individual would not experience reality as a net of obtrusive and vexing constraints, thereby feeling truly free and happy.

We may say that the modern way of tackling the inherent ambivalence of the 'disembedded' or 'disencumbered' identity set afloat with the demise of the self-reproducing premodern setting was to adjust individual wants to what the designed, legally framed social setting rendered 'realistic'. To this strategy we can also trace the roots of the modernity's hidden, yet notorious totalitarian tendency: within the framework of that strategy, harmony between wants and abilities could be truly achieved, if at all, only under conditions of concentrated legislative power, ubiquitous and comprehensive normative regulation, and the delegalization and disempowerment (and in the end elimination) of all countervailing authorities (collective, as well as those rooted in the benighted depths of not-fully-tamed individuality).

In our own times, two things are becoming increasingly clear: that this strategy failed to achieve its purpose, and that it has been by and large abandoned – perhaps even reversed. It was abandoned, let me add, not *because* of its failure; abandonment came *first*, and only then, in retrospect, could the inevitability of failure be fully and clearly seen.

The modern strategy of fighting ambivalence failed mostly because of its conservative, restrictive impact, which clashed with other, inherently dynamic aspects of modernity – the continuous 'new beginning' and 'creative destruction' as the way of life. The 'steady state', the 'balanced state', the 'state of equilibrium', the state of the full satisfaction of the (supposedly invariable) sum total of human needs, that state set by early modern economists as the final condition of humanity to which 'the invisible hand' of the market was leading, proved to be a constantly receding horizon, pushed ever further by the relentless power of the needs rising faster than the capacity to satisfy them. The modern strategy of fighting ambivalence could be applied with however meagre a chance of success only if needs/wants/desires were consistently assigned to play second fiddle to the 'objective possibility' of gratifying them.

That strategy is still applied today – but solely to the 'underclass', the 'new poor', the 'welfare recipients' – to people who by common consent are incapable of managing the endemic conflict between their wants and their abilities; only in respect of their case does the argument 'we cannot afford it' strike a receptive chord. As to the rest – the majority, the main body, the pattern-setting part of society – it is the wants that have been assigned an unqualified priority and given the role of the initiating and driving force as far as the potentialities of society are concerned. We measure 'economic growth' and the overall 'health' of the economy by a rising demand for commodities, and economic success by a rising 'power to spend'. In times of recession and falling output, we hear of 'consumer-led recovery'. As Pierre Bourdieu indicated in *Distinction*, his eye-opening study of contemporary culture, needs creation is today taking the place of normative regulation, advertising replaces ideological indoctrination and seduction is substituted for policing and coercion. We may say that the bulk of the population is integrated into contemporary society in their role of consumers, not producers; and integration of that sort can only hold fast as long as the wants exceed the level of their current satisfaction.

This is why the modern strategy of fighting ambivalence has been all but abandoned (except, let us repeat, in dealings with the margins of society – whose marginality consists precisely in their practical, yet supposedly organic, inability to cope with the ambivalence born of the wants/abilities gap). The permanent disharmony between 'I want' and 'I can', and more exactly the excess of wants over the present ability to gratify them, is turning into the guiding principle of the social setting at all three of its 'analytical levels' – identity formation, social integration and systemic reproduction. But such disharmony spells ambivalence and ever more ambivalence; one may say that the postmodern/consumerist/deregulated society has a powerful stake in maintaining a high level of ambivalence in individual life. Ambiguity of life context, if I am allowed to use that blatantly modernist notion, is for the postmodern condition 'functional'.

There is another reason why the modern strategy was bound to fail. Short of following their inborn totalitarian tendency to the end (cases fortunately few and rare in modernity's history), modern societies could only apply that strategy locally, 'to one problem at a time', 'as the problems arise' – more in the style of crisis management than of a comprehensive, overall plan. Each effort to streamline and clarify a particularly vexing confusion had therefore to bring forth new 'grey areas', no man's lands and situations without unambiguous definition in places where precarious and as a rule uncoordinated local orders interfaced or, worse still, overlapped.

As Ulrich Beck admirably showed in his description of the *Risk Society*, that 'archipelago' character of the modern social order(s) and the relative autonomy of every single island of order have created the man-made confusion which has by and large now replaced the 'natural confusion' which modernity set out to replace with the clarity and transparency of the thoroughly legislated order. We speak of 'risks' whenever it is impossible to precisely predict the outcome of actions we intend to undertake, and hence every decision is ambiguous, and every wish to act ambivalent; in other words, 'risk' stands for the incurable unclarity of the situation. The present-day unclarity is itself a product of the urge to clarify; most of the acutely felt ambivalence stems today from the disparate and diffuse efforts to eliminate equivocality from selected, separate and always confined localities. But, as Beck convincingly argues, the continuous, expanding and redoubtable ambivalence ruling this *Risk Society* of ours has its uses. It lubricates the wheels of science and technology, the two major vehicles of contemporary development. It has itself become, to deploy another discredited modernist concept, a formidable agent of *progress*.

We may conclude that ambivalence is now fast losing its societal/systemic sting; it ceases to be a 'public enemy'. Which does not mean, however, that it ceases, or is likely to cease, to be a 'private enemy'; an adversary, perhaps the most frightening among many, of the human individual in his or her unstoppable effort of identity formation. Like so many other aspects of contemporary society, the dangers of ambivalence have undergone a process of deregulation, and the task of coping with the results (though not necessarily the resources which the task requires) has been privatized. Ambivalence may be, as before, a social phenomenon, but each one of us faces it alone, as a *personal problem* (and, as many counsellors in our 'counselling boom' era would keenly suggest, as our personal fault or ailment). We are – most of us – free to enjoy our freedom, but unfree to avoid the consequences of that enjoyment. To tackle the consequences, we are bound to turn to the self-same market of commodified goods, services and ideas (thus also, presumably, of counsels and therapies), which is the major production plant of ambivalence and its zealous and resourceful supplier. The market keeps ambivalence alive, and ambivalence keeps the market alive. From this closed circle there is no obvious exit. But since the times of the Gordian knot every close circle breeds the temptation to cut and the demand for sharp knives...

Hence the neo-tribal and fundamentalist sentiments which inescapably accompany the current privatization of ambivalence. Their allure is the promise to put paid to the agony of individual choice by abolishing the choice itself; to heal the pain of individual uncertainty and hesitation by finishing off the cacophony of voices which makes one unsure of the wisdom of one's decisions. Their bait is that of the long-lost *Eindeutigkeit* – of a world unambiguous again, sending unequivocal signals; that is, of an identity no longer multilayered, multidimensional and 'until-further-notice'. Like everything else in the deregulated world of the lonely consumer, these sentiments (to use an apt metaphor from Iuri Lotman, the great Russian philosopher) do not coalesce into one powerful flow of a river, rushing in one direction and dissolving and carrying away every obstacle on its way, but erupt suddenly in places that are scattered and difficult to predict, like mines in a vast minefield.

The modern romance with clarity is not over – it has only changed its form. The great, three-hundred-year modern war against ambivalence is no longer conducted by regular conscript armies, but by guerrilla units coming together and disappearing again in the dark blind alleys which intersperse the brightly lit avenues of the postmodern disneylands of free consumers.

5

Am I my brother's keeper?

Professor van der Laan kindly sent me a number of thoughtful and insightful studies dealing, as he pointed out, with 'important issues in social work in the Netherlands'. I am grateful – I learned from him quite a lot about the problems which occupy the attention of social workers in this country. But I am particularly grateful for the reassurance I got from my readings: that the worries of Dutch social workers are no different from what people engaged in social work in other European countries feel. In his own article Professor van der Laan encapsulated that widespread feeling of unease very well, when he indicated that the welfare state is under attack, accused of providing its wards with a hammock, whereas a genuine safety net ought to act more like a springboard. In other words, the welfare state is charged with not working itself out of the job.

The proper task of social work ought to be, we are told, getting rid of the unemployed, the handicapped, invalids and other indolent people who for one reason or another cannot eke out their own living and so depend on social help and care for their survival; and this evidently is not happening. As social work, we are told, ought to be judged like any other human action by its cost-and-effects balance sheet – it does not, in its present form, 'make economic sense'. It could only justify its continued existence if it made dependent people independent and made lame people walk on their own feet. The tacit, rarely spelled-out assumption is that for not-independent people, such people as do not join the game of selling and buying, there is no room in the society of players. 'Dependence' has become a dirty word: it refers to something which decent people should be ashamed of.

When God asked Cain where Abel was, Cain replied, angrily, with another question: 'Am I my brother's keeper?' The greatest ethical philosopher of our century, Emmanuel Levinas, commented: from that angry Cain's question all immorality began. Of course I am my brother's keeper; and I am and remain a moral person as long as I do not ask for a special reason to be one. Whether I admit it or not, I am my brother's keeper because my brother's well-being *depends* on what I do or refrain from doing. And I am a moral person because I recognize that dependence and accept the responsibility that follows. The moment I question that dependence, and demand as Cain did to be given reasons why I should care, I renounce my responsibility and am no longer a moral self. My brother's dependence is what makes me an ethical being. Dependence and ethics stand together and together they fall.

To think of it, Levinas's blunt verdict is not news. It simply reiterates in somewhat different terms what was, for millennia, the kernel of Judaeo-Christian teachings, nurturing and casting further afield our common understanding of humanity and civilized being. What Levinas spelled out made the need of the other, and the responsibility for meeting that need, into the cornerstone of morality – and the acceptance of that responsibility into the birth-act of the moral person. But if Levinas's verdict is not news, then the derision and contempt for dependence and the stigma attached to it must be news; perhaps even the most profound and radical of novelties which Judaeo-Christian civilization has confronted in its long history. It is worth our while to give some thought to that novelty and its causes, when we celebrate the anniversary of the daring initiative which today, a hundred years later, is pressed to apologize for its results...

If Cain's question is asked today in various updated forms all over Europe and if the welfare state comes under attack everywhere, it is because the unique combination of factors which led to its establishment, and made it look and feel like the natural state of modern society, has by now fallen apart. We may say that at its birth the welfare state was 'overdetermined'. But now it is the resentment towards welfare state institutions, and their gradual dismantling, which are similarly 'overdetermined'.

It has been said by some people that the emergence of the welfare state was a triumph of ethical intentions: recasting them among the constitutive principles of modern civilized society. It has been said by some others that the introduction of the welfare state was the result of the prolonged struggle waged by trade unions and labour parties demanding collective and state-endorsed insurance for livelihoods threatened by the uneven and erratic course of capitalist development. Still other analysts have emphasized the wish of the political establishment to defuse dissent and avert the possible rebellion against that threat. All these explanations have a credible ring, but each one captures but a part of the truth. None of the named factors would be likely to be able to carry the weight of the welfare state on its own; it was, rather, their coincidence that paved the way for the creation of the welfare state and assured nearly universal support for its provisions, and a similarly universal readiness to share its costs.

But even that combination of factors could have proved insufficient had it not been for that buckle which held them together: the need to keep both capital and labour in a 'market-ready' state, and the responsibilities for this which had fallen on the state. For the capitalist economy to function, capital had to be able to buy labour, and labour had to be in an attractive enough condition to appear to its prospective buyers as a wanted commodity. Under the circumstances, the major task of the state and the key to the proper fulfilment of all its other functions was the 'commodification of capital–labour relations'; seeing to it that the transaction of buying and selling labour could go on unhindered.

At that stage of capitalist development (now by and large over) the rate of growth and of profits was proportionate to the volume of labour engaged in the productive process. The working of the capitalist market was notorious for its ups and downs, for periods of boom followed by protracted depressions; not all the labour resources potentially available could therefore be employed at all times. But those currently idle were the active labour force of tomorrow: currently, but only temporarily, they were unemployed, people in an abnormal but also transient and rectifiable condition. They were the 'reserve army of labour' – their status was defined by what they were not at that moment but would be ready to become when the time came. As every general will tell you, care for the military strength of the nation requires that reservists are well nourished and kept in good health, so as to be ready to face the strains of army life when called into active service. And since that was the era of massive labour and mass conscript armies, the nation could be confident of its strength only if everyone – if the need arose – could be drawn into the ranks of industrial labour or the army. The working and fighting capacity of its citizens was the *conditio sine qua non* of the state's sovereignty and of the well-being of the state's subjects. Regarded as the duty of society as a whole and as a matter of the well-understood interests of the nation as a whole, the task of keeping the poor and the handicapped, the impoverished and the indolent ready to rejoin the ranks at any moment was fully and truly an issue 'beyond left and right'. No one needed much convincing that the money spent on welfare provisions was money well spent.

The times of mass-employment industry are now over, at least in our part of the world, and the mass conscript army also belongs to the past. Modern weapons mean few professional soldiers, and technological progress in goods production consists nowadays in cutting down the need for employment; investment means fewer, not more, jobs, and stock exchanges all over the world promptly reward the 'slimming down' and 'downsizing' companies and react nervously to news of a falling unemployment rate.

Let us be clear about it: people traditionally called 'unemployed' are no longer a 'reserve army of labour', just as an adult man in Holland or England is no longer an army reservist about to rejoin the troops in case of military need. We are fooling ourselves if we expect industry to recall the people it made redundant. Such an eventuality would go against the grain of everything relevant to the present-day economic prosperity: the principles of flexibility, competitiveness and productivity measured by falling labour costs. And let us face the truth – that even if the new rules of the market game promise a rise in the total wealth of the nation, they also, inevitably, make virtually inescapable the widening gap between those in the game and the rest who are left out.

This is not the end of the story, though. People left out of the game are also left without a function which by any stretch of the imagination could be seen as 'useful', let alone indispensable, for the smooth and profitable running of the economy. They are not needed as the would-be producers; but in a society in which consumers, not producers, are cast as the driving force of economic prosperity (it is the 'consumer-led' recovery that we expect to take us out of economic troubles), the poor are also worthless as consumers: they won't be tempted by market blandishments, they carry no credit cards and can count on no bank overdrafts, and the commodities they most need bring little or no profit to the traders. No wonder they are being reclassified as an 'underclass': no longer a temporary abnormality waiting to be rectified and brought back in line, but a class outside the classes, a category cast permanently off-limits from the 'social system', a category the rest of us would be better off and more comfortable without.

Ulrich Beck, the insightful and perspicacious German sociologist, recently published a book under the title *Schöne neue Arbeitswelt* (*The Brave New World of Work*); the major thesis of that thoughtful book is that in ten years or so only one in two work-capable Europeans will be boasting full-time, regular employment, and even this half will hardly enjoy the degree of long-term security which the union-protected jobs entailed just a quarter of a century ago (as the noted economist from the Sorbonne, Daniel Cohen, pointed out, anyone joining the Ford or Renault factories could have counted on staying there till the end of their working life, while people who get their lucrative jobs in Bill Gates's enterprises have not the slightest idea where they will be next year). The rest of us will get our living 'Brazilian style': through occasional, short-term, casual work, with no contractual guarantees and no pension or compensation rights, though with the distinct possibility of being terminated shortly and at the employer's whim. If Ulrich Beck is right (and his predictions carry a widespread support of facts and learned opinion), then the recently popular 'welfare to workfare' schemes meant to make the welfare state redundant are not measures aimed at improving the lot of the poor and unprivileged, but a statistical exercise meant to wipe them off the register of social, and indeed ethical, problems through the simple trick of reclassification.

The preachers of the so-called 'third way' may be right when they proclaim the *dismantling* of the 'welfare state as we know it' to be an issue 'beyond left and right', as once upon a time the *creation* of the welfare state used to be.[1] Indeed, governments of the left and right alike can hardly curry favour with the electorate otherwise than by cajoling global, exterritorial and free-floating capital and finance to come in and stay. From the point of view of the latter, keeping the local poor in decent human conditions, that principal objective of the welfare state, is utterly devoid of 'economic sense'.

No wonder the welfare state has a 'bad press'. One hardly reads or hears nowadays of those hundreds or thousands of human beings whom caring social workers have drawn back from the brink of ultimate despair or collapse; or of those millions for whom welfare provisions made all the difference between wretched poverty and a decent life; or of those tens of millions who found that the awareness that help would come if it were needed meant that they could face the risks of life with that courage and determination without which successful, let alone dignified, life is unthinkable. But one reads and hears quite a lot about those hundreds or thousands who sponge and cheat and abuse the patience and benevolence of public authorities; and of those hundreds of thousands or perhaps millions whom 'life on the dole' has apparently transformed into inept and lazy idlers not just unable but unwilling to take up work when it comes their way, preferring to live at the hard-working taxpayer's expense. In the popular American definitions of the members of the 'underclass', poverty-stricken people, single mothers, school dropouts, drug addicts and criminals on parole stand side by side and are no longer easy to set apart. What unites them and justifies piling them together is that all of them, for whatever reason, are a 'burden on society'. We would all be better off and happier if they somehow, miraculously, disappeared.

There is one more, and powerful, reason, why the contemporary poor – the 'social services clients' – may turn from objects of pity and compassion into objects of resentment and anger. We all, to a greater or smaller degree, experience the world we inhabit as full of risks, uncertain and insecure. Our social standing, our jobs, the market value of our skills, our partnerships, our neighbourhoods and the networks of friends we can rely on are all unstable and vulnerable – unsafe harbours for anchoring our trust. A life of constant consumer choice is not tranquil either: what about the perpetual anxiety about the wisdom of the choices we are bound daily to make; what about the objects of desire fast losing their attractions, and the objects of pride turning overnight into stigmas of shame; what about the identity we all desperately seek, which has the nasty habit of falling out of fashion and esteem well before we have found it? Indeed, life is full of anxiety and fear, and few people would say that they would change nothing in it if given the chance. Our *Risk Society* faces an awesome task when it comes to reconciling its members to the hazards and dreads of daily life. It is this task that the poor presented as an underclass of outcasts makes a little easier. If their kind of life is the sole alternative to 'staying in the game', then the risks and horrors of a flexible world and lifelong uncertainty seem a little less repulsive and unendurable: that is, they feel better than all other thinkable options could. One may say, a bit cynically, that our peace of mind, our reconciliation with life, and whatever happiness we may derive from the life to which we have reconciled ourselves, all depend psychologically on the wretchedness and the misery of the outcast poor. And the more miserable and wretched the lot of the outcast poor is, the less miserable we feel.

And so making the lot of the poor even worse than it is makes the fate of all the rest of us look better. This is bad news for prospects of solidarity with the poor – that solidarity which came easily and naturally in the times when the major oppression suffered by the bulk of the population was the grinding routine of daily work and the relentless chores of the daily struggle for survival. Between the plight of the employed and the plight of the unemployed poor there was a close and intimate kinship, and the insight into the situation of the people out-of-work did not present those in-work with any difficulty. If the first and the second were both miserable, both were miserable for essentially similar reasons and the difference in their suffering was a matter of degree, not kind. Today, on the contrary, the empathy with 'people on the dole' does not come easily to the rest of us. They and we may be unhappy, but obviously we are unhappy for different reasons – our miseries have distinctly different shapes and do not readily translate.

The fears which haunt most of us daily arise from too little security of well-being; they, the poor, are on the contrary much too secure in their misery. If we suffer, it is because of the flexibility and instability of our livelihood; but instability is the last thing which people condemned to a life of poverty would complain about. They suffer because of the scarcity of their chances in a world which boasts of offering unprecedented opportunities to anyone else; we, however, tend to view their lack of chances as freedom from the risks which torment us. Their income may be meagre – but it is, at least, secure; the welfare cheques come regularly, whatever happens, and so those people do not need to prove themselves daily in order to be sure of their tomorrows. Doing nothing at all, they obtain and enjoy that certainty which we lean over backwards, but in vain, to achieve. This is why 'from welfare to workfare' schemes may count on the outspoken, or at least a tacit support of the majority of the 'flexibly employed': let them, like us, be buffeted by the shifting waves of the labour market, let them be haunted by the same uncertainty we are all tormented by...

And so, the welfare state's falling out of favour is *overdetermined*. The rich and powerful see it as a bad investment and money wasted, while the less rich and powerless feel no solidarity with the 'welfare clients' and no longer see in their predicament a mirror-reflection of their own troubles. The welfare state is on the defensive. It must apologize and argue daily, over and over again, for its *raison d'être*. And while arguing, it can hardly use the most popular language of our times, that of interest and profitability. More can be said in fact: no *rational* arguments can be raised in favour of the continuing existence of the welfare state. The care of the well-being of the 'reserve army of labour' could be presented as a rational step to take, indeed as a command of reason. Keeping the 'underclass' alive and well defies all rationality and serves no visible purpose.

And so we are back to square one. After a century or so of a happy marital cohabitation between ethics and rational-instrumental reason, the second partner opted out from the wedlock and ethics remained alone in charge of the once shared household. And when alone, ethics is vulnerable and does not find it easy to stand its ground.

The question 'Am I my brother's keeper?', which not long ago was thought to have been answered once and for all and so was seldom heard, is asked again, more vociferously and belligerently by the day. And people wishing for a 'yes' answer try desperately, yet with no evident success, to make it sound convincing in the cool and businesslike language of interests. What they should do instead is reassert, boldly and explicitly, the ethical reason for the welfare state – the only reason needed by the welfare state to justify its presence in a humane and civilized society. There is no guarantee whatsoever that the ethical argument will cut much ice in a society in which competitiveness, cost-and-effects calculations, profitability and other free market commandments rule supreme and join forces in what according to Pierre Bourdieu is fast becoming our *pensée unique*, the belief beyond all questioning; but the issue of guarantee is neither here nor there, since the ethical argument is the welfare state's only remaining line of defence.

One measures the carrying capacity of a bridge by the strength of its weakest pillar. The human quality of a society ought to be measured by the quality of life of its weakest members. And since the essence of all morality is the responsibility which people take for the humanity of others, this is also the measure of a society's ethical standard. This is, I propose, the only measure the welfare state can afford, but also the only one it needs. This measure may prove insufficient to endear the welfare state to all of us on whose support its fate depends – but this is also the sole measure which resolutely and unambiguously speaks in the welfare state's favour.

The needed return to ethical foundations is likely to encounter other obstacles as well, in addition to the obvious one, which is its lack of resonance with the dominant discourse of the time. These other obstacles are *internal* to social work; they stem from the long bureaucratization of social work which for many years could proceed unabated precisely because the ethical substance of welfare work, having been taken for granted, could be relegated to the seldom explored background of its daily practices. Professor van der Laan puts his finger on the most invidious and vexing of such self-inflicted difficulties when he points out that in welfare practice 'moral assessment has been replaced by the procedural execution of rules.' The propriety of social work came to be assessed by conformity to the rules. This was perhaps unavoidable, given the large and constantly rising number of cases with which social workers needed to deal, and the necessity of making comparisons and finding 'common denominators' for human sufferings whose uniqueness defied comparison and neat classification. The tendency might have had its good reasons, but its results made the daily practice of social work ever more distant from its original ethical impulse; the objects of care turned more and more into specimens of legal categories and the process of 'effacing the face', endemic to all bureaucracy, was set in motion.

No wonder that social workers, in the Netherlands as much as in other countries, have been trained to believe that the secret of success and defeats in their work should be sought and could be found in the letter of procedural rules and in the proper interpretation of their spirit. When 'procedural execution' takes over from 'moral assessment' as the guide to job performance, one of the most conspicuous and seminal consequences is the urge to make the rules more precise and less ambiguous than they are, to taper the range of their possible interpretations, to make the decisions in each case fully determined and predictable 'by the book'; along with the expectation that all this can be done, and that if it has not been done it is the sloppiness, neglect and short-sightedness of the social workers and their bosses which are to blame. Such beliefs prompt social workers to be inward-looking and seek the explanation of the rising tide of anti-welfare state criticism in their own failings. They come to believe that whatever the critics say is wrong with the welfare state could be rectified, and the critics could be placated, if only they, the social workers, could design and write down in the statute books a clear inventory of the clients' entitlements and an *eindeutig* code of our conduct...

I put it to you that the beliefs and expectations in question are illusions; and that just how illusionary they are becomes clear the moment we recall that social work, whatever else it may be, is also the ethical gesture of taking responsibility for our ineradicable responsibility for the fate and the well-being of the Other; and that the weaker and less able to demand, to litigate and to sue the Other is, the greater is our responsibility. We are all our brothers' keepers; but what that means is far from being clear and can hardly be made transparent and *eindeutig*. Clarity and unambiguity may be the ideal of a world in which 'procedural execution' is the rule. For the ethical world, however, ambivalence and uncertainty are its daily bread and cannot be stamped out without destroying the moral substance of responsibility, the foundation on which that world rests.

The uncertainty which haunts social work is nothing more and nothing less than the uncertainty endemic to moral responsibility. It is there to stay forever; it may be neutralized only together with the ethical conscience. As another great moral philosopher of our times, the Aarhus theologian Knud Løgstrup, put it – when it comes to what he calls the 'unspoken command' to care, 'conflict is always possible'. We are doomed to steer uneasily between two extremes, each presenting a danger of its own. On the one hand, Løgstrup warns, 'the situation may be such that I am challenged to oppose the very thing which the other person expects and wishes me to do for him or her, because this alone will serve his or her best interest.' On the other hand, though, 'if it were merely a matter of fulfilling the other person's expectations and granting his or her wishes, our association would mean nothing less than – irresponsibly – making oneself the tool of another person.' 'Simply trying to please one another while always dodging the issue' is one tempting and so common distortion of the moral relationship; having 'definite opinions about how to do things and how others ought to be', and wishing 'that we not be distracted by too much understanding of those who are to be changed' is another. Both distortions are morbid and we should do all we can to avoid them. The point is, however, that the possibility of slipping into one or the other of the traps will always be with us: the dangers are endemic to all moral relationships – our responsibility is firmly placed in the frame fixed by these two dangers. If the demand for responsibility and care 'could be spelled out in detail', as – tired of perpetual uncertainty – we so often dream, 'the demand would be purely an external matter' 'without any responsibility on our part, without any investment of our own humanity, imagination, or insight'. 'Absolute certainty', concludes Løgstrup, 'is the same as absolute irresponsibility.' 'No one is more thoughtless than he who makes a point of applying and realizing previously issued directives.'

All this is bad news for the seekers of peace and tranquillity. Being one's brother's keeper is a life sentence of hard labour and moral anxiety, which no amount of trying would ever be able to put to rest. But this is good news for the moral person: it is precisely in the situations social workers are in daily, in situations of difficult choices, of choices without guarantee and without an authoritative reassurance of propriety, that the responsibility for the Other, that foundation of all morality, comes into its own.

Let me sum up the message which, I think, needs to be pondered when we commemorate the pioneers of social work in the Netherlands. The future of social work and, more generally, of the welfare state does not depend today on sharpening up, narrowing down and better focusing the rules, the classifications, the procedure; nor on reducing the variety and complexity of human needs and problems. It depends, instead, on the ethical standards of the society we all inhabit. It is those ethical standards which, much more than the rationality and diligence of social workers, are today in crisis and under threat.

The future of the welfare state, one of the greatest gains of humanity and achievements of civilized society, lies on the front-line of the ethical crusade. That crusade might be lost – all wars involve the risk of defeat. Without it, however, no effort stands a chance of success. Rational arguments won't help; there is, let us be frank, no 'good reason' why we should be our brothers' keepers, why we should care, why we should be moral – and in a utility-oriented society the useless and functionless poor and indolent cannot count on rational proofs of their right to happiness. Yes, let us admit it – there is nothing 'reasonable' about taking responsibility, about caring and being moral. Morality has only itself to support it: it is *better* to care than to wash one's hands, better to be solidary with the unhappiness of the other than indifferent, and altogether better to be moral, even if this does not make people wealthier and companies more profitable.

It is a hundred-year-old decision to take responsibility for our responsibility, a decision to measure the quality of a society by the quality of its ethical standards, that we celebrate today.

6

United in difference

Many a distinctive mark of contemporary living contributes to an overwhelming feeling of *uncertainty*: to a view of the future of the 'world as such', *and* the future of the private world, the 'world within reach', as essentially undecidable, uncontrollable and hence *frightening*; and to a suspicion that the present, already familiar frames of action will not remain constant long enough to allow a correct calculation of the effects of one's actions... We live today, to borrow an expression coined by Marcus Doel and David Clarke, in an atmosphere of *ambient fear*.

Let me name just a few of the many factors responsible for that feeling of uncertainty.

(1) 'Order matters most when it is lost or in the process of being lost.' So James Der Derian reminds us, and then he explains *why* it matters so much *today* – by quoting George Bush's declaration, after the collapse of the Soviet empire, that the new enemy is *uncertainty, unpredictability and instability*. We may add that in our modern times order came to be identified, for all practical intents and purposes, with *control and administration*, which in their turn came to mean an established code of practice and the ability to enforce obedience to the code. In other words, the idea of order related not so much to the things themselves, as to the ways of managing them; to the *capacity* of *ordering*, rather than to any immanent quality of things as they happened to be at that moment.

What George Bush must have meant was not so much the dissipation of the 'order of things', as the disappearance of the means and the know-how needed to *put things in order* and keep them there.

After half a century of neat divisions and clear purposes a world came that was devoid of visible structure, and any – however sinister – logic. The power bloc politics which dominated the world not so long ago was frightening because of the horrifying things the world powers could do. Whatever it is that has come to replace it frightens by its lack of consistency and direction, and its ever more obvious incapacity to do anything, to mitigate poverty, prevent genocide or curb violence. Hans Magnus Erzensberger of Germany fears the impending era of the civil war (he has counted about forty such wars being waged – from Bosnia through Afghanistan to Bougainville). In France, Alain Minc writes of the coming of the New Dark Ages. In Britain, Norman Stone asks whether we are not back in the medieval world of beggars, plagues, conflagrations and superstitions. Whether this is or is not the tendency of our time remains, of course, an open question – but what truly matters now is that auguries like these can be publicly made from the most prestigious sites of contemporary intellectual life, listened to, pondered and debated.

Today twenty or so wealthy, but troubled, worried and confidence-lacking countries confront a rest of the world which is no longer inclined to look up to their definitions of progress and happiness, yet grows by the day ever more dependent on them for preserving whatever happiness or merely survival it can scrape together by its own means. The former civilizational centre appears ever more often in the role not of a pacifying or policing force, but of a supplier of the weapons needed to conduct tribal wars in the innumerable Afghanistans, Senegals, Rwandas and Sierra Leones of the globe. Perhaps the concept of a 'secondary barbarization' best sums up the overall impact of the present-day metropolises on the world periphery.

(2) Then there is the universal deregulation – the unqualified priority awarded to the irrationality and moral blindness of market competition, the unbound freedom granted to capital and finance at the expense of all other freedoms, the tearing up of societally maintained safety nets, and the neglect of all but economic considerations, all these gave a new push to the relentless

process of polarization both inside and between societies. Inequality – intercontinental, interstate and, most seminally, intrasocietal – is once more reaching a scale such as yesterday's world, confident of its ability to self-regulate and to self-correct, seemed to have left behind once and for all. By cautious and, if anything, conservative calculations, rich Europe counts among its citizens about 3 million homeless, 20 million people evicted from the labour market, 30 million living below the poverty line. The ever more explicit surrender of their traditional duties by nation-states, switching from the project of national community as the guardian of the universal right to a decent and dignified life, and endorsing instead the promotion of the market as a sufficient guarantee of a universal chance for self-enrichment, deepens further the suffering of the new poor – adding insult to their injury, glossing poverty with humiliation and with a denial of consumer freedom, now identified with humanity.

The present-day wealth of the top 358 'global billionaires' equals the combined riches of 2.3 billion of the poorest people (45 per cent of the world's population). Global finance, global trade and the global information industry depend for their liberty of movement and for their unconstrained freedom to pursue their ends on the political fragmentation of the world scene. Global capital, one may say, has developed a vested interest in 'weak states' – that is, in such states as are *weak* but nevertheless remain *states*. Deliberately or subconsciously, such interstate institutions as there are exert coordinated pressures on all member or dependent states to systematically destroy everything which could slow down the free movement of capital and limit market liberty. Throwing wide open the gates and abandoning any thought of an autonomous economic policy is the preliminary condition of eligibility for financial assistance from world banks and monetary funds. Weak states are precisely what the New World Order, which looks suspiciously like the new world *disorder*, needs to sustain and reproduce itself. Weak states can be easily reduced to the (useful) role of local police precincts, securing the modicum of order required for the conduct of business, but not needing to be feared as an effective brake on global companies' freedom.

The psychological effects of all this reach far beyond the swelling ranks of the people already dispossessed and redundant. Only a few people among us can be really sure that their homes, however solid and prosperous they may seem today, are not haunted by the spectre of tomorrow's downfall. No jobs are guaranteed, no positions are foolproof, no skills are of lasting utility; experience and know-how turn into liabilities as soon as they become assets, while seductive careers all too often prove to be suicide tracks. In their present rendering, human rights do not entail the acquisition of a right to a job, however well performed, or – more generally – the right to care and consideration on account of past merits. Livelihood, social position, acknowledgement of usefulness and entitlement to self-dignity may all vanish together, overnight and without notice.

(3)   The other safety nets, of the self-woven and self-maintained kind – these second lines of trenches once offered by the neighbourhood or the family, where one could withdraw to heal the bruises left by the marketplace skirmishes – have fallen apart, or have been considerably weakened. The changing pragmatics of interpersonal relations (the new style of 'life politics', as described with great conviction by Anthony Giddens), now permeated by the spirit of consumerism and casting the Other as the potential source of pleasurable experience, is partly to blame: whatever else the new pragmatics is good at, it cannot generate lasting bonds, and most certainly not the bonds which are *presumed* to be lasting and *treated* as such. The bonds it does generate have inbuilt until-further-notice and withdrawal-at-will clauses and promise neither the granting nor the acquisition of rights and obligations.

The slow yet relentless dissipation and forgetting of social skills bear another part of the blame. What used to be put together and kept together by people's own skills and with the use of indigenous resources tends to be mediated now by technologically produced tools purchasable at the market. In the absence of such tools, partnerships and groups disintegrate, even if they had the chance to emerge in the first place. Not just the satisfaction of individual needs, but the presence and resilience of teams and collectivities become to an ever greater extent market-dependent, and so duly reflect the capriciousness and unpredictability of the marketplace.

(4)   As David Bennett recently observed, 'radical uncertainty about the material and social worlds we inhabit and our modes of political agency within them...is what the image-industry

offers us . . .' Indeed, the message conveyed today with great power of persuasion by the most effective cultural media, the message easily read out by its recipients against the background of their own experience, is a message of the essential indeterminacy and softness of the world: in this world, everything may happen and everything can be done, but nothing can be done once and for all – and whatever it is that happens comes unannounced and goes away without notice. In this world, human bonds are split into successive encounters, identities into successively worn masks, life history into a series of episodes that last only in the equally ephemeral memory. Nothing can be known for sure, and what is known can be known in different ways – one way of knowing being as good or as bad (and certainly as volatile and precarious) as any other. Betting is now the rule where once certainty was sought, while risk-taking replaces the stubborn pursuit of goals. And thus there is little in the world which one can consider solid and reliable, nothing reminiscent of a tough canvas into which one could weave one's own life itinerary.

Like everything else, human identities – their self-images – split into collections of snapshots, each one having to conjure up, carry and express its own meaning, more often than not without reference to other snapshots. Instead of constructing one's identity gradually and patiently, as one builds a house – through the slow accretion of ceilings, floors, rooms, connecting passages – a series of 'new beginnings', one experiments with instantly assembled yet easily dismantled shapes, painted one over the other; this is a truly *palimpsest identity*. This is the kind of identity which fits a world in which the art of forgetting is an asset no less, if no more, important than the art of memorizing, in which forgetting rather than learning is the condition of continuous fitness, in which ever new things and people enter and exit the field of vision of the stationary camera of attention, and where the memory itself is like video-tape, always ready to be wiped clean in order to admit new images.

These are some, though certainly not all, of the dimensions of postmodern uncertainty. Living under conditions of overwhelming, perpetual and self-perpetuating uncertainty is an unnerving experience; one shivers in front of the endless possibilities as one hesitates when facing choice; one trembles at the thought that the sensible reasons of today may prove costly mistakes tomorrow; one does not know any more what the future may bring, and even less how to force it to deliver what one wishes it to offer. Uncertainty, hesitation, lack of control – all result in anxiety. This anxiety is the price paid for new individual freedoms and new responsibility. However enjoyable such freedoms may be in other respects, many people find the price too high to be paid gladly. They would rather opt for a world less complex and so less frightening; for a world in which choices are simple, rewards for good choices assured and the signs of a good choice clear and unmistakable. For a world in which one knows what to do to be in the right. A world which hides no mysteries and does not take one by surprise. For many people cast into freedom without being asked, the offer of a 'great simplification' is one they find tempting and difficult to refuse.

But there is little chance of things getting transparent and simple for us, the residents of modern cities. Since the beginning of modern times cities have been gatherings of anonymous crowds, meeting places of strangers – genuine 'universal otherhoods', as Benjamin Nelson called them. Strangers mean a lack of clarity: one cannot be sure what they will do, how they would respond to one's acts; one cannot tell whether they are friends or enemies – and so one cannot help but view them with suspicion. If they stay in the same place for a long time, one can establish certain rules of cohabitation which mitigate the fear: strangers – the 'aliens', the people 'not like us' – can be confined to their own quarters, so one can go around them and avoid them; they can be assigned to certain jobs and services, to be used only at clearly defined times and places; and they can be otherwise held separate, at a safe distance from the flow of normal, daily life. This 'normalization' or 'ritualization' of the alien presence, practised with some success in all modern cities, would not help much, however, in our present era of great migrations, of a genuine *Völkerwanderung*. Strangers come in such numbers that one can hardly assign them to marginal places and functions; their presence is much too fresh to allow for any degree of habituation and ritualization; in an increasingly 'deregulated' world, one cannot hope to confine them to any particular places and tasks, or hold them at a distance; one cannot even force them to obey local custom, since – unlike the ethnic or cultural strangers of the past – they are proud of their own traditions and customs and do not genuflect to the habits and fads and prejudices of their hosts as unambiguously superior to their own. No wonder that the fears and anxieties of postmodern men and women tend to focus on those 'new strangers'. It stands to reason, does it not? Before the cities were flooded by those strange, insubordinate and cheeky people, life used to be simpler and not as nerve-wracking an affair as it is today...

This is a general picture; but the city today is anything but a uniform, homogeneous space. It is, rather, an aggregate of qualitatively distinct areas whose attractions are highly selective, each area being distinguished not only by the type of its permanent dwellers but also by the type of incidental strangers likely to visit it or pass through. The borderlines between the areas are sometimes clearly drawn and guarded, but much more often blurred or poorly signposted; in most cases they are contested and in need of constant realignment through borderline skirmishes and reconnaissance forays. Under these circumstances, the odiousness, the 'nuisance power' of strangers is a matter of degree; it is experienced with different intensities in different quarters of the city and by different categories of city residents. In the city, one person's home ground is another person's hostile environment. This is the case because freedom of movement within the city has become today, one may say, the principal *stratifying* factor. A position in the social hierarchy of the city may best be measured by the degree to which confinement to a single area may be avoided (or not), and whether the 'no go' areas may or may not be ignored or securely bypassed.

In other words, city dwellers are stratified according to the degree to which they can *ignore* the presence of strangers and defuse the dangers that presence portends. The point is that the resources necessary to do just that are unevenly distributed among city dwellers. Many residents of the contemporary city are left without a feasible 'avoidance strategy' and more often than not must confine their map of livable (or, indeed, 'public' – freely accessible) space to a strictly circumscribed 'ghettoized' area. They can, at best, try to keep the rest of the city's inhabitants off-limits. The famous 'no go areas' look different depending on from which side one looks at them: for those lucky enough to circulate outside they are 'no *go in* areas', but for the insiders 'no go' means 'no going out'. The rest of the city dwellers, who enjoy the freedom to bypass areas they do not wish to visit, can with a bit of care eliminate the ghetto-dwellers from the inventory of strangers they are likely to encounter. The network of inner-city motorways, thoroughfares and throughways, and of course the secure fortresses of burglar-proof private cars with reinforced glass and anti-theft locks, allow them to stay away from the spaces where such strangers are likely to be met. Much of the bewildering 'messiness' of the strangers-infested city is for them, to all practical intents and purposes, invisible – and has no need of being calculated when their own actions are plotted. To sum up: city life has different meanings for different people – and so does the figure of the stranger and the set of entities to which it refers. Whenever the experience of postmodern city-dwellers is interpreted, one should keep in mind that the double freedom to *move everywhere* and to *ignore selectively* is its baseline condition.

Different experiences give birth to different worldviews and different life strategies. As long as the freedom of mobility and the 'avoidance power' are maintained, the presence of strangers neither constrains, irritates nor confuses, while the chances of variegated, exciting experiences which that presence offers may be welcomed and enjoyed. In this condition, the sweet fruits of freedom of choice can be gathered and tasted in full. 'Transgression of borders' may be a tremendous pleasure, providing one can do that at will while barring the others from doing the same... As Jonathan Freedman suggests in his profound reassessment of the currently fashionable 'cultural hybridization' theories, 'Mixed culture is a product of identifications from above/outside the lives of those whose existences are so ordered. And as this outside/above is a social position, the question of class becomes crucial in understanding just what is going on.' He sums up: 'The logic that develops in underclass neighbourhoods is likely to be of a different nature than those that develop among the highly educated world travellers of the culture industries.' The 'hybridity' experienced by the elite 'is quite opposed to the balkanisation and tribalisation experienced at the bottom of the system'.

Let me repeat. For some residents of the modern city, secure in their burglar-proof homes in leafy suburbs, in their fortified offices in the heavily policed business centres, with cars full of security gadgets to take them from homes to offices and back – the 'stranger' is as pleasurable as the surfing beach, and not at all threatening. The strangers run restaurants promising unusual, exciting experiences to the taste-buds, sell curious-looking, mysterious objects fit to be talking points at the next party, offer services other people would not stoop or deign to offer, dangle morsels of wisdom refreshingly different from the routine and boring. The strangers are people you pay for the services they rendered and for the right to terminate their services once they no longer bring pleasure. At no point do the strangers compromise the freedom of the consumer of their services. As the tourist, the patron, the client, the consumer of services is always in charge: she or he demands, sets the rules, and above all decides when the encounter starts and when it ends. In that life, the strangers are purveyors of pleasures. Their presence is a break in the tedium. One should thank God that they are here. So what is all that uproar and outcry for?

The uproar and the outcry come, let there be no mistake, from other areas of the city, ones which the pleasure-seeking consumers never visit, let alone live in. Those areas are populated by people not able to choose whom they meet and for how long and unable to pay for having their choices respected; by powerless people, who experience the world as a trap, not an adventure park; who are incarcerated in a territory from which there is no exit *for them*, but which *others* may enter or leave at will. Since money, the only tokens for securing freedom of choice which are legal tender in the consumer society, is in short supply or denied to them altogether, they need to resort to the only resources they possess in quantities large enough to impress; they defend the territory under siege (to use Dick Hebdidge's pithy description) through 'rituals, dressing strangely, striking bizarre attitudes, breaking rules, breaking bottles, windows, heads, issuing rhetorical challenges to the law'. They react in a wild, rabid, distraught and flustered fashion to the dangers which are at the same time ubiquitous and intangible. Their enemies – the alien intruders – look so potent and powerful thanks to their own incapacitating weakness; the ostensible resourcefulness and ill-will of the strangers is the reflection of their own powerlessness. It is their own lack of power that crystallizes in their eyes as the awesome might of the strangers. The weak meets and confronts the weak; but both feel like Davids fighting Goliaths.

In his seminal study of contemporary chauvinism and racism, Phil Cohen suggests that all xenophobia, ethnic or racist, all positing of the stranger as an enemy and of an outer boundary and limit to individual or collective sovereignty, has the idealized conception of *secure home* as its sense-giving metaphor. The image of secure home transforms the street, the 'outside of the home', into a terrain fraught with danger; the inhabitants of that outside turn into the carriers of threat – they need to be contained, chased away and kept away: 'the external environment can come to be seen as uniformly undesirable and dangerous, whilst behind the symbolic lace curtains, "personal standards can be maintained". The sense of home shrinks to that space where some sense of inherent "order and decency" can be imposed on that small part of a chaotic world which the subject can directly own and control.' It is that dream of a 'defensible space', a place with secure and effectively guarded borders, a territory well marked and legible, a site cleansed of risk, and particularly of uncalculable risks – which transforms the merely 'unfamiliar people' into 'dangerous elements', if not into downright enemies. And city life, with all the intricate skills, taxing efforts and strenuous vigilance but also considerable resources it calls for, cannot but render those dreams of home ever more intense.

The 'home' of that dream derives its meaning from the oppositions between risk and control, danger and security, combat and peace, episode and perpetuity, fragmentation and the whole. That home, in other words, is the craved-for remedy for the pains and distress of city life, that life of strangers among strangers. The trouble is, though, that the remedy can only be imagined and postulated; in its craved-for shape it is unattainable – much as the vexing features of city life are unavoidable. It is the irreality of the postulated remedy, the yawning gap between the dreamt-of home and every given building of bricks and mortar, every 'watched neighbourhood', that makes the continuous territorial warfare into the only modality of home, and border skirmishes into the only practical means of making the borders, and the home itself, 'real'. The stranger is constantly *ante portas* – at the gate; but it is the presumed ill-will of the stranger, of a stranger conspiring to trespass, to break in and invade, that makes the gate tangible.

I propose that *the specifically postmodern forms of violence arise from the privatization, deregulation and decentralization of identity problems*. The dismantling of the collective, institutionalized and centralized frames of identity-building which is taking place in the postmodern world might have come about by design or by default; it may be welcomed or bewailed. But it certainly has this effect, that – as Peter Wagner recently pointed out – the site from which an intervention on behalf of common interests that override the localized animosities 'could be undertaken, previously held by the state, is seen as non-existent or empty'. What is needed, says Wagner, is a 'communicative process about what it is that various social groups... have in common under current social practices, and to find out whether they have to commonly regulate the impacts of these practices'.

Let us observe, however, that so far this need is seeking anchorage in vain, because of – as Hannah Arendt put it – 'the emptiness of political space'. What Hannah Arendt meant was that in our times there are no longer obvious sites in the *body politic* from which meaningful and effective interventions can be made into the way our collective life is lived. Partial, segmental, task-oriented, time-limited interventions – yes, of these we have no shortage. But more often than not they do not add up to any meaningful totality: like everything else they are fragmentary and discontinuous, quite often clashing with each other – and no one can claim with any degree of self-assurance to know in advance the possible outcome of such clashes. Such human interventions as are undertaken peter out in the intricacies of the opaque and impenetrable 'global disorder', only to rebound later in a form more reminiscent of natural catastrophes than of deliberate human actions. On the other hand, it seems to be obvious that – due to the nature of the choices we confront now – privatized initiatives and deregulated intervention simply won't do; they are, if anything, part of the problem, not its solutions. Evidently, some sort of coordinated and concerted action is imperative. And the name of such action is politics; the promotion of new and badly needed ethics for the new age can only be approached as a *political* issue and task. The void left by the receding nation-state is now being filled by the neo-tribal, postulated or imagined, would-be communities: and if it is not filled by them, then it remains a political void, densely populated by individuals lost in the hubbub of conflicting noises, with a lot of opportunity for violence, and little chance, perhaps none at all, for argument.

Contemporary humanity speaks in many voices and we know now that it will continue to do so for a very long time to come. The central issue of our times is how to reforge that polyphony into harmony and prevent it from degenerating into cacophony. Harmony is not uniformity; it is always an interplay of a number of different motifs, each retaining its separate identity and sustaining the resulting melody through, and thanks to, that identity.

Hannah Arendt saw that capacity for interplay to be the quality of the *polis* – a site where we can meet each other as *equals*, while recognizing our diversity, and taking the preservation of that diversity as the very purpose of our meeting...How can this be achieved (how can *we* achieve it)? *Through making sure that separate identities stop short of exclusivity*, of a refusal to cohabit with other identities; this in turn requires abandoning the tendency to suppress other identities in the name of the self-assertion of one's own, while accepting, on the contrary, that it is precisely the guarding of other identities that maintains the diversity in which one's own uniqueness can thrive. The citizens who used to meet in the public spaces of the *polis* managed by and large to do it quite well. But they met there with the overt intention of discussing public matters, for which they, and they alone, bore responsibility: the things would not be done anywhere else if they did not do them...Whatever 'overlapping consensus' there was, it was their common achievement, not a gift they received – they made and made again that consensus as they met, and talked, and argued. In Jeffrey Weeks's apt phrase, 'humanity is not an essence to be realised, but a pragmatic construction, a perspective, to be developed through the articulation of the variety of individual projects, of differences, which constitute our humanity in the broadest sense.'

'Humanity' enjoys no existential privilege over antagonistic and belligerent tribes. Like them, it is but 'postulated'; like them, it exists but in the future tense; like them, it has but human affection and dedication for its sole bricks and mortar. *And* like them, it needs to have its hands carefully watched – so that those around the table are not cheated, as they used to be so many times before, into mistaking the ad hoc interest of the bank-holder for the sought-after universal rules. Finally, like them, it faces the task of finding *unity in diversity*. An attempt known for being undertaken many times before, but always stronger in its declaration of intent than reliable in its delivery. In the past, up to now, either unity or diversity had to give way. And there is no guarantee of any kind that history won't repeat itself this time. As before, we need to act without victory being assured in advance. By the way, this was always the case. Only now we know that it was, and that it is.

And yet there seems to be a genuine emancipatory chance in that postmodern condition of ours; the chance of laying down arms, suspending border battles waged to keep the stranger away, taking apart the mini-Berlin Walls erected daily and meant to keep people at a distance and to separate. This chance does not lie in a celebration of a born-again ethnicity and in genuine or invented tribal tradition, but in bringing to its conclusion the 'disembedding' work of modernity, through focusing on *the right to choose one's identity as the sole universality of the citizen/human*, on the ultimate, inalienable individual responsibility for the choice – and through unmasking and laying bare the complex state- or tribe-managed mechanisms aimed at depriving the individual of that freedom of choice and that responsibility. The chance of human togetherness depends on the rights of the stranger, not on the question of who – the state or the ad hoc patched-up tribe – is entitled to decide who the strangers are.

When interviewed by Robert Maggiori for *Libération* on 24 November 1994, Jacques Derrida appealed for *rethinking*, rather than *abandoning*, the modern idea of humanism. The 'human right', as we begin to see it today, but above all as we may and ought to see it, is not the product of legislation, but precisely the opposite: it is what sets the limit 'to force, declared laws, political discourses' and to all 'founded' rights (regardless of who has, or demands, or usurps the prerogative to 'found' them authoritatively). 'The human' of traditional humanist philosophy, including the Kantian subject, is – so suggests Derrida – 'still too "fraternal", subliminally virile, familial, ethnic, national, etc.'

That rethinking is a philosophical task. But saving the possibility of emancipation from being stillborn also sets, besides the philosophical, a political task. We have noted that the threatening/frightening potential of the stranger progresses as the freedom of individuals, faced with the duty of self-assertion, declines. We have also noted that the postmodern setting does not so much increase the total volume of individual freedom as redistribute it, in an increasingly polarized fashion: intensifies it among the joyfully and willingly seduced, while tapering it almost beyond existence among the deprived and normatively regulated. With this polarization uncurbed, one can expect the present duality of the socially produced status of strangers to continue unabated. At one pole, strangerhood (and difference in general) will go on being constructed as a source of pleasurable experience and aesthetic satisfaction; at the other, the strangers as a terrifying incarnation of the fragility and uncertainty of the human condition – as a natural effigy for all future ritual burnings of its horrors. And power politics would offer its usual share of opportunities for short-circuiting that duality: to protect their own emancipation-through-seduction, those close to the first pole would seek domination-through-fear over those close to the second pole, and so endorse and sponsor their cottage industry of horrors.

The fear of strangers, tribal militancy and the politics of exclusion all stem from the ongoing polarization of freedom and security. This is the case because for large sections of people that polarization means growing impotence and insecurity that prevent in practice what the new individualism hails in theory and promises, but fails, to deliver: the genuine and radical freedom of self-constitution and self-assertion. It is not merely income and wealth, life expectation and life conditions, but also – and perhaps most seminally – the right to individuality that is being increasingly polarized. And as long as it stays this way, there is little chance of the 'detoxification' of strangers, but ample opportunity for the tribalization of politics, ethnic cleansing and the balkanization of human coexistence.

The Way We Think

7

Critique – privatized and disarmed

What is wrong with the society we live in – said Cornelius Castoriadis – is that it has stopped questioning itself. This is a kind of society which no longer recognizes any alternative to itself and thereby feels absolved from the duty to examine, demonstrate, justify (let alone prove) the validity of its outspoken and tacit assumptions. This society did not suppress critical thought as such, neither did it make its members afraid of voicing it. The opposite is the case: it made the critique of reality, the disaffection with 'what is', both an unavoidable and an obligatory part of every member's life business. We are all engaged in 'life politics' – we are 'reflexive beings' who look closely at every move we take and are seldom satisfied with its results. Somehow, however, that reflexion does not reach far enough to embrace the conditions which connect our moves with their results and decide their outcomes. We are critically predisposed, but our critique is, so to speak, 'toothless', unable to affect the agenda set for our 'life-political' choices. The unprecedented freedom which our society offers its members has arrived, as Leo Strauss warned a long while ago, together with unprecedented impotence.

One sometimes hears the opinion that contemporary society (late modern or postmodern society, or, as Ulrich Beck has recently suggested, the society of 'second modernity') is inhospitable to critique. That opinion seems, however, to miss the nature of the ongoing change by assuming that the meaning of 'hospitality' itself is invariant. The point is, rather, that contemporary society has given 'hospitality to critique' an entirely new sense and invented a way to accommodate critical thought and action while itself remaining immune to the consequences of that accommodation and emerging unaffected and unscathed from the tests and trials of the open-house policy.

One can think of the kind of 'hospitality to critique' characteristic of present-day modern society as having the pattern of a camping site. The place is open to everyone who has their own caravan and money to pay the rent. Guests come and go, none taking much interest in how the site is run, providing that they have been allocated a plot big enough to park the caravan, that the electric sockets and water taps are in good order and that the passengers in nearby caravans do not make too much noise and turn down their portable hi-fi and TV speakers after 10 p.m. Drivers bring their own homes attached to their cars, equipped with all the appliances they need for the short stay. Each driver has his or her own plans and own schedule, and wants from the site managers nothing more than to be left alone and not to be interfered with, promising in exchange not to break the site rules and to pay the rent. They pay and they demand. They tend to be quite adamant in claiming their rights to go their own ways and to demand that the promised services are on offer. On occasion, they may clamour for better service; if they are outspoken, vociferous and resolute enough, they may even obtain it. If they feel they are being short-changed or find that the managers' promises are not kept, campers may complain and demand their due – but it won't occur to them to challenge and renegotiate the managerial philosophy of the site. They may, at the utmost, make a mental note never to use the facilities again and not to recommend using them to their friends. When they leave, following their own itinerary, the site remains much as it was before their arrival – unaffected by past campers and waiting for the next to come – though if certain complaints go on being lodged repeatedly, the services provided may be modified to prevent similar discontents in the future.

As far as 'hospitality to critique' goes, our society follows the pattern of the *camping site* – while at the time 'critical theory' was put into shape by Adorno and Horkheimer it was another model – of a shared household, with its norms and rules, assignment of duties and supervised performance – in which, not without good reason, the idea of critique was inscribed. While hospitable to critique after the fashion of the camping site's hospitality to caravan owners, our society is definitely and resolutely *not* hospitable to critique in the mode which the founders of the critical school assumed and to which they addressed their theory. To put it in a nutshell, we may say that 'consumer-style critique' has come to replace the 'producer-style' one. That fateful shift cannot be explained merely by reference to a change of public mood, a waning of the appetite for social reform, a fading interest in the common good and images of the good society, a fall in the popularity of political engagement or a rising tide of hedonistic and 'me first' sentiments – though all such phenomena are indeed signs of our times. The causes of the shift go deeper; they are rooted in a profound transformation of the public space and, more generally, in the fashion in which modern society works and self-perpetuates.

The kind of modernity which was the target, but also the cognitive frame, of classical critical theory appears in retrospect 'heavy' as against the contemporary 'light' modernity; better still, 'solid' as distinct from 'liquid' or 'liquefied'; condensed as against capillary; finally, *systemic* as distinct from *network-style*.

That was a kind of modernity pregnant with a totalitarian tendency; totalitarian society of compulsory and enforced homogeneity loomed constantly on the horizon as its ultimate destination, ineradicable threat or never fully exorcised spectre. That modernity was the sworn enemy of contingency, variety, ambiguity, waywardness and idiosyncrasy, and was bent on their annihilation; in the last account, it was freedom and autonomy that was expected to be the prime casualty of the crusade. The principal icons of that modernity were the *Fordist factory*, which reduced human activities to simple and routine and by and large predesigned moves, meant to be followed unquestioningly and mechanically without engaging mental faculties while keeping all spontaneity and individual initiative off-limits; *bureaucracy*, akin at least in its innate tendency to Max Weber's ideal model, in which the identities and social bonds of the officials were deposited in the cloakrooms on entry, together with hats, umbrellas and overcoats, so that solely the command and the statute book could guide the actions of the insiders so long as they stayed inside; the *panopticon*, with its watch-towers and residents who could never count on their surveillants having a momentary lapse of vigilance;

the *Big Brother* who never dozes off, always quick and expeditious
to reward the faithful and punish the infidels; and – finally – the
concentration camp (later to be joined in the anti-Pantheon of
modern demons by the *gulag*), the site at which the limits of
human malleability are tested under laboratory conditions, while
all those presumed not to be malleable enough are selected for gas
chambers and Auschwitz crematoria.

   Again in retrospect, we can say that critical theory was aimed at
defusing, neutralizing and best of all turning off the totalitarian
tendency of a society presumed to be contaminated with that
tendency endemically and permanently. Defending human autonomy and the freedom to choose and self-assert was critical theory's principal target. Much as the early Hollywood melodramas
presumed that the moment when the lovers find each other again
and take marriage vows was the end of the drama and the beginning of the blissful 'living happily ever after', early critical theory
saw the wrenching of individual liberty from the iron grip – or
letting the individual out of the iron cage – of a society afflicted
with insatiable totalitarian, homogenizing and uniformizing appe-
tites as the ultimate task of emancipation and the end to human
misery. Critique was to serve that purpose; it need not look beyond
the moment of its attainment.

   George Orwell's *1984* was at its time the canonical inventory of
the fears and apprehensions which haunted modernity in its 'heavy'
stage; once projected upon diagnoses of current troubles and causes
of current sufferings, these fears set the horizons of the emancipatory programmes of the era. Come the real 1984, and Orwell's
vision was expectedly drawn back into public debate and given
once more (perhaps for the last time) a thorough venting. Most
writers, again expectedly, sharpened their pens to pinpoint the truth
and untruth in Orwell's prophecy as tested by the stretch of time
Orwell gave his words to turn into flesh. In our times, when even the
immortality of the greatest monuments of human cultural history is
subject to continuous recycling, as they surface in public attention
on the occasion of anniversaries or retrospective exhibitions, only
to vanish from view and thought again once the exhibitions are
over, the 'Orwell event' was not much different from the treatment
accorded intermittently to the likes of Tutankhamen, Vermeer,
Picasso or Monet. Even so, the brevity of *1984* celebration, the
tepidness and rapid cooling of the interest it aroused and the

speed with which Orwell's *chef d'oeuvre* sank into oblivion once the press hype ended – all that makes one pause and think; this book, after all, served for many decades (and still not that long ago) as the most authoritative catalogue of public fears, forebodings and nightmares; so why only passing interest in its brief flare-up? The only reasonable explanation is that those who discussed the book in 1984 felt lukewarm towards their subject because they no longer recognized their own chagrins and agonies in Orwell's dystopia. The book reappeared fleetingly in public debate, carrying a status plotted somewhere between that of Pliny the Elder's *Historia naturalis* and that of Nostradamus's prophecies.

For many years Orwell's dystopia, much like the sinister potentials of the Enlightenment unravelled by Adorno and Horkheimer, Bentham/Foucault's panopticon, or recurrent signals of a gathering totalitarian tide, came to be identified with the idea of 'modernity'. No wonder that once new fears, quite unlike the horrors of an impending *Gleichschaltung* and loss of freedom, came to the fore and forced their way into public debate, many observers hastened to proclaim the 'end of modernity' (or even, more boldly, the end of history itself – arguing that it had already reached its *telos* and made freedom, at least the type of freedom exemplified by consumer choice, immune to all further threats). And yet, to repeat after Mark Twain, the news of modernity's death is grossly exaggerated: the profusion of its obituaries does not make them any less premature. It seems that the kind of society which has been diagnosed and put on trial by the founders of Critical Theory (or, for that matter, by Orwell's dystopia) was but one of the forms modern society was to take. Its waning does not augur the end of modernity. Nor does it herald the end of human suffering. Least of all does it presage the end of critique as intellectual task and vocation – even less does it render such critique redundant.

The society which enters the twenty-first century is no less 'modern' than the society which entered the twentieth; the most one can say is that it is modern in a somewhat different way. What makes it modern is what sets modernity apart from all other historical forms of human cohabitation: compulsive and obsessive, continuous and unstoppable *modernization*, the overwhelming and endemic urge for creative destruction (or destructive creativity, as the case might be: to 'clear the site' in the name of 'new and improved' design; to 'dismantle', 'cut out', 'phase out', 'downsize' for the sake of greater productivity or competitiveness). As Gotthold Lessing pointed out long ago, at the threshold of modern times we were emancipated from belief in the act of creation, in revelation and eternal condemnation; with such belief out of the way we, the humans, are 'on our own' – which means that there are no limits to improvement and self-improvement other than our own inherited or acquired gifts, nerve, resolve and determination. And whatever is man-made can be man-unmade. Being modern means being unable to stop, let alone to stand still. We move and are bound to keep moving not so much because of the 'delay of gratification', as Max Weber suggested – but due to the *impossibility* of being gratified: the horizon of satisfaction, the end of effort and restful self-congratulation move away faster than the fastest of the runners. Fulfilment is always in the future, and achievements lose their attraction and , satisfying potential once achieved. Being modern means being perpetually ahead of oneself, in a state of constant transgression; it also means having an identity which can exist only as an unfulfilled project. In these respects, there is not much to distinguish between our grandfathers' and our own plights. Two features, nonetheless, make our situation – our form of modernity – novel and different.

The first is the collapse and decline of early modern illusions: namely, that there is an end to the road along which we proceed – a state of perfection to be reached tomorrow, next year or in the next millennium – something like a good society, just society, conflict-free society in any of its visualized forms: a state of steady equilibrium between supply and demand, of the satisfaction of all needs; a state of perfect order, in which everything is allocated to its right place and no place is in doubt; a state of affairs totally transparent, a state of knowing everything there was to know; a state of complete control over the future, free from contingency, contention, ambivalence and unanticipated consequences of human undertakings.

The second seminal change is the deregulation and privatization of modernizing tasks and duties. What used to be seen as a task standing before human reason, seen as the collective endowment and property of the human species, has been fragmented – 'individualized', left to individual guts and stamina – and assigned to individually administered resources. Though the idea of improvement (or the modernization of the status quo) through legislating actions of the society as a whole has not been completely abandoned, the emphasis has shifted decisively towards the self-assertion of the individual. This fateful departure has been reflected in the shift of the ethical/political discourse from the 'just society' to 'human rights': that is, to the right of individuals to stay different and to pick and choose at will their own models of happiness and proper lifestyle.

Instead of big money in governmental coffers, small change in the 'taxpayers' pockets'. The original modernity was top-heavy. The present-day modernity is light at the top at the expense of the middle and bottom layers, to which most of the burden of continuous modernization has been relegated. 'No more salvation by society,' famously proclaimed the spokesman for the new business spirit, Peter Drucker; 'there is no such thing as society,' declared yet more bluntly Margaret Thatcher. Do not look behind your back, or up; look inside, wherever your own cunning, will and power reside. There is no longer a 'Big Brother watching you'; it is now your task to watch Big Brothers and Big Sisters, closely and avidly, in the hope of finding a pattern to follow and guidance for coping with your problems, which, like their problems, need to be coped with individually and only individually. No more great Leaders to tell you what to do and to relieve you from responsibility for the consequences of your doings; in the world of the individuals, there are but other individuals from whom you may draw examples of how to go about your own life business, bearing full responsibility for the consequences of investing your trust in this rather than that example.

We are all individuals now; not by choice, though, but by necessity. We are individuals *de jure* regardless of whether we are or are not individuals *de facto*: self-identification, self-management and self-assertion, and above all self-sufficiency in the performance of all these three tasks, are our duty whether or not we command the resources which the performance of the new duty demands (a duty by default rather than by design: simply, there is no other agency to do the job for us). Many of us have been individualized without truly becoming individuals, and many more yet are haunted by the suspicion that they are not really individuals enough to face up to the consequences of individualization. For most of us – as Ulrich Beck poignantly put it in *Risikogesellschaft* (*Risk Society*) – individualization amounts to 'the experts dumping their contradictions and conflicts at the feet of the individual and leaving him or her with the well-intentioned invitation to judge all of this critically on the

basis of his or her own notions'. As a result, most of us are compelled to seek 'biographic solutions to systemic contradictions'.

The modernizing impulse, in any of its renditions, means a
compulsive critique of reality. The privatization of the impulse
means compulsive *self-critique*: being an individual *de jure*
means having no one to blame for one's own misery, seeking
causes of one's own defeats nowhere except in one's own indolence
and sloth, and looking for no remedies other than trying harder
and harder still. Living daily with the risk of self-reprobation and
self-contempt is not an easy matter. It generates ever greater supplies of the painful feeling of *Unsicherheit*. With eyes focused on
one's own performance and thus diverted from the social space
where the contradictions of individual existence are collectively
produced, men and women are naturally tempted to reduce the
complexity of their predicament. Not that they find 'biographic
solutions' onerous and cumbersome: there are, simply, no 'biographic solutions to systemic contradictions', and so the dearth of
solutions at their disposal needs to be compensated for by imaginary ones. Yet – imaginary or genuine – all 'solutions', to at least
seem sensible and viable, must be in line and on a par with the
'individualization' of tasks and responsibilities. There is therefore
a demand for individual pegs on which frightened individuals can
collectively hang their individual fears, if only for a brief moment.
Our time is auspicious for scapegoats – be they politicians making
a mess of their private lives, criminals swarming out of the mean
streets and rough districts, or 'foreigners in our midst'. Ours is a
time of patented locks, burglar alarms, barbed fences, 'neighbourhood watches' and vigilantes, as well as 'investigative' tabloid
journalists fishing for conspiracies to fill the threateningly empty
public space and for plausible new causes for 'moral panics' to
release the pent-up fear and anger.

There is a wide and growing gap between the plight of the
'individuals *de jure*' and their chances to become 'individuals *de
facto*': to be in control of their fate and take the choices they truly
desire. It is from that abysmal gap that the most poisonous effluvia
contaminating the lives of contemporary individuals emanate. And
that gap cannot be filled by individual efforts alone: not by the
means and resources available within 'life politics'. Bridging that
gap is a matter of politics. We may say that the gap has emerged
and grown precisely because of the emptying of the public space,

and particularly the *agora*, that public/private, intermediary site where 'life politics' meets Politics with a capital 'P': where private problems are translated as public issues and public solutions are sought, negotiated and agreed for private troubles.

The table has been turned; the task of critical theory has been reversed. It used to be the defence of private autonomy from the advancing troops of the public domain, almost wholly subsumed under the rule of the all-powerful, impersonal State and its many bureaucratic tentacles or smaller-scale replicas. It is now the defence of the vanishing public realm, or rather the refurnishing of the public space fast emptying due to desertion on both sides: the exit of the 'interested citizen' and the escape of real power into a territory which, for all the extant democratic institutions are capable of doing, can only be described as outer space.

It is no longer true that the 'public' is set on colonizing the 'private'. The opposite is the case: it is the private that colonizes the public space, squeezing out and chasing away everything which cannot be fully, without residue, translated into the vocabulary of private interests and pursuits. As de Tocqueville observed as much as two centuries ago – the individual is the citizen's worst enemy. Told repeatedly that he or she is the master of his or her own fate, the individual has little reason to accord 'topical relevancy' (Alfred Schütz's term) to anything which resists being engulfed within the self and being dealt with by the self's facilities; but having such a reason and acting upon it is precisely the trademark of the citizen.

For the individual, the public space is not much more than a giant screen on which private worries are projected without, in the course of magnification, ceasing to be private: the public space is where public confession of private secrets and intimacies is made. From the daily guided tours of the public space individuals return reinforced in their *de jure* individuality and reassured that the solitary fashion in which they go about their life business is what other 'individuals like them' do, and – again like them – do with their own measure of stumblings and (hopefully transient) defeats.

As to the power – it sails away from the street and the market-place, from assembly halls and parliaments, local and national governments, and beyond the reach of citizens' control, into the exterritoriality of electronic networks. Its strategic principles are nowadays escape, avoidance, disengagement and invisibility. Attempts to anticipate its moves and predict the unanticipated consequences of its moves (let alone to avert the undesirable among them) have all the practical effectiveness of a League to Prevent the Changes of Weather.

And so the public space is increasingly empty of public issues. It fails to perform its former role of a meeting-and-dialogue place for private troubles and public issues. On the receiving end of the individualizing pressures, individuals have been gradually but consistently stripped of the protective armour of citizenship and had their citizen skills and interests expropriated. As a result, the prospect of the individual-*de-jure* ever turning into the individual-*de-facto* (that is, one who commands the resources indispensable for genuine self-determination) becomes ever more remote.

The 'individual *de jure*' cannot turn into the 'individual *de facto*' without first turning into the *citizen*. There are no autonomous individuals without an autonomous society, and the autonomy of society requires deliberate and deliberated self-constitution, which may only be a shared accomplishment of its members. 'Society' has always stood in an ambiguous relation to individual autonomy: it has been, simultaneously, its enemy and its *sine qua non* condition. But the relative proportions of threats and chances in what is bound to remain an ambivalent relationship have radically changed in the course of modern history. Less than an enemy, society is the condition individuals strongly need yet badly miss in their vain and frustrating struggle to reforge their *de jure* status into a genuine autonomy and capacity for self-assertion.

This is, in the broadest of outlines, the predicament setting the present-day tasks of critical theory – and social critique in general. They boil down to once more tying together what the combination of formal individualization and the divorce between power and politics have torn asunder. In other words, to redesigning and repopulating the now largely vacant *agora* – the site of meeting, debate and negotiation between the individual and the common, private and public good. If the old objective of critical theory – human emancipation – means anything today, it means to reconnect the two edges of the abyss which has opened between the reality of the 'individual *de jure*' and the prospects of the 'individual *de facto*'. And individuals who have relearned the forgotten citizen skills and reappropriated the lost citizen tools are the only builders who are up to the task of this particular bridge-making.

8

Progress: the same and different

The town hall of Leeds, the city in which I have spent the last thirty years, is a majestic monument to the ambitions and matching self-confidence of the captains of the industrial revolution. Built in the middle of the nineteenth century, grand and opulent, architecturally a mixture of the Parthenon and a pharaoh's temple, it contains as its centrepiece a huge assembly hall designed for the burghers to meet regularly to discuss and decide further steps on the road to the city's and the British Empire's greater glory. Under the ceiling of the assembly hall, in gold and purple letters, the rules binding anyone joining that road are spelled out. Among the sacrosanct principles of homespun ethics, like 'Honesty is the best policy', 'Auspicium melioris aevi' or 'Law and order', one precept is striking for its self-assured and uncompromising brevity: 'Forward'. Unlike the contemporary visitor to the town hall, those who composed the code must have had no doubts as to its meaning. They knew the difference between 'forward' and 'backward'. And they felt strong enough to stay on track and stick to the chosen direction.

On 25 May 1916 Henry Ford told the correspondent of the *Chicago Tribune*: 'History is more or less bunk. We don't want tradition. We want to live in the present and the only history that is worth a tinker's damn is the history we make today.' Ford was famous for saying loudly and bluntly what others would think twice before admitting. Progress? Do not think of it as the 'work of history'. It is our work, the work of *us* who live in the *present*. The sole history that counts is one not-yet-made-but-being-made at the moment and bound-to-be-made: that is, the *future* (of which another pragmatic and down-to-earth American, Ambrose Bierce, wrote ten years before, in *The Devil's Dictionary*, that it is 'that period of time in which our affairs prosper, our friends are true and our happiness is assured'). Ford would proclaim triumphantly what Pierre Bourdieu has recently sadly concluded (in *Contre-feu* – *Acts of Resistance*): 'to master the future, one needs a hold on the present.' The person who keeps the present in their grip can be confident of being able to force the future to make their affairs prosper, and for this very reason may ignore the past: that person can truly *make* past history into 'bunk' – nonsense, idle boast, humbug. Or at least give it no more attention than things of such a kind deserve. Progress does not elevate or ennoble history. 'Progress' is a declaration of intent to devalue and cancel it.

This is the point. 'Progress' stands not for any attributes of history but for the *self-confidence of the present*. The deepest, perhaps the sole meaning of progress is the feeling that time is on our side because *we are the ones who make things happen*. All the rest we tend to say about the 'essence' of the idea of progress is an understandable, yet misleading and futile effort to 'ontologize' that feeling. Indeed – is history a march towards better living and more happiness? Were that true, how would we know? We, who say that, did not live in the past, those who lived in the past do not live today – so who is to make the comparison? Whether, as Benjamin/Klee Angel of History, we flee into the future pushed by the horrors of the past, or we hurry into the future pulled by the hope that 'our affairs will prosper', the sole evidence to go by is the play of memory and imagination, and what links them or separates is our self-confidence or its absence. For people confident of their power to change things, 'progress' is an axiom. To people who feel that things fall out of their hands, the idea of progress would not occur and would look laughable if offered. Between the two polar conditions, there is little room for a *sine ira et studio* debate, let alone consensus. Ford would perhaps apply to progress the opinion he expressed on exercise: 'Exercise is bunk. If you are healthy, you don't need it; if you are sick, you won't do it.'

But if self-confidence – the reassuring feeling of 'keeping a hold on the present' – is the sole foundation on which trust in progress rests, then it's no wonder that in our times that trust is bound to be wobbly. The reasons why it should be so are not difficult to find.

First, the conspicuous absence of an *agency* able to 'move the world forward'. The most painful and least answerable question of our late modern or postmodern times is not 'what is to be done' (in order to make the world better or happier), but 'who is going to do it'. In *New World Disorder*, Ken Jowitt announced the collapse of the 'Joshua discourse', which used to shape our thoughts about the world and its prospects until quite recently and which held the world to be 'centrally organized, rigidly bounded, and hysterically concerned with impenetrable boundaries'. In such a world the question of agency could hardly arise: the world of the 'Joshua discourse' was but a conjunction of a powerful agency and the residues/effects of its actions. That image had its epistemological bases in the Fordist factory and the order-designing-and-adminis-tering sovereign state (if not in their reality, at least in their ambition and determination). Both bases are today losing their grip, together with their sovereignty and their ambitions. The jading of the modern state is perhaps felt the more acutely, since it means that the power to do things is taken away from politics – which is meant to decide what things ought to be done. While all the agencies of political life stay put, tied to their localities, power flows and so stays well beyond their reach. Ours is an experience akin to that of passengers in a plane who discover, high in the sky, that the cockpit is empty.

Secondly, it gets less and less clear what it is an agency should do to improve on the shape of the world – in the unlikely event of being powerful enough to do it. The visions of the happy society painted in many colours and by many brushes in the course of the last two centuries all proved to be either unattainable pipe-dreams or – if their arrival was declared – unlivable. Each form of social design was found to produce as much, if not more, misery than happiness. That applies in equal measure to both the principal antagonists – the now defunct Marxism and the now ruling eco-nomic liberalism. As to other serious competitors, the question put by François Lyotard, 'What kind of thought is able to sublate Auschwitz in a general... process towards a universal emancipa-tion', still stays unanswered and will remain so. The time of the 'Joshua discourse' is over: all the visions of a made-to-measure world already painted feel unpalatable, and those not yet painted feel suspicious. We now travel without any idea of a destination to guide us, neither looking for a 'good society' nor hoping ever to arrive at one. Peter Drucker's verdict of 'no more salvation by society' aptly captured the mood of the time.

The modern romance with progress – with life that can be and is to be remade and made ever 'new and improved' – is not over, though, and unlikely to end soon. Modernity knows of no other life but 'made': the life of modern men and women is a task, not a given, and a task ever incomplete and forever calling for more care and effort. The human condition in its 'late modern' or 'postmodern' rendition made that modality of life yet more obtrusive: progress is no longer an interim matter, leading eventually to a state of perfection, that is, a state in which whatever had to be done has been done and no other change is called for – but a perpetual state, the very meaning of 'staying alive'.

If the idea of progress in its present shape looks unfamiliar to the point of wondering whether it is still with us – it is because progress, like so many other parameters of modern life, has been *deregulated* and *privatized*. It is deregulated – since the question of whether a particular 'new' means improvement has been left to be freely contested and is bound to remain contentious even after the choices have been made. And it is privatized – since it is each man and woman on their own who is expected to use, individually, their own wits, resources and industry to lift themselves up to a more satisfactory condition and leave behind whatever aspect of their present condition they may resent.

The issue of the *feasibility* of progress remains, however, very much as it was before deregulation and privatization set in – and exactly as Pierre Bourdieu articulated it: to design the future, a hold on the present is needed. Only now it is the individual's hold on her or his own present which matters. And for many – perhaps most – contemporary individuals, a 'hold on the present' is shaky or blatantly absent. We live in a world of universal flexibility, under conditions of acute and prospectless *Unsicherheit*, penetrating all aspects of individual life – sources of livelihood as much as partnerships of love or commonality of interests, parameters of professional as much as cultural identity, modes of the presentation of self in public as much as patterns of health and fitness, values worth pursuing as much as the ways of pursuing them. Safe havens for trust are few and far between, and most of the time trust remains unanchored.

When *Unsicherheit* becomes permanent and is seen as such, plans for the future become transient and fickle. The less hold one has on the present, the less of the 'future' can be embraced in design – the stretches of time labelled 'future' get shorter, and the timespan of life as a whole is sliced into episodes faced and tackled 'one at a time'. Continuity is no longer a mark of improvement: the cumulative and long-term nature of progress is giving way to the demands addressed to every successive episode separately: the merit of each episode must be revealed and consumed in full before the episode is ended and the next episode started. In a life ruled by the precept of flexibility – life strategies, plans and desires can be but short-term.

The cultural and ethical consequences of that great transformation have not yet started to be explored in earnest and can only be adumbrated.

9

Uses of poverty

Freed from political reins and local constraints, the fast globalizing and increasingly exterritorial economy is known to produce the ever deepening wealth-and-income gaps between the better off and the worse off sections of the world population, and inside every single society. It is also known for laying off ever wider chunks of the population as not just living in poverty, misery and destitution, but also permanently evicted from whatever has been socially recognized as economically rational and socially useful work, and so made economically and socially *redundant*.

According to the most recent report of the United Nations Development Programme,[1] while the global consumption of goods and services was twice as big in 1997 as in 1975 and had multiplied by a factor of six since 1950, 1 billion people 'cannot satisfy even their elementary needs'. Among 4.5 billion of the residents of the 'developing' countries, three in every five are deprived of access to basic infrastructures: a third have no access to drinkable water, a quarter have no accommodation worthy of its name, one-fifth have no use of sanitary and medical services. One in five children spend less than five years in any form of schooling; a similar proportion is permanently undernourished. In seventy to eighty of the hundred or so 'developing' countries the average income per head of population is today lower than ten or even thirty years ago: 120 million people live on less than one dollar a day.

At the same time, in the USA, by far the richest country in the world and the homeland of the world's wealthiest people, 16.5 per cent of the population live in poverty; one-fifth of adult men and women can neither read nor write, while 13 per cent have a life expectancy shorter than sixty years.

On the other hand, the three richest men on the globe have private assets bigger than the combined national product of the forty-eight poorest countries; the fortune of the fifteen richest persons exceeds the total product of the whole of sub-Saharan Africa. According to the report, less than 4 per cent of the personal wealth of the 225 richest people would suffice to offer all the poor of the world access to elementary medical and educational amenities, as well as adequate nutrition.

The effects of growing inter- and intrasocietal polarization of wealth, income and life chances – this undoubtedly most worrying of contemporary tendencies – have been and are widely studied and discussed; though little – except for a few ad hoc, fragmentary and irresolute measures – has been undertaken to roll back these effects, let alone to arrest the tendency. The ongoing story of concern and inaction has been told and retold many times over, with no visible benefit thus far. It is not my intention to repeat the story once more – but to question the cognitive frame and the value-set in which it is as a rule contained; a frame and a set which are a bar to the full comprehension of the gravity of the situation and so also to the search for its feasible alternatives.

The cognitive frame in which the discussion of growing poverty is commonly placed is purely economic (in the dominant sense of 'economy' as primarily the aggregate of money-mediated transactions) – that of the distribution of wealth and income and the access to paid employment. The value-set which informs the choice of relevant data and their interpretation is most often that of pity, compassion and solicitude for the lot of the poor. Occasionally, concern with the safety of social order is also expressed, though – rightly – seldom in full voice, since few sober minds would sense in the plight of the contemporary poor and destitute a tangible threat of rebellion. Neither the cognitive set nor the value-set are wrong in themselves. More precisely – they are wrong not in what they focus on, but in what they gloss over in silence and leave out of sight.

And the facts they suppress are the role played by the new poor in the reproduction and reinforcement of the kind of global order which is the cause of their destitution, but also of the ambient fear making the life of all the rest miserable; and the extent to which the global order depends on that destitution and that ambient fear for its own self-perpetuation. Karl Marx said once – in the times of the up-and-coming, savage and as yet untamed capitalism, still too illiterate to decipher the writings on the wall – that the workers cannot liberate themselves without liberating the rest of society. It could be said now, in the times of capitalism triumphant, with no more heeding of the writings on any wall (or the walls themselves, for that matter), that *the rest of human society cannot be liberated from its ambient fear and impotence unless its poorest part is liberated from its penury.*

To put it in a nutshell: the presence of the large army of the poor and the widely publicized egregiousness of their condition are a countervailing factor of great, perhaps crucial, importance to the extant order. Its importance lies in an offsetting of the otherwise repelling and revolting effects of the consumer's life lived in the shadow of perpetual uncertainty. The more destitute and dehumanized the poor of the world and the poor in the next street are shown and seen to be, the better they play that role in the drama which they did not script and did not audition for.

Once upon a time people were induced to meekly endure their lot, however harsh it might have been, by being shown vividly painted pictures of hell ready to ingest everyone guilty of rebellion. Like all other things otherworldly and eternal, the netherworld meant to achieve a similar effect has now been brought to earth, placed firmly within the confines of earthly life and presented in a form ready for instant consumption. The poor are today the collective 'Other' of the frightened consumers; they are now the 'others' who much more tangibly and with more conviction than those of Sartre's *In Camera* are fully and truly their hell. In one vital respect the poor are what the non-poor rest of the world would dearly like to be (though would not dare to try): free from uncertainty. But the certainty they got in exchange comes in the shape of disease-crime-and-drug-infested mean streets (if they happen to live in Washington DC) or a slow death of malnutrition (if they inhabit the Sudan). The lesson one learns when hearing about the poor is that *certainty is most certainly to be feared more than the detested uncertainty*, and that the punishment for rebellion against the discomforts of daily uncertainty is swift and merciless.

The sight of the poor keeps the non-poor at bay and in step. It thereby perpetuates their life of uncertainty. It prompts them to tolerate or bear resignedly the unstoppable 'flexibilization' of the world and growing precariousness of their condition. The sight incarcerates their imagination and shackles their arms. They do not dare to imagine a different world; they are much too chary to try to change this one. And as long as this is the case, the chances of an autonomous, self-constituting society, of democratic republic and citizenship, are – to say the least – slim and dim.

This is a good enough reason for the political economy of uncertainty to include, as one of its indispensable ingredients, the casting of 'the problem of the poor' as, alternatively, the issue of law and order or the object of humanitarian concern – but nothing else and no more than that. When the first representation is used, the popular condemnation of the poor – depraved rather than deprived – comes as close as conceivable to the burning of popular fear in effigy. When the second representation is deployed, the wrath against the cruelty and callousness of the vagaries of fate can be safely channelled into innocuous carnivals of charity, and the shame of impassivity can be evaporated in short-lived explosions of human solidarity.

Day by day, though, the world poor and the country poor do their silent work in undermining the confidence and resolution of all those still in work and on regular incomes. The link between the poverty of the poor and the surrender of the non-poor has nothing irrational about it. The sight of the destitute is a timely reminder to all sober and sensible beings that even the prosperous life is insecure, and that today's success is not a guarantee against tomorrow's fall. There is a well-founded feeling that the world is increasingly overcrowded; that the sole choice open to the governments of countries is, at best, one between widespread poverty with high unemployment, as in most European countries, and widespread poverty with a little less unemployment, as in the USA. Scholarly research confirms the feeling: there is less and less paid work around. This time round, unemployment looks more sinister than ever before. It does not seem a product of a cyclical 'economic depression'; no more a temporary condensation of misery, to be dissipated and wiped out by the next economic boom. Politicians' promises to settle the issue by a 'return to work' bear an uncanny similarity to Barry Goldwater's apocryphal response to the nuclear threat: 'let us put the wagons in a circle' ... As Jean-Paul Maréchal argues,[2] during the era of 'heavy industrialization' the need to construct huge industrial infrastructures and to build bulky machinery saw to it that more new jobs were regularly created than old ones were destroyed as a result of the annihilation of traditional crafts and skills: but this is, evidently, no longer the case. Until the 1970s the relationship between the growth of productivity and the level of employment was still positive; since then the relation grows more negative by the year. An important threshold seems to have been crossed in the 1970s. Recent figures speak volumes about the reasons to feel insecure in even the most stable and regular of jobs.

The shrinking volume of employment is not, though, the sole reason to feel insecure. Such jobs as are still to be had are no longer fortified against the unpredictable hazards of the future; work is today, one may say, a daily rehearsal of redundancy. The 'political economy of insecurity' has seen to it that the orthodox defences have been dismantled and the troops manning them have been dismantled too. Labour has become 'flexible', which in unadorned speech means that it is easy now for the employer to fire employees at will and without compensation, and that solidary – and effective – trade union action in defence of the wrongly dismissed looks increasingly like a pipe-dream. 'Flexibility' means as well the denial of security: the growing number of available jobs are part-time or fixed term, most contracts are 'rolling' or 'renewable' at intervals frequent enough to prevent the rights to relative stability from acquiring force. 'Flexibility' means also that the old life strategy of investing time and effort in specialist skills in the hope of a steady inflow of interest makes ever less sense – and so, that once most common rational choice of people wishing for the life of security is no longer available.

Livelihood, that rock on which all life projects and aspirations must rest to be feasible – to make sense and to muster energy they need to be fulfilled or at least have a go at being fulfilled – has become wobbly, erratic and unreliable. What the advocates of 'welfare to work' programmes leave out of account is that the function of livelihood is not just to provide day-to-day sustenance for the employees and their dependants, but – no less importantly – to offer the existential security without which neither freedom nor the will to self-assertion are conceivable, and which is the starting point of all autonomy. Work in its present shape cannot offer such security even if it manages time and again to cover the costs of staying alive. The road from welfare to work leads from security to insecurity, or from lesser to greater insecurity. That road being what it is, prompting as many people as possible to take it chimes well with the principles of the political economy of insecurity.

The political economy of uncertainty is the set of 'rules to end all rules' imposed on local political authorities by extra-territorial financial, capital and trade powers. Its principles have found full expression in the ill-famed 'Multilateral Agreement on Investment'; in the constraints it imposed on the governments' freedom to constrain capital's freedom of movement, as well as in the clandestine way in which it was negotiated and the secrecy in which it was kept by common consent of political and economic powers – until discovered and brought to light by a group of investigative journalists. The principles are simple, since they are mostly negative: they are not meant to establish a new order, only to take apart the extant ones; and to prevent the state governments of the day from replacing the dismantled regulations with new ones. The political economy of uncertainty boils down essentially to the prohibition of politically established and guaranteed rules and regulations, and the disarming of the defensive institutions and associations which used to stand in the way of capital and finance becoming truly *sans frontières*. The overall outcome of both measures is the state of permanent and ubiquitous uncertainty which is to replace the rule of coercive law and legitimating formulae as the grounds for obedience (or, rather, warranty for the lack of resistance) to the new, this time suprastate and global, powers.

The political economy of uncertainty is good for business. It makes the orthodox, bulky, unwieldy and costly instruments of discipline redundant – replacing them not so much with the self-control of trained, drilled and disciplined objects, as with the inability of privatized and endemically insecure individuals to act in a concerted way; the kind of inability which is made all the more profound by their disbelief that any such action might be effective and that private grievances might be recast into collective issues, let alone into the shared projects of an alternative order of things. As far as eliciting the passive submission to the rules of the game, or to a game without rules, is concerned, endemic uncertainty from the bottom to the top of the social ladder is a neat and cheap, yet highly efficient substitution for normative regulation, censorship and surveillance. Apart from the margins of the excluded and redundant, who are much too certain of their exclusion and redundancy to be receptive to the policies of uncertainty, panopticons in either the old and heavy or the updated, high-tech and lightweight versions are not needed. Freedom alone, in its consumer market rendition and under the conditions of market-sustained precariousness, can be relied upon completely to elicit all human conduct needed to keep the global economy going.

The truly potent powers of today are essentially exterritorial, while the sites of political action remain local – and so the action is unable to reach the quarters where the limits of sovereignty are drawn and the essential premises of political endeavours are – by design or by default – decided.

This separation of power from politics is often referred to under the name of 'globalization'. As I have pointed out elsewhere,[3] the term 'globalization' has settled in the current discourse in the place occupied throughout the modern era by the term 'universalization' – and it did so mainly because 'globalization' refers to *what is happening to us, rather than – like 'universalization' did – to what we need, or ought, or intend to do*. 'Globalization' signals a 'naturalization' of sorts of the course that world affairs are taking: their staying essentially out of bounds and out of control, acquiring a quasi-elemental, unplanned, unanticipated, spontaneous and contingent character. Just as the user of the world wide web can only select from the choices on offer, and can hardly influence the rules by which the internet operates or expand the range of choices available under these rules – so the individual nation-states cast in the globalized environment have to play the game by its rules, or risk severe retribution, or at best total ineffectiveness for their undertakings, if the rules are ignored.

Once the powers that preside over the growing 'flexibility' of life situations, and so the ever more profound uncertainty saturating the whole course of human lives, have become *de facto* global (or at least suprastate), the preliminary condition of an effective action aimed at mitigating the level of the first two elements of the triad – of insecurity, uncertainty and safety – is raising politics to the level that is as genuinely international as that on which the present-day powers operate. Politics must catch up with power which has cut itself free to roam in the politically uncontrolled space – and for that purpose it must develop instruments allowing it to reach the spaces through which those powers 'flow' (to deploy Manuel Castells's term). Nothing less is needed than an international republican institution on a scale commensurate with the scale of operation of the transnational powers. Or, as Alain Gresh put it recently in an article commemorating the 150th anniversary of the *Communist Manifesto*, what is needed is a 'new internationalism'.[4]

There are few signs to suggest that anything like a new internationalist spirit is indeed emerging. The outbursts of supranational solidarity are notoriously carnival-like, sporadic and short-lived. The media coined the telling-it-all term 'the aid fatigue' to denote the persistent tendency of international solidarity to wear off and evaporate in a matter of days rather than weeks. As Gresh points out, Bosnia was not a late twentieth-century replay of the Spanish War; while in the face of the ongoing wars-of-attrition in Algeria and dozens of other gory civil wars or government-orchestrated massacres of 'aliens', unwelcome tribal or ethnic minorities and infidels, only half-hearted noises are made in conference rooms, but virtually no action is taken on the ground. There are noble exceptions like Amnesty International or Greenpeace – but on the whole the few idealist efforts to break through the wall of indifference muster at best a token or perfunctory support from some state governments (but subterranean or overt hostility from quite a few others), and virtually no popular movement to back the attitude they selflessly promote and exemplify. The activists of Médecins sans Frontières have bitterly complained that their initiative, cast by the media as 'humanitarian action', has been cynically exploited by the powers-that-be to justify their own inactivity in, for instance, Bosnia or Rwanda, and to clear 'by proxy' the consciences of their subjects.

The need for global agencies powerful enough to match the condensed strength of global markets and finance capital is beyond doubt. A moot question, though, is whether the extant political institutions – state governments and state-bound political parties – can transform themselves into, or generate through negotiation, agencies of such a type. It is a moot question since the governments and the parties are necessarily homeward-looking and bound to remain local. Perhaps the associations unbound by such limitations – able to acquire a truly across-the-boundaries character and focus their action on what most pains most of the people most of the time – have better prospects. They stand little chance, though, without the notion of the 'common good' striking its roots in the collectively guaranteed security of the would-be political actors.

Utopia, after all, as Victor Hugo once said, 'is tomorrow's truth'.

10

Education: under, for and in spite of postmodernity

Summing up dozens of years dedicated to the study of the ways of life practised by many and different, far and near societies, Margaret Mead came to the following conclusion:

> The social structure of a society and the way learning is structured – the way it passes from mother to daughter, from father to son, from mother's brother to sister's son, from shaman to novice, from mythological specialists to aspirant specialist – determine far beyond the actual content of the learning both how individuals will learn to think and how the store of learning, the sum total of separate pieces of skill and knowledge...is shared and used.[1]

In this statement Mead did not invoke the concept of 'deutero-learning' or 'learning to learn', forged a quarter of a century earlier by Gregory Bateson, her life companion, yet she clearly pays tribute to Bateson's vision when assigning the primal and decisive role in the process of teaching and learning to the social context and the mode in which the message is conveyed, rather than to the contents of instruction. The contents – the subject-matter of what Bateson calls 'proto-learning' (primary learning or 'first degree learning') – can be seen with a naked eye, monitored and recorded, even designed and planned; but deutero-learning is so to speak a subterranean process, hardly ever consciously noticed and even less frequently monitored by its participants and only loosely related to the ostensible topic of education. It is in the course of deutero-learning, seldom in the conscious control of the appointed or self-proclaimed educators, that the objects of educational action acquire skills incomparably more important for their future life than even the most carefully preselected bits and pieces of knowledge which combine into written or uncontrived curricula. They acquire

> a habit of looking for contexts and sequences of one type rather than another, a habit of 'punctuating' the stream of events to give repetitions of a certain type of meaningful sentence... The states of mind which we call 'free will', instrumental thinking, dominance, passivity, etc., are acquired by a process which we may equate with 'learning to learn'.[2]

Later Bateson would dot the i's and cross the t's, asserting that deutero-learning, that 'learning how to learn', is not only unavoidable, but an indispensable complement of all proto-learning;[3] without deutero-learning, 'first degree learning' would result in a desiccated and ossified mind incapable of assimilating a changed situation, or simply one unthought of in advance. Later still, much later, as a kind of afterthought, Bateson would feel the need to cap the idea of 'second degree learning' with the concept of 'learning of a third degree', 'tertiary learning' – when the subject of education acquires the skills to modify the set of alternatives which they have learned to expect and handle in the course of deutero-learning.

Deutero-learning retains its adaptive value and renders all the service necessary only so long as the learners have good reason to expect that the contingencies they encounter do plot themselves into a certain stable pattern; to put it differently – the usefulness or harmfulness of the habits acquired in the course of deutero-learning depends not so much on the diligence and talents of the learners and the competence and assiduity of their teachers, as on the attributes of the world in which the former pupils are bound to live their lives. In Bateson's view, the first two degrees of learning concord with the nature òf the human species, as it has been formed in the course of evolution, and so they appear in one shape or another in every known culture; third degree learning, however, may have, and often does have, *pathogenic* consequences, resulting in a listless, drifting, *schizophrenic* personality.

One can say about our times, fitted out by now with many names like 'late modernity', 'reflexive modernity', 'sur-modernity' or 'postmodernity', that they elevate to the rank of the *norm* what Bateson in the last years of his life could still view, or rather adumbrate, as *abnormality* – a kind of condition dissonant with the inherited and innate equipment of the human species and, from the point of view of human nature, pathological. Every single orientation point that made the world look solid and favoured logic in selecting life strategies: the jobs, the skills, human partnerships, models of propriety and decorum, visions of health and disease, values thought to be worth pursuing and the proved ways of pursuing them – all these and many more once stable orientation points seem to be in flux. Many games seem to be going on at the same time, and each game changes its rules while being played. These times of ours excel in dismantling frames and liquidizing patterns – all frames and all patterns, at random and without advance warning. Under such circumstances 'tertiary learning' – learning how to break the regularity, how to get free from habits and prevent habitualization, how to rearrange fragmentary experiences into heretofore unfamiliar patterns while treating all patterns as acceptable solely 'until further notice' – far from being a distortion of the educational process and a deviation from its true purpose, acquires a supreme adaptational value and fast becomes central to what is indispensable 'equipment for life'. Postmodern humans are denied the luxury of assuming, with the Shakespearian hero, that 'there is a method in this madness'. If they expect to find a cohesive and coherent structure in the mangle of contingent events, they are in for costly errors and painful frustrations. If the habits acquired in the course of training prompt them to seek such cohesive and coherent structures and make their actions dependent on finding them – they are in real trouble. Postmodern humans must therefore be capable not so much of unearthing a hidden logic in the pile of events or concealed patterns in random collections of colourful spots, but of undoing their mental patterns at short notice and tearing down artful canvases in one sharp move of the mind; briefly – to handle their experience the way a child plays with a kaleidoscope found under the Christmas tree. The life success (and so the *rationality*) of postmodern men and women depends on the speed with which they manage to get rid of old habits, rather than on the quick acquisition of new ones. Best of all not to bother at all with the business of patterning; the kind of habit acquired in 'tertiary learning' is the habit of doing without the habits...

Deutero-learning, as we remember, is only obliquely and in part under the control of the education professionals, the 'people in charge', the composers of curricula and the teachers. And yet conscious control over deutero-learning and its purposeful management seem straightforward and easy when compared with the flow of 'tertiary learning'. Margaret Mead was fully aware of a certain degree of intransigence and unruliness in deutero-learning, but this knowledge did not stop her from considering the phenomenon of education in terms of 'from' 'to' – from mother to daughter, from the master to his apprentices. Whatever it is that is being transmitted in this picture of the educational event has clear labels with the addresses of the sender and the recipient; the division of roles is not in question. What is missing in Margaret Mead's perceptive analysis is a situation in which it is far from clear who acts as the teacher and who acts as the pupil, who owns the knowledge to be transmitted and who is placed at the receiving end of the transmission, and who decides which knowledge needs to be passed over and is worth appropriating. In other words, a situation *devoid of structure*, or another situation with equally confusing consequences – one marked by an *excess of structures*, overlapping and criss-crossing, mutually independent and uncoordinated structures, a situation in which educational processes are anything but neatly separated from the rest of life engagements and intercourses and so no one is truly 'in charge'. Education having been understood since at least the Age of Enlightenment as a tightly structured setting with its supervisors firmly in the saddle and having all the initiative, the ungoverned and in all probability ungovernable setting cannot but give the theorists and the practitioners of education pause and be seen as a cause for worry. A sketchy, yet vivid description of such an educational context, ever more prominent, noticeable and acknowledged by the analysts of our times, was provided a few years ago by Cornelius Castoriadis. Having first observed that 'the democratic society is one huge pedagogical institution, the place of an unstoppable self-education of its citizens', Castoriadis points out, sadly, that 'an exactly opposite situation has now arisen':

City walls, books, spectacles, events educate – yet now they mostly *miseducate* their residents. Compare the lessons, taken by the citizens of Athens (women and slaves included), during the performances of Greek tragedies with the kind of knowledge which is today consumed by the spectator of *Dynasty* or *Perdue de vue*.[4]

I suggest that the overwhelming feeling of crisis experienced by philosophers, theorists and the practitioners of education alike, in a greater or smaller measure, that current version of the 'living at the crossroads' feeling, the feverish search for a new self-definition and, ideally, a new identity as well – these have little to do with the faults, errors or negligence of the professional pedagogues or failures of educational theory, but quite a lot to do with the universal melting of identities, with the deregulation and privatization of the identity-formation processes, the dispersal of authorities, the polyphony of value messages and the ensuing fragmentariness of life which characterize the world we live in – the world I prefer to call 'postmodern' (though, I repeat, I would not mind calling it late, reflexive or sur-modern, or by any other name for that matter, providing we agree on what the name stands for). The postmodern condition has split the one big game of modern times into many little and poorly coordinated games, played havoc with the rules of all the games and shortened sharply the lifespan of any set of rules. Beyond all this slicing and splicing, one can sense the crumbling of time, no longer continuous, cumulative and directional as it seemed a hundred or so years ago; postmodern fragmentary life is lived in *episodic* time, and once the events become episodes they can be plotted into a cohesive historical narrative only posthumously; as long as it is being lived, each episode has only itself to supply all the sense and purpose it needs or is able to muster to keep it on course and to see it through. All in all, the world in which postmodern men and women need to live and to shape their life strategies puts a premium on 'tertiary learning' – a kind of learning which our inherited educational institutions, born and matured in the modern ordering bustle, are ill prepared to handle; and one which educational theory, developed as a reflection on modern ambitions and their institutional embodiments, can only view with a mixture of bewilderment and horror, as a pathological growth or a portent of advancing schizophrenia.

The present educational crisis is first and foremost a crisis of inherited institutions and inherited philosophies. Meant for a different kind of reality, they find it increasingly difficult to absorb, accommodate and hold the changes without a thorough revision of the conceptual frames they deploy, and such a revision, as we know from Thomas Kuhn, is the most overpowering and deadly of all the challenges thought may encounter. Short of designing different frames, philosophical orthodoxy can only set aside and dismiss the rising pile of new phenomena as so many anomalies and deviations.

The postmodern crisis afflicts all established educational institutions from the top to the bottom, yet at each level, given the peculiarity of the assigned tasks and educational briefings, it gives birth to somewhat different misgivings and worries. Let me focus the more detailed analysis that follows on the form in which the present crisis presents itself at one institutional level of education, that of the universities. Such a focus is warranted by the role of educational pace-setter and tune-caller assigned to, claimed and to some extent carried by the universities throughout modern history.

Though the roots of European universities are sunk deep in the Middle Ages, our received idea of the university and its role in society is a *modern creation*. Among many aspects distinguishing modern civilization from other modes of human cohabitation, the marriage between knowledge and power is perhaps the most conspicuous and seminal. Modern power seeks enlightenment and guidance in scholarship, while modern knowledge follows August Comte's succinct yet precise recipe *savoir pour prévoir, prévoir pour pouvoir* – to know in order to have the power to act. And since modern civilization has been all along mostly about acting, about making things different from what they were and about using power to enforce change – the marriage placed the practitioners of knowledge, the discoverers of new truths and disseminators of the old ones, either close to or in competition with the rulers, but in both cases at the very centre of the institutional network and in the top rank of spiritual authority.

The institutional centrality of knowledge and its practitioners was anchored, on the one side, in a state-national reliance on *legitimation* (Max Weber), a *ruling formula* (Gaetano Mosca), or a *central cluster of values* (Talcott Parsons) for the translation of domination into authority and discipline; on the other, in the practice of culture (education, *Bildung*) which was meant to shape individual members of society into *social* beings fit to perform, and willing to abide by, the socially assigned roles. Both anchors were serviced by the universities – the crucial sites where the values instrumental in social integration were generated, and the training ground where the educators meant to disseminate them and translate them into social skills were trained. Both anchors, though, are today afloat. This is why the ostensibly programmatic statement of the *Magna Carta of European Universities*, recently signed in Bologna – that the universities be 'autonomous institutions at the centre of society' – is redolent of nostalgia for a fast disappearing state of affairs, and why the image of the university painted with the brushes of historical memory inclines us to define the present realities as pregnant with crisis. After all, both the autonomy, and the centrality of the universities and the scholarship as such are today in question.

The list of the social/cultural/political transformations which brought about the crisis is long. The most decisive among them, however, are intimately related to the rapid weakening of the orthodox institutional bases/guarantees of the universities' authority.

On the one hand, contemporary nation-states all over the globe and on both sides of the recent global divide have all but abandoned most of the integrative functions which the paradigmatic nation-state claimed in modern times, and ceded them to forces which they do not control and which stay by and large outside the reach of the political process. Having done that, present-day states lose interest in ideological conversion and mobilization, in cultural policy, in the promotion of cultural patterns stamped as superior to other patterns, which because of their inferiority are condemned to extinction. By the same token, they leave the formation of cultural hierarchies (or, indeed, the very question of their feasibility) to the mercy of diffuse and uncoordinated market forces. As a result, the prerogative to distribute and apportion knowledge-generated authority upon the individuals active in the production and dissemination of knowledge – a prerogative once bestowed by the state exclusively on the universities – has also been challenged and successfully contested by other agencies. Reputations are made and unmade by and large outside the walls of universities, with a diminishing role assigned to the once crucial judgement of peers. In shaping hierarchies of influence, notoriety replaced fame, public visibility elbowed out scholarly credentials, and so the process is not so much *controlled*, as *buffeted* by agencies specializing in the management of public attention (Régis Debray speaks of 'mediocracy'; the pun entailed is clearly intentional). It is the media value of the news, rather than the orthodox university standards of scholarly significance, which determines the hierarchy of authority – as unstable and short-lived as the 'news value' of the messages.

On the other hand, with the prospect of cultural universality receding and no longer arousing enthusiasm or dedication, and with cultural plurality having no serious adversaries while enjoying ample institutional support – the monopolistic, or even privileged role of the universities in value creation and selection is now no longer tenable. Universities have to compete on allegedly equal terms with numerous other agencies, many of which are much more skilful in 'getting their message across' and much more in tune with the cravings and fears of contemporary consumers. It is not clear why individuals attracted by the assumed 'enabling' capacity of skills and knowledge, and thus wishing to acquire them, should look for assistance to the universities, rather than to their competitors.

As if this were not a heavy enough blow to the status and prestige of the university, the institutionalized institutions of every degree of learning find the once unquestioned right to decide the canons of professional skill and competence fast slipping out of their hands. At a time when everyone – students, teachers and teachers' teachers alike – has equal access to VDUs connected to the internet, when the latest thoughts of science, duly bowdlerized, trimmed to the curriculum requirements, user-friendly and tamely interactive, are available in every game shop, while access to the latest fads and foibles of scholarship depends on money had, rather than the degree held – who can claim that his or her pretence to instruct the ignorant and to guide the perplexed is his or her *natural* right? It was the opening of the information superhighway that revealed, in retrospect, just how much the claimed, and yet more the genuine, authority of the teachers used to rest on their collectively exercised, exclusive control over the sources of knowledge and the no-appeal-allowed policing of all roads leading to such sources. It has also shown to what extent that authority depended on the unshared right of the teachers to shape the 'logic of learning' – the time sequence in which various bits and pieces of knowledge can and need to be ingested and digested. With those once exclusive properties now deregulated, privatized, floated on the publicity stock exchange and up for grabs, the claim of academia to be the only and the natural seat for those 'in pursuit of higher learning' sounds increasingly hollow to the ears of everybody except those who voice it.

This is not, though, the whole story. The permanent and continuing technological revolution transforms the acquired know-how and learned habits from assets into a handicap, and sharply shortens the lifespan of useful skills, which often lose their utility and 'enabling power' in less time than it takes to acquire them and certify them through a university diploma. Under such circumstances, the ad hoc, short-term professional training administered by employers and oriented directly to prospective jobs, or flexible courses and (quickly updated) teach-yourself kits offered through the market by the extra-university media become more attractive (and, indeed, more reasonable a choice) than a fully fledged university education which is no longer capable of promising, let alone guaranteeing, a lifelong career. The burden of occupational training is shifting gradually yet steadily away from the universities, reflected everywhere in the waning willingness of the state to subsidize them from the public purse. One is inclined to suspect that if the intake of universities is not yet falling sharply, it is to a large extent due to their unanticipated and unbargained-for role as a temporary shelter in a society afflicted by structural unemployment; a device allowing the newcomers to postpone for a few years the moment of truth that arrives when the harsh realities of the labour market need to be faced.

Like all other value-adding monopolies, the monopoly of the institutional 'commodification' of acquired or assumed skills also needs a regulated environment to be effective; but the kind of regulation required here, like the tango, takes two. In the case under discussion, the condition of effectiveness is a relatively stable coordination between job descriptions and skills descriptions, both stable enough to be measured by the average timespan of the 'pursuit of higher education'. In our increasingly 'flexible' and thoroughly deregulated job market this condition is seldom met, and all prospects of arresting the rot, let alone restoring the fast vanishing framework of prospective planning, grow bleaker by the hour. The process of higher learning historically institution-alized by university practice cannot easily adopt the job market pace of flexible experiment, and even less can it accommodate the all-too-apparent normlessness and thus unpredictability of muta-tion which the drifting called flexibility cannot but spawn. Besides, the types of skills required to practise flexible occupations do not on the whole demand long-term and systematic learning. More often than not, they transform a well profiled, logically coherent body of acquired skills and habits from the asset it used to be into the handicap it is now. And this severely dents the commodity value of the degree certificate. The latter may find it difficult to compete with the market value of in-job training, short courses and weekend seminars. The loss of its after-Robbins universal availability and relative cheapness deprived university education of one more – perhaps even the decisive – competitive advantage. With its fast-rising fees and living costs it is not entirely fanciful to suppose that a university education may soon be discovered not to be offering, in market terms, value for money – and may even price itself out of the competition altogether...

In a world characterized by the episodicity and fragmentation of social and individual time, the universities, burdened as they are with a sense of history and linear time, fit ill and must feel ill at ease. Everything the universities have been doing for the last nine hundred years made sense either within the time of *eternity* or the time of *progress*; if modernity got rid of the first, postmodernity put paid to the second. And the episodic time hovering among the two-tiered ruins of eternity and progress proves inhospitable to everything we grew up to treat as the mark of the university, that defined by the *OED* as the 'coming together in pursuit of higher learning'. Inhospitable not just to lifelong academic tenure, but to all those ideas which used to underpin and justify it: that *auspicium melioris aevi*; that experience, like wine, acquires nobility with age; that skills, like houses, are built floor by floor; that reputations can be accumulated like savings and, like savings, yield more interest the longer they are kept.

Régis Debray has pointed out the gradual, yet relentless shifting of the grounds on which academic reputations, public fame and influence are made and unmade.[5] Those grounds used to be the cooperative property of academic peers, but as early as the first half of the twentieth century had been transferred to the administration of the publishing houses. The new owners did not manage their property for long, though; it took just a few dozen years for the property to shift again, this time to the ownership of the mass media. Intellectual authority, says Debray, was once measured solely by the size of the crowd of disciples flocking in from far and wide to hear the master; then also, and in a rising degree, by the number of copies sold and the critical accolade the *oeuvre* received; but both measurements, though not entirely extinct, have been dwarfed now by television time and newspaper space. For intellectual authority, the appropriate version of Descartes's *cogito* would be today: I am talked about, therefore I am.

Let us note that this is not just a story of property changing hands and new controllers taking over. The property itself could not emerge unscathed from the change of management, and the shift in control could not but transform the controlled object beyond recognition. Publishing houses cultivate a kind of intellectual authority quite different from that sprouting on university private plots; and the authority emerging out of the information-processing plants of the mass media bears but a vague resemblance to either of its two predecessors. According to the witty remark of a French journalist – if Émile Zola was allowed to state his case on TV, he would be given just enough time to shout 'J'accuse!' With public attention turning now into the scarcest of commodities, the media have nothing like the amount of time required to cultivate *fame* – what they are good at growing is the fast harvested and fast disposed of crop of *notoriety*. 'Maximal impact and instant obsolescence', as George Steiner put it, has become the most effective technique of its production. Whoever enters the game of notoriety must play by its rules. And the rules do not privilege the intellectual pursuits which once made academics famous and the universities imperious; the relentless, but slow and circumspect search for truth or justice is ill fitted for being conducted under the public gaze, unlikely to attract, let alone to hold, public attention and most certainly not calculated for instant applause. Once notoriety takes over from fame, college dons find themselves in competition with sportsmen, pop stars, lottery winners, terrorists, bank robbers and mass killers – and in this competition they have little, if any, chance of winning.

The very titles of academia and its members to superior prestige and exclusive treatment are being gnawed at at the roots. One of the most resplendent feathers in the modern universities' cap used to be the assumed link between the acquisition of knowledge and moral refinement. Science – so it was believed – was a most potent *humanizing* factor; so was aesthetic discernment, and culture in general; culture ennobles the human person and pacifies human societies. After the scientifically assisted horrors of the twentieth century this faith seems laughably, perhaps even criminally, naive. Rather than entrusting ourselves gratefully to the care of know-ledge-carriers, we are inclined to watch their hands with growing suspicion and fear. The new apprehension found its spectacular expression in Michel Foucault's exceedingly popular hypothesis of the intimate link between the development of scientific discourse and the tightening of all-penetrating surveillance and control; rather than praised for promoting enlightenment, technoscience has been charged with responsibility for the new, refined version of constraint and dependency. The 'mad scientist' bugbear of yester-year is now casting a gigantic shadow on the popular image of science as such. Most recently, and to worldwide acclaim, Ulrich Beck proposed that it is the metastatically and chaotically self-propagating technoscience that stands behind the awesome and terrifying risks that mankind is facing today on a scale never faced before. The equation mark put traditionally between knowledge, civilization, the moral quality of human cohabitation and (social as well as individual) well-being has been brutally effaced; a most crucial argument in the universities' bid for social resources and deference has been thereby made invalid.

This is, roughly, the gist of the present crisis: with virtually all orthodox grounds and justifications of their once elevated position either gone or considerably weakened, universities (at least in the developed and affluent countries – in the 'modernizing' countries they may still play the traditional role of factories supplying a heretofore missing educated elite) face the need to rethink and articulate anew their role in a world that has no use for their traditional services, sets new rules for the game of prestige and influence, and views with growing suspicion the values they stood for.

One obvious strategy is to accept the new rules and play the game accordingly. In practice, this means submission to the stern criteria of the market and measuring the 'social usefulness' of university products by the presence of 'clearing demand', treating the know-how universities may offer as one more commodity that still has to fight for a place on overcrowded supermarket shelves, as one more commodity among other commodities, still to be tested for quality by its merchandising success. Many an academic embraces the new reality with gusto, looking forward to making the university into a business enterprise and spying out an exhilarating opportunity where previously threats were sighted. Particularly in the US, but also to a great extent in Britain and less blatantly in other European countries, the ranks of the university professors praising the salutary effects of market competition for money and positions grow unstoppably. The entitlement of the knowledge-bearers to claim superiority for their explicit judgements over those emerging implicitly from the supply-and-demand game are questioned and disparaged from inside academia. In a desperate attempt to make a virtue out of necessity, or to steal the thunder, the intellectuals collectively downgraded by market competition convert into zealous promoters of market criteria in university life: this or that course or project is good and sound since it stands a good market chance, it sells well – and the sellability ('meeting the demand'; 'satisfying the manpower needs'; 'offering the services industry requires') is to be elevated as the supreme criterion of proper curricula, courses and degrees. Spiritual leadership is a mirage; the task of the intellectuals is to follow the world out there, not to legislate for standards of propriety, truth and good taste.

The opposite strategy, counting no fewer supporters and practitioners, is to burn the bridges: to withdraw from the no-win situation of the market into a fortress built of esoteric language and obscure, impervious theory; to hide behind the secure walls of a competition-free mini-market, if the supermarkets are out of bounds or unpromising. The withdrawal and implosion, rather than outward movement and explosion, may be a viable strategy in a country which, like the United States, is densely populated with academic professionals to the extent of supporting a well-nigh self-sufficient and self-feeding (one is tempted to say incestuous) producing/consuming milieu for products too obscure and nebulous for the wider public exposed to the 'general' market. In such a country, yet only in such a country, there may be no limit to

The Way We Think

the incomprehensibility and social irrelevance beyond which a product would find no clients and, therefore, no publishers or distributors.

Each in its own way, both strategies renounce the traditional role which the universities claimed, were assigned, and have tried to fulfil throughout the modern era. Both spell an end to the 'autonomy' of university activity (note that a splendid isolation from all engagement with the world, preached by the second strategy, is not autonomy but irrelevance) and to the 'centrality' of intellectual work. Both strategies, each in its own way, mean surrender: the first strategy, the acceptance of the subordinated, derivative position of a servant in a hierarchy of relevance shaped and presided over by market forces; the second, the acceptance of social/cultural irrelevance imposed by the unchallenged rule of those forces. Both strategies make the prospect of the *Magna Carta* of the universities becoming anything more than a pious wish look bleak indeed.

The present-day version of the theory of evolution tells us that 'generalistic', that is unchoosy, species have a much greater capacity for survival than species that are splendidly accommodated to a particular ecological niche, and thus environmentally selective and whimsical. It is tempting to say that the universities have fallen victim to their own perfect fit and adjustment; it just happened that what they adjusted to was a different, now vanishing, world. That was a world marked first and foremost by the slow, sluggish by present standards, flow of time. A world in which it took quite a while for skills to become obsolete, for specialisms to be relabelled as blinkers, for bold heresies to turn into retrograde orthodoxies, and all in all for assets to turn into liabilities and for the spade to stop being a spade. Such a world, let me repeat once more, is now vanishing, and the sheer speed of its vanishing is far in excess of the capacity for readjustment and redeployment the universities have acquired over the centuries. Besides, it is not just that the situation in which the universities operate is changing; the most difficult thing to cope with adequately is, so to speak, the 'metachange' – the change in the fashion in which the situation is changing...

The world to which the institution adjusts leaves its imprint on the shape of the institutionalized routine, on the monotony of pattern reproduction. But it also shapes the institution's way of coping with crises, reacting to the change in the environment, articulating problems and seeking solutions. Whenever they are in crisis and well before the nature of the crisis has been fathomed and understood, institutions tend to resort instinctively to their repertory of tried and thus habitualized responses. This is one, the insider's, way of putting it; another, an outsider's, way would be to observe that crises are joint products of the perception of the situation as critical, and proceeding to act in a fashion jarring with what the situation renders possible and/or desirable. What the outsider's perspective reveals therefore is the sad yet all-too-real suicidal tendency of any evolutionary success story. The more successful an institution has been in fighting off certain kinds of crises, the less apt it becomes to react sensibly and effectively to crises of a different and heretofore unexperienced kind. I suppose that if applied to the universities this rather banal rule would go some way towards a better comprehension of their present-day predicament – not a small part of which derives from their institutionalized reluctance or learned incapacity to recognize the present environmental change as an essentially novel event – novel enough to call for a revision of strategic ends and the rules of their pursuits.

I submit that the chance of adjusting to the new postmodern situation, that paradoxical situation which renders a perfect adjustment a liability, lies precisely in that selfsame all-too-often bewailed plurality and multivocality of the present-day collection of 'gatherings for the sake of the pursuit of higher learning' which jar with the legislators' love of cohesion and harmony and which they, the legislators, approach with the kind of disgust and contempt with which one treats public threats and personal offences. It is this multivocality that offers the universities the chance of emerging successfully from the present challenge. It is good luck for the universities that there are so many of them, that there are not two of them exactly alike, and that inside every university there is a mind-boggling variety of departments, schools, styles of thought, styles of conversation and even styles of stylistic concerns. It is good luck for the universities that despite all the efforts of the self-proclaimed saviours, know-betters and well-wishers to prove the contrary, they are not comparable, not measurable by the same yardstick and – most important of all – not speaking in unison. Only such universities have something of value to offer to a multivocal world of uncoordinated needs, self-procreating possibilities and self-multiplying choices. In a world in which no one can (though many do, with consequences ranging from the irrelevant to the disastrous) anticipate the kind of expertise that may be needed tomorrow, the debates that may need mediation and the beliefs that may need interpretation – the recognition of many and varied ways to, and many and varied canons of, higher learning is the condition *sine qua non* of a university system capable of rising to the postmodern challenge.

What has been said here of the universities applies to present-day education as a whole. Coordination (perhaps even pre-ordained harmony) between the effort to 'rationalize' the world and the effort to groom rational beings fit to inhabit it, that underlying assumption of the modern educational project, seems no longer credible. And with the hope of rational control over the social habitat of human life fading, the adaptive value of 'tertiary learning' becomes all the more evident. 'Preparing for life' – that perennial, invariable task of all education – must mean first and foremost cultivating the ability to live daily and at peace with uncertainty and ambivalence, with a variety of standpoints and the absence of unerring and trustworthy authorities; must mean instilling tolerance of difference and the will to respect the right to be different; must mean fortifying critical and self-critical faculties and the courage needed to assume responsibility for one's choices and their consequences; must mean training the capacity for 'changing the frames' and for resisting the temptation to escape from freedom, with the anxiety of indecision it brings alongside the joys of the new and the unexplored.

The point is, though, that such qualities can hardly be developed in full through that aspect of the educational process which lends itself best to the designing and controlling powers of the theorists and professional practitioners of education: through the verbally explicit contents of curricula and vested in what Bateson called 'proto-learning'. One could attach more hope to the 'deutero-learning' aspect of education, which, however, is notoriously less amenable to planning and to comprehensive, all-out control. The qualities in question can be expected to emerge, though, primarily out of the 'tertiary learning' aspect of educational processes, related not to one particular curriculum and the setting of one particular educational event, but precisely to the variety of criss-crossing and competing curricula and events.

In as far as the above observation holds true, educational philosophy and theory[6] face the unfamiliar and challenging task of theorizing a formative process which is not guided from the start by the target form designed in advance; modelling without the model to be arrived at in the end being known or clearly visualized; a process which can at best adumbrate, never enforce, its results and which builds that limitation into its own structure; in short, an open-ended process, concerned more with remaining open-ended than with any specific product, and fearing all premature closure more than it shuns the prospect of staying forever inconclusive.

This is perhaps the greatest challenge which the philosophers of education, together with the rest of their philosophical colleagues, have encountered in the modern history of their discipline.

11

Identity in the globalizing world

'There has been a veritable discursive explosion in recent years around the concept of "identity",' observed Stuart Hall in the introduction to a volume of studies published in 1996.[1] A few years have passed since that observation was made, during which the explosion has triggered an avalanche. No other aspect of contemporary life, it seems, attracts the same amount of attention these days from philosophers, social scientists and psychologists. It is not just that 'identity studies' are fast becoming a thriving industry in their own right; more than that is happening – one may say that 'identity' has now become a prism through which other topical aspects of contemporary life are spotted, grasped and examined. Established issues of social analysis are being rehashed and refurbished to fit the discourse now rotating around the 'identity' axis. For instance, the discussion of justice and equality tends to be conducted in terms of 'recognition', culture is debated in terms of individual, group or categorial difference, creolization and hybridity, while the political process is ever more often theorized around the issues of human rights (that is, the right to a separate identity) and of 'life politics' (that is, identity construction, negotiation and assertion).

I suggest that the spectacular rise of the 'identity discourse' can tell us more about the present-day state of human society than its conceptual and analytical results have told us thus far. And so, rather than composing another 'career report' of contentions and controversies which combine into that discourse, I intend to focus on the tracing of the experiential grounds, and through them the structural roots, of that remarkable shift in intellectual concerns of which the new centrality of the 'identity discourse' is a most salient symptom.

We know from Hegel that the owl of Minerva, the goddess of wisdom, spreads its wings, prudently, at dusk; knowledge, or whatever passes under that name, arrives by the end of the day when the sun has set and things are no longer brightly lit and easily found and handled (long before Hegel coined the tarrying-owl metaphor, Sophocles made clarity of sight into the monopoly of blind Teiresias). Martin Heidegger gave a new twist to Hegel's aphorism in his discussion of the priority of *Zuhandenheit* over *Vorhandenheit* and of the 'catastrophic' origin of the second: good lighting is the true blindness – one does not see what is all-too-visible, one does not note what is 'always there', things are noticed when they disappear or go bust, they must first fall out from the routinely 'given' for the search after their essences to start and the questions about their origin, whereabouts, use or value to be asked. In Arland Ussher's succinct summary, 'The world as world is only revealed to me when things go wrong.'[2] Or, in Vincent Vycinas's rendition,[3] whatever my world consists of is brought to my attention only when it goes missing, or when it suddenly stops behaving as, monotonously, it did before, loses its usefulness or shows itself to be 'unready' for my attempts to use it. It is the awkward and unwieldy, unreliable, resistant and otherwise *frustrating* things that force themselves into our vision, attention and thought.

Let us note that the discovery that things do not keep their shape once and for all and may be different from what they are is an ambiguous experience. Unpredictability breeds anxiety and fear: the world is full of accidents and surprises, one must never let vigilance lapse and should never lay down arms. But the unsteadiness, softness and pliability of things may also trigger ambition and resolve: one can make things better than they are, and need not settle for what there is since no verdict of nature is final, no resistance of reality is unbreakable. One can now dream of a different life – more decent, bearable or enjoyable. And if in addition one has confidence in one's power of thought and in the strength of one's muscles, one can also act on those dreams and perhaps even force them to come true...Alain Peyrefitte has suggested that the remarkable, unprecedented and unique dynamism of our modern capitalist society, all the spectacular advances made by 'Western civilization' over the last two or three centuries, would be unthinkable without such confidence: the triple trust – in oneself,[4] in others, and in the jointly built, durable institutions in which one can confidently inscribe one's long-term plans and actions.

Anxiety and audacity, fear and courage, despair and hope are born together. But the proportion in which they are mixed depends on the resources in one's possession. Owners of foolproof vessels and skilled navigators view the sea as the site of exciting adventure; those condemned to unsound and hazardous dinghies would rather hide behind breakwaters and think of sailing with trepidation. Fears and joys emanating from the instability of things are distributed highly unequally.

Modernity, we may say, specialized in making *zuhanden* things into *vorhanden*. By 'setting the world in motion', it exposed the fragility and unsteadiness of things and threw open the possibility (and the need) of reshaping them. Marx and Engels praised the capitalists, the bourgeois revolutionaries, for 'melting the solids and profaning the sacreds' which had for long centuries cramped human creative powers. Alexis de Tocqueville thought rather that the solids picked for melting in the heat of modernization were already in a state of advanced decomposition and so beyond salvation well before the modern overhaul of nature and society started. Whichever was the case, human nature, once seen as a lasting and not to be revoked legacy of one-off Divine creation, was thrown, together with the rest of Divine creation, into a melting pot. No more was it seen, no more could it be seen, as 'given'. Instead, it turned into a *task*, and a task which every man and woman had no choice but to face up to and perform to the best of their ability. 'Predestination' was replaced with 'life project', fate with vocation – and a 'human nature' into which one was born was replaced with 'identity' which one needs to saw up and make fit.

Philosophers of the Renaissance celebrated the new breathtaking vistas that the 'unfinishedness' of human nature opened up before the resourceful and the bold. 'Men can do all things if they will,' declared Leon Battista Alberti with pride. 'We can become what we will,' announced Pico della Mirandola with joy and relish. Ovid's Proteus – who could turn at will from a young man into a lion, a wild boar or a snake, a stone or a tree – and the chameleon, that grandmaster of instant reincarnation, became the paragons of the newly discovered human virtue of self-constitution and self-assertion.[5] A few decades later Jean-Jacques Rousseau would name *perfectibility* as the sole no-choice attribute with which nature had endowed the human race; he would insist that the capacity of self-transformation is the only 'human essence' and the only trait common to us all.[6] Humans are free to self-create. What they are does not depend on a no-appeal-allowed verdict of Providence, is not a matter of predestination.

Which did not mean necessarily that humans are doomed to float and drift: Proteus may be a symbol of the potency of self-creation, but protean existence is not necessarily the first choice of free human beings. Solids may be melted, but they are melted in order to mould new solids better shaped and better fitted for human happiness than the old ones – but also more solid and so more 'certain' than the old solids managed to be. Melting the solids was to be but the preliminary, site-clearing stage of the modern undertaking to make the world more suitable for human habitation. Designing a new – tough, durable, reliable and trustworthy – setting for human life was to be the second stage, a stage that truly counted since it was to give meaning to the whole enterprise. One order needed to be dismantled so that it could be replaced with another, purpose-built and up to the standards of reason and logic.

As Immanuel Kant insisted, we all – each one of us – are endowed with the faculty of reason, that powerful tool which allows us to compare the options on offer and make our individual choices; but if we use that tool properly, we will all arrive at similar conclusions and will all accept one code of cohabitation which reason tells us is the best. Not all thinkers would be as sanguine as Kant was: not all were sure that each one of us would follow the guidance of reason of their own accord. Perhaps people need to be forced to be free, as Rousseau suspected? Perhaps the newly acquired freedom needs to be used *for* the people rather than *by* people? Perhaps we still need the despots, though ones who are 'enlightened' and so less erratic, more resolute and effective than the despots of yore, to design and fix reason-dictated patterns which would guarantee that people make right and proper uses of their freedom? Both suppositions sounded plausible and both had their enthusiasts, prophets and preachers. The idea of human self-construction and self-assertion carried, as it were, the seeds of democracy mixed with the spores of totalitarianism. The new era of flexible realities and freedom of choice was to be pregnant with unlikely twins: with human rights – but also with what Hannah Arendt called 'totalitarian temptation'.

These comments are on the face of it unrelated to our theme; if I made them here, I did it with the intention of showing that the ostensible unrelatedness is but an illusion, if not a grave mistake. Incompleteness of identity, and particularly the individual responsibility for its completion, are in fact intimately related to all other aspects of the modern condition. However it has been posited in our times and however it presents itself in our reflections, 'identity' is not a 'private matter' and a 'private worry'. That our individuality is socially produced is by now a trivial truth; but the obverse of that truth still needs to be repeated more often: the shape of our sociality, and so of the society we share, depends in its turn on the way in which the task of 'individualization' is framed and responded to.

What the idea of 'individualization' carries is the emancipation of the individual from the ascribed, inherited and inborn determination of his or her social character: a departure rightly seen as a most conspicuous and seminal feature of the modern condition. To put it in a nutshell, 'individualization' consists in transforming human 'identity' from a 'given' into a 'task' – and charging the actors with the responsibility for performing that task and for the consequences (also the side-effects) of their performance; in other words, it consists in establishing a 'de jure' autonomy (though not necessarily a *de facto* one). One's place in society, one's 'social definition', has ceased to be *zuhanden* and become *vorhanden* instead. One's place in society no longer comes as a (wanted or unwanted) gift. (As Jean-Paul Sartre famously put it: it is not enough to be born a bourgeois – one must live one's life as a bourgeois. The same did not need to be said, and could not be said, about princes, knights, serfs or townsmen of the premodern era.) Needing to *become* what one *is* is the feature of modern living (not of 'modern individualization' – that expression being evidently pleonastic; to speak of individualization and of modernity is to speak of the same social condition). Modernity replaces the *determination* of social standing with a compulsive and obligatory *self*-determination.

This, let me repeat, holds for the whole of the modern era: for all periods and for all sectors of society. If so – then why has 'the veritable explosion' of concerns with identity occurred in recent years only? What, if anything, happened that was new to affect a problem as old as modernity itself?

Yes, there is something new in the old problem – and this explains the current alarm about the tasks which past generations seemed to handle routinely in a 'matter-of-fact' way. Within the shared predicament of identity-builders there are significant variations setting successive periods of modern history apart from each other. The 'self-identification' task put before men and women once the stiff frames of estates had been broken in the early modern era boiled down to the challenge of living 'true to kind' ('keeping up with the Joneses'): of actively conforming to the established social types and models of conduct, of imitating, following the pattern, 'acculturating', not falling out of step, not deviating from the norm. The falling apart of 'estates' did not set individuals drifting. 'Estates' came to be replaced by 'classes'.

While the estates were a matter of ascription, class membership entailed a large measure of achievement; classes, unlike the estates, had to be 'joined', and the membership had to be continuously renewed, reconfirmed and documented in day-by-day conduct. In other words, the 'disembedded' individuals were prompted and prodded to deploy their new powers and new right to self-determination in the frantic search for 're-embeddedness'. And there was no shortage of 'beds' waiting and ready to accommodate them. Class allocation, though formed and negotiable rather than inherited or simply 'born into' in the way the *estates*, *Stände* or *états* used to be, tended to become as solid, unalterable and resistant to individual manipulation as the premodern assignment to the estate. Class and gender hung heavily over the individual range of choices; to escape their constraint was not much easier than challenging one's place in the 'divine chain of beings'. If not in theory, then at least for *practical* intents and purposes, class and gender looked uncannily like 'facts of nature' and the task left to most self-assertive individuals was to 'fit in' into the allocated niche through behaving as its established residents did.

This is, precisely, what distinguished the 'individualization' of yore from the form it has taken now, in our own times of 'liquid' modernity, when not just the individual *placements* in society, but the *places* to which the individuals may gain access and in which they may wish to settle are melting fast and can hardly serve as targets for 'life projects'. This new restlessness and fragility of goals affects us all, unskilled and skilled, uneducated and educated, work-shy and hard-working alike. There is little or nothing we can do to 'bind the future' through following diligently the current standards.

As Daniel Cohen has pointed out, 'Qui débute sa carrière chez Microsoft n'a aucune idée de là où il la terminera. La commencer chez Ford ou Renault s'était au contraire la quasi-certitude de la finir au même endroit.'[7] It is not just the individuals who are on the move but also the finishing lines of the tracks they run and the running tracks themselves. 'Disembeddedness' is now an experience which is likely to be repeated an unknown number of times in the course of an individual life since few if any 'beds' for 're-embedding' look solid enough to augur the stability of long occupation. The 'beds' in view look rather like 'musical chairs' of various sizes and styles as well as of changing numbers and mobile positions, forcing men and women to be constantly on the run, promising no rest and none of the satisfaction of 'arriving', none of the comfort of reaching the destination where one can lay down one's arms, relax and stop worrying. There is no prospect of a 'final re-embeddedness' at the end of the road; being on the road has become the permanent way of life of the (now chronically) disembedded individuals.

Writing at the beginning of the twentieth century, Max Weber suggested that 'instrumental rationality' is the main factor regulating human behaviour in the era of modernity – perhaps the only one likely to emerge unscathed from the battle of motivational forces. The matter of ends seemed then to have been settled, and the remaining task of modern men and women was to select the best means to the ends. One could say that uncertainty as to the relative efficiency of means and their availability would be, as long as Weber's proposition held true, the main source of insecurity and anxiety characteristic of modern life. I suggest, though, that whether or not Weber's view was correct at the start of the twentieth century, its truth gradually yet relentlessly evaporated as the century drew to its close. Nowadays, it is not the *means* that are the prime source of insecurity and anxiety.

The twentieth century excelled in the overproduction of means; means have been produced at a constantly accelerating speed, overtaking the known, let alone acutely felt, needs. Abundant means came to seek the ends which they could serve; it was the turn of the solutions to search desperately for not-yet-articulated problems which they could resolve. On the other hand, though, the ends have become ever more diffuse, scattered and uncertain: the most profuse source of anxiety, the great unknown of men's and women's lives. If you look for a short, sharp yet apt and poignant expression of that new predicament in which people tend to find themselves these days, you could do worse than remember a small ad published recently in the 'jobs sought' column of an English daily: 'Have car, can travel; awaiting propositions.'

And so the 'problem of identity', haunting men and women since the advent of modern times, has changed its shape and content. It used to be the kind of problem which pilgrims confront and struggle to resolve: a problem of 'how to get there?' It is now more like a problem with which the vagabonds, people without fixed addresses and *sans papiers*, struggle daily: 'Where could I, or should I, go? And where will this road I've taken bring me?' The task is no longer to muster enough strength and determination to proceed, through trials and errors, triumphs and defeats, along the beaten track stretching ahead. The task is to pick the least risky turn at the nearest crossroads, to change direction before the road ahead gets impassable or before the road scheme has been redesigned, or before the coveted destination is moved else- where or has lost its past glitter. In other words, the quandary tormenting men and women at the turn of the century is not so much how to obtain the identities of their choice and how to have them recognized by people around – but *which* identity to choose and how to keep alert and vigilant so that *another* choice can be made in case the previously chosen identity is with- drawn from the market or stripped of its seductive powers. The main, the most nerve-wracking worry is not how to find a place inside a solid frame of social class or category, and – having found it – how to guard it and avoid eviction; what makes one worry is the suspicion that the hard-won frame will soon be torn apart or melted.

In his by now classic statement of about forty years ago, Erik H. Erikson diagnosed the confusion suffered by the adolescents of that time as 'identity crisis' (a term first coined during the war to describe the condition of some mental patients who 'lost a sense of personal sameness and historical continuity'). 'Identity crisis' in adults, as Erikson put it, is a pathological condition which requires medical intervention; it is also a common yet passing stage in 'normal' personal development, which in all probability will come to its natural end as an adolescent matures. To the question of what the healthy state of a person should be, 'what identity feels like when you become aware of the fact that you do undoubtedly *have* one', Erikson answered: it makes itself felt 'as a *subjective sense* of an *invigorating sameness* and *continuity*'.[8]

Either Erikson's opinion has aged, as opinions usually do, or the 'identity crisis' has become today more than a rare condition of mental patients or a passing condition of adolescence: that 'sameness' and 'continuity' are feelings seldom experienced nowadays either by the young or by adults. Furthermore, they are no longer coveted – and if desired, the dream is as a rule contaminated with sinister premonitions and fears. As the two prominent cultural analysts Zbyszko Melosik and Tomasz Szkudlarek have pointed out,[9] it is a curse of all identity construction that 'I lose my freedom, when I reach the goal; I am not myself, when I become somebody.' And in a kaleidoscopic world of reshuffled values, of moving tracks and melting frames, freedom of manoeuvre rises to the rank of the topmost value – indeed, the *meta* value, condition of access to all other values: past, present and above all those yet to come. Rational conduct in such a world demands that the options, as many as possible, are kept open, and gaining an identity which fits too tightly, an identity that once and for all offers 'sameness' and 'continuity', results in the closing of options or forfeiting them in advance. As Christopher Lasch famously observed, the 'identities' sought these days are such as 'can be adopted and discarded like a change of costume'; if they are 'freely chosen', the choice 'no longer implies commitments and consequences' – and so 'the freedom to choose amounts in practice to an abstention from choice',[10] at least, let me add, from a *binding* choice.

In Grenoble in December 1997, Pierre Bourdieu spoke of 'précarité', which 'est aujourd'hui partout' and 'hante les consciences et les inconscients'. The fragility of all conceivable points of refer-

ence and endemic uncertainty about the future prof
those who have already been hit and all the rest of us
be certain that future blows will pass us by. 'En
l'avenir incertain,' says Bourdieu, 'la précarité in___ ___ ___ ___ toute
anticipation rationnelle et, en particulier, ce minimum de croyance
et d'espérance en l'avenir qu'il faut avoir pour se révolter, surtout
collectivement, contre le présent, même le plus intolérable.' 'Pour
concevoir un projet révolutionnaire, c'est-à-dire une ambition rai-
sonnée de transformer le présent par référence à un avenir projeté,
il faut avoir un minimum de prise sur le présent'[11] – and the grip
on the present, the confidence of being in control of one's destiny,
is what men and women in our type of society most conspicuously
lack. Less and less we hope that by joining forces and standing arm
in arm we may force a change in the rules of the game; perhaps the
risks which make us afraid and the catastrophes which make us
suffer have collective, social origins – but they seem to fall upon
each one of us at random, as individual problems, of the kind that
could be confronted only individually, and repaired, if at all, only
by individual efforts.

There seems to be little point in designing alternative modes of
togetherness, in stretching the imagination to visualize a society
better serving the cause of freedom and security, in drawing blueprints of socially administered justice, if a collective agency capable of making the words flesh is nowhere in sight. Our
dependencies are now truly global, our actions however are, as
before, local. The powers which shape the conditions under which
we confront our problems are beyond the reach of all the agencies
invented by modern democracy in the two centuries of its history;
as Manuel Castells put it – real power, the exterritorial global
power, flows, but politics, confined now as in the past to the
framework of nation-states, stays as before attached to the ground.

A vicious circle, indeed. The fast globalization of the power
network seems to conspire and collaborate with a privatized life
politics; they stimulate, sustain and reinforce each other. If globalization saps the capacity of established political institutions to act
effectively, the massive retreat from the 'body politic' to the narrow concerns of life politics prevents the crystallization of alternative modes of collective action on a par with the globality of the
network of dependencies. Everything seems to be in place to make
both the globalization of life conditions *and* the 'morcellement',

the atomization and privatization of life struggles, self-propelling and self-perpetuating. It is against this background that the logic and the endemic illogicality of contemporary 'identity concerns' and the actions they trigger needs to be scrutinized and understood.

As Ulrich Beck has pointed out, there are no biographical solutions to systemic contradiction – though it is such solutions that we are pressed or cajoled to discover or invent. There can be no rational response to the rising *précarité* of human conditions so long as such a response is to be confined to the individual's action; the irrationality of possible responses is inescapable, given that the scope of life politics and of the network of forces which determine its conditions are, purely and simply, incomparable and widely disproportionate.

If you cannot, or don't believe you can, do what truly matters, you turn to things which matter less or perhaps not at all, but which you can do or believe you can; and by turning your attention and energy to such things, you may even make them matter – for a time at least...'Having no hope', says Christopher Lasch,

> of improving their lives in any of the ways that matter, people have convinced themselves that what matters is psychic self-improvement; getting in touch with their feelings, eating health food, taking lessons in ballet or belly-dancing, immersing themselves in the wisdom of the East, jogging, learning how to 'relate', overcoming the 'fear of pleasure'. Harmless in themselves, these pursuits, elevated to a programme and wrapped in the rhetoric of authenticity and awareness, signify a retreat from politics...'[12]

There is a wide and widening spectrum of 'substitute pastimes', symptomatic of the shift from things that matter but about which nothing can be done to things that matter less or do not matter, but which can be dealt with and handled. Compulsive shopping figures prominently among them. Mikhail Bakhtin's 'carnivals' used to be celebrated inside the home territory where 'routine life' was at other times conducted, and so allowed to lay bare the normally hidden alternatives which daily life contained. Unlike them, the trips to the shopping malls are expeditions to *another world* starkly different from the rest of daily life, to that 'elsewhere' where one can experience briefly that self-confidence and 'authenticity' which one is seeking in vain in routine daily pursuits. Shopping expeditions fill the void left by the travels no longer undertaken by the imagination to an alternative, more secure, humane and just society.

The time-and-effort-consuming activity of putting together, dismantling and rearranging self-identity is another of the 'substitute pastimes'. That activity is, as we have already seen, conducted under conditions of acute insecurity: the targets of action are as precarious as its effects are uncertain. Efforts lead to frustration often enough for the fear of ultimate failure to poison the joy of temporary triumphs. No wonder that to dissolve personal fears in the 'might of numbers', to try to make them inaudible in the hubbub of a boisterous crowd, is a constant temptation which many a lonely 'identity-builder' finds it difficult to resist. Even stronger is the temptation to pretend that it is the similarity of individual fears that 'makes a community' and so one can make company out of solitude.

As Eric Hobsbawm recently observed, 'never was the word "community" used more indiscriminately and emptily than in the decades when communities in the sociological sense became hard to find in real life';[13] 'Men and women look for groups to which they can belong, certainly and forever, in a world in which all else is moving and shifting, in which nothing else is certain.'[14] Jock Young supplies a succinct and poignant gloss: 'Just as community collapses, identity is invented.'[15] 'Identity' owes the attention it attracts and the passions it begets to being a *surrogate of community*: of that allegedly 'natural home' which is no longer available in the rapidly privatized and individualized, fast globalizing world, and which for that reason can be safely imagined as a cosy shelter of security and confidence, and as such hotly desired. The paradox, though, is that in order to offer even a modicum of security and so to perform its healing role, identity must belie its origin, must deny being just a surrogate, and best of all needs to conjure up a phantom of the self-same community which it has come to replace. Identity sprouts on the graveyard of communities, but flourishes thanks to its promise to resurrect the dead.

The 'era of identity' is full of sound and fury. The search for identity divides and separates; yet the precariousness of the solitary identity-building prompts the identity-builders to seek pegs on which they can hang together their individually experienced fears and anxieties and perform the exorcism rites in the company of others, similarly afraid and anxious individuals. Whether such 'peg communities' provide what they are hoped to offer – a collective insurance against individually confronted risks – is a moot question; but mounting a barricade in the company of others does supply a momentary respite from loneliness. Effective or not, something has been done, and one can at least console oneself that the blows are not being taken with hands down. As Jonathan Friedman put it, in our globalizing world 'one thing that is not happening is that boundaries are disappearing. Rather, they seem to be erected on every new street corner of every declining neighbourhood of our world.'[16]

Boundaries are not drawn to fence off and protect already existing identities. As the great Norwegian anthropologist Frederick Barth explained – it is exactly the other way round: the ostensibly shared, 'communal' identities are by-products of feverish boundary-drawing. It is only after the border-posts have been dug in that the myths of their antiquity are spun and the fresh cultural/political origins of identity are carefully covered up by the genesis stories. This stratagem attempts to belie the fact that (to quote Stuart Hall again) what the idea of identity does *not* signal is a 'stable core of the self, unfolding from the beginning to end through all the vicissitudes of history without change'.[17]

Perhaps instead of talking about identities, inherited or acquired, it would be more in keeping with the realities of the globalizing world to speak of *identification*, a never-ending, always incomplete, unfinished and open-ended activity in which we all, by necessity or by choice, are engaged. There is little chance that the tensions, confrontations and conflicts which that activity generates will subside. The frantic search for identity is not a residue of preglobalization times which are not yet fully extirpated but bound to become extinct as the globalization progresses; it is, on the contrary, the side-effect and by-product of the combination of globalizing and individualizing pressures and the tensions they spawn. The identification wars are neither contrary to nor stand in the way of the globalizing tendency: they are a legitimate offspring and natural companion of globalization and, far from arresting it, lubricate its wheels.

12

Faith and instant gratification

The ancients already knew the truth. In his dialogue *On Happy Life* Lucius Anneus Seneca pointed out that in stark opposition to the pleasures of virtue, the delights of rapture cool off when at their hottest; their capacity is so small that it fills up to exhaustion in no time. Invigorated but for a fleeting moment, the seekers of sensual pleasure quickly fall into languor and apathy. In other words, their happiness is short-lived and their dreams self-destructive. Seneca warned: the gratification quickest to come is also the one that dies first.

The ancient sage had also guessed what kind of people tend to choose a life dedicated to the search for the pleasures that bring gratification instantly. In another dialogue, on the *Brevity of Life*, he noted that this kind of life was the lot of people who had forgotten the past, did not care about the present, and were afraid of the future.

True observations about the human predicament stay true for a long time. Their truth is not affected by the trials of history. Seneca's insights, no doubt, belong to this category. The endemic frailty of instant gratification, and the close link between the obsession for instant delight, indifference to what has been and distrust of what is to come, tend to be confirmed today just as they were two millennia ago. What has changed are the numbers of people who experience at first hand the misery of living in a flattened and sliced time. What for Seneca seemed to be but a sign of regrettable deviation from the right path – of the way lost and life wasted – has turned into the norm. What used to be a choice of the few is now the fate of the many. In order to understand why this has happened, we could do worse than follow Seneca's hunches.

The title of a paper given in December 1997 by one of the most perceptive social analysts of our times, Pierre Bourdieu, was *Le précarité est aujourd'hui partout*. The title told it all: precariousness – instability, vulnerability – is a widespread (as well as the most painfully felt) feature of contemporary life conditions. The French theorists speak of *précarité*, the German of *Unsicherheit* and *Risikogesellschaft*, the Italians of *incertezza* and the English of *insecurity*. All have in mind the same aspect of the human predicament, experienced all over the highly developed, modernized and well-off part of the globe, and felt there to be especially unnerving and depressing because it is new and in many ways unprecedented: the phenomenon they try to grasp is the combined experience of *insecurity* of position, entitlements and livelihood, of *uncertainty* as to their continuation and future stability, and of *lack of safety* of one's body, one's self and their extensions – possessions, neighbourhood, community. The tendency to forget the past, to care not about the present and to fear the future Seneca deprecated as his contemporaries' personal failings; but we may say today that in our fellow humans' experience, the past does not count for much since it does not offer secure foundations for life's prospects, the present is not given proper care since it is virtually out of control, and there are good reasons to be afraid that the future has in store further unpleasant surprises, trials and tribulations. Nowadays, precariousness is not a matter of choice; it is fate.

To have faith means to have trust in the meaning of life and to expect what one does or desists from doing to be of long-lasting importance. Faith comes easy when life experience confirms that this trust is well founded. Only in a relatively stable world, in which things and acts retain their value over a long period of time, a period commensurate with the length of a human life, is such confirmation likely to be offered. In a logical and consistent world human actions also acquire logic and consistency. Living in such a world, as the eminent ethical philosopher Hans Jonas has put it, we count days and the days count. Our times are hard for faith –

any faith, sacred or secular; for belief in Providence, a Divine Chain of Beings, as much as for belief in a mundane utopia, in a perfect society to come. Our times are inhospitable for trust, and more generally for long-haul purposes and efforts, because of the evident transience and vulnerability of everything (or almost everything) that counts in earthly life.

To start with the preliminary condition of all the rest: a person's livelihood. This has become exceedingly fragile. German economists write of 'zwei-Drittel Gesellschaft' and expect it soon to become an 'ein-Drittel' one, meaning that everything needed to satisfy market demand can now be produced by two-thirds of the population, and soon one-third will be enough – leaving all the other men and women without employment, making them *economically* useless and *socially* redundant. However brave the faces the politicians put on and however audacious their promises, unemployment in the affluent countries has become 'structural': there is simply not enough work for everybody.

How brittle and uncertain the lives of those directly affected have become as a result can be easily imagined. The point is, though, that everybody else is also, if for the time being indirectly, affected. In a world of structural unemployment no one can feel secure. There is no such thing any more as secure jobs in secure companies; nor are there many skills and kinds of experience which, once acquired, would guarantee that a job will be offered, and once offered, will be lasting. No one may reasonably assume they are insured against the next round of 'downsizing', 'streamlining' or 'rationalizing', against erratic shifts of market demand and whimsical yet powerful pressures of 'competitiveness' and 'effectiveness'. 'Flexibility' is the catchword of the day. It augurs jobs without inbuilt security of entitlements: fixed-term or rolling contracts, dismissal without notice or compensation.

No one can feel truly irreplaceable; even the most privileged position may prove to be but temporary and 'until further notice'. And if human beings do not count, neither do the days of their lives. In the absence of long-term security, 'instant gratification' looks enticingly like a reasonable strategy. Whatever life may offer, let it offer it *hic et nunc* – right away. Who knows what tomorrow may bring? Delay of satisfaction has lost its allure: it is, after all, highly uncertain whether the labour and effort invested today will count as assets for as long as it takes to reach reward; it is far from certain, moreover, that the prizes which look attractive today will still be desirable when they at long last come. Assets tend to become liabilities, glittering prizes turn into badges of shame, fashions come and go with mind-boggling speed, all objects of desire become obsolete and off-putting before they have time to be fully enjoyed. Styles of life which are 'chic' today will tomorrow become targets of ridicule.

If this is the case, then to avoid frustration one would do better to refrain from developing habits and attachments or entering into lasting commitments. The objects of desire are better enjoyed on the spot and then disposed of; markets see to it that they are made in such a way that both the gratification and the obsoleteness are instant. Not just the contents of the wardrobe need to be changed every season – cars need to be replaced because their body design has become old-fashioned and hurts the eye, good computers are thrown on the scrapheap because new gadgets have made them out-of-date, splendid and cherished music collections on long-playing records are replaced by cassettes only to be replaced again by CDs simply because new recordings are no longer available in previous forms.

Men and women are thereby trained (made to learn the hard way) to perceive of the world as of a container full of disposable objects, objects for one-off use. The whole world – including other human beings. Every item is replaceable, and had better be replaceable: what if greener grass appears in sight, if better – as yet untried – joys beckon from afar? In a world in which the future is full of dangers, any chance not taken here and now is a chance missed; not taking it is thus unforgivable and cannot be justified. Since present-day commitments stand in the way of the next day's opportunities, the lighter and more superficial they are, the less is the damage. 'Now' is the keyword of life strategy, whatever that strategy may refer to. Through such an insecure and unpredictable world smart and clever wanderers travel light and would shed no tears for anything that cramped their moves.

And so the policy of 'precarization' conducted by the operators of labour markets is aided and abetted by life policies. Both converge on the same result: the fading and wilting, falling apart and decomposing of human bonds, communities and partnerships. Commitments of the 'till death us do part' type become contracts 'until satisfaction fades', temporal by definition and design – and amenable to be broken unilaterally whenever one of the partners sniffs better value in opting out rather than continuing the relationship.

Bonds and partnerships are viewed, in other words, as things to be *consumed*, not produced; they are subject to the same criteria of evaluation as all other objects of consumption. In the consumer market, ostensibly durable products are as a rule offered for a 'trial period', and return of money is promised if the purchaser is less than fully satisfied. If the partner in a partnership is seen in these terms, then it is no longer the task of both partners to 'make the relationship work' – to see it work through thick and thin, to help each other through good and bad patches, to trim if need be one's own preferences, to compromise and make sacrifices for the sake of lasting union. It is instead a matter of obtaining satisfaction from a ready-to-use product; if the pleasure derived is not up to the standard promised and expected, or if the novelty wears off together with the joy, there is no reason to stick to the inferior or aged product rather than find another, 'new and improved', in the shop.

What follows is that the assumed temporariness of partnerships tends to turn into a self-fulfilling prophecy. If the human bond is, like all other consumer objects, not something to be worked out through protracted effort and occasional sacrifice, but something which one expects to bring satisfaction right away, something that one rejects if it does not do that and keeps and uses only as long as (and no longer than) it continues to gratify – then there is not much point in trying hard and harder still, let alone in suffering discomfort and unease in order to save the partnership. Even a minor stumble may cause the partnership to overturn; trifling disagreements turn into bitter conflicts, slight frictions are taken to signal essential incompatibility. As the American sociologist W. I. Thomas would say, if people assume their commitments to be temporary and until further notice, these commitments do tend to become such in consequence of people's own actions.

In these times of uncertainty and precariousness, transience acquires a 'strategic edge' over durability. It is no longer clear what is the cause and what is the effect. Are the fragility and vulnerability of the human condition the summary result of common life policies that do not recognize long-term purposes and values that are hard to earn and preserve? Or is it rather that people tend to prefer short-term satisfactions because little in the world is truly durable and few objectives may be relied on to outlive the effort needed to fulfil them? Both suppositions are partly true and each conveys a part of the truth. A world saturated with uncertainty, and lives sliced into the short-lived episodes required to bring instant gratification, aid and abet, support and reinforce each other.

A crucial part of any faith is the investment of value in something more durable than the evanescent and endemically mortal individual life; something lasting, resistant to the eroding impact of time, perhaps even immortal and eternal. Individual death is unavoidable, but life may be used to negotiate and earn a place in eternity; life may be lived in such a fashion that individual mortality is transcended – that the trace left by life is not completely effaced. Faith may be a spiritual matter, but in order to hold firm it needs mundane anchoring; its fastenings must reach deep into the experience of daily life.

Family served for a long time as one of the principal links connecting mortal beings to immortality: from individual life pursuits to lasting values. Yellowing photographs in family albums, and before that the long lists of birth, wedding and funeral dates in family bibles, testified to the longevity of the family, which individual members should do nothing to jeopardize and everything to make secure. Family albums, though, have now been replaced by camcorders with video-cassettes, and video-tapes differ from photographic paper in being eminently effaceable and meant to be effaced again and again to make room for new, similarly temporary recordings. The substitution of videos for photographs has symbolic significance; it fits the changing status of the family life, which has now become, for a growing number of men and women, an event that does not necessarily last longer than an individual life. Families tend to be made and unmade a number of times during the lifespan of a single individual. The family can hardly serve as a material, solid and reliable bridge to immortality.

However enormous the consequences of this development have been, it is not alone; what happens nowadays to the family mirrors profound changes taking place in the other aspects of the human condition which once upon a time provided bridges leading from individual mortality to durable, even immortal, values. One may say that immortality itself tends to become 'instant'. One can hear the broadcasters of sporting events or pop music festivals announcing, in voices choked with excitement, that they (and the viewers) 'witness history being made'. In its new rendition, immortality is not something to be earned the hard way, through lifelong effort; it is, rather, something to be enjoyed on the spot, without giving much thought to the consequences – without asking how really eternal that instantly relished 'immortality' will prove to be. Artists used to take the greatest care to ensure their murals and canvases were durable, architects used to erect buildings meant to last for centuries to come. Now the favoured art materials are those that brandish and flaunt their perishability; the favourite form of visual art is a 'happening' or installation – patched together as a one-off event, for the duration of an exhibition, and destined to be disassembled the night after the gallery closes. In all fields of culture (including science – concerned allegedly with *eternal* truths) *notoriety* replaces *fame*; and notoriety is, admittedly and unashamedly, the instant version of immortality, oblivious and indifferent to all other versions.

If dedication to lasting values is today in crisis, it is because the very idea of duration, of immortality, is in crisis too. But immortality is in crisis because the basic, daily trust in the durability of things towards which and by which human life may be oriented is undermined by daily human experience. That erosion of trust is, in turn, perpetrated by the endemic precariousness, fragility, insecurity and uncertainty of the human place in human society.

The promotion of competitiveness, and of a 'free for all' pursuit of the highest gain, to the rank of the main (even a monopolistic) criterion to distinguish between proper and improper, right and wrong actions is the factor that bears the ultimate responsibility for the 'ambient fear' which permeates the life of most contemporary men and women, for their widespread, perhaps universally shared, feeling of insecurity. Society no longer guarantees, or even promises, a collective remedy for individual misfortunes. Individuals have been offered (or, rather, have been cast into) freedom of unprecedented proportions – but at the price of similarly unprecedented insecurity. And when there is insecurity, little time is left for caring for values that hover above the level of daily concerns – or, for that matter, for whatever lasts longer than the fleeting moment.

Fragmented life tends to be lived in episodes, in a series of unconnected events. Insecurity is a point at which being breaks down into fragments, and life into episodes. Unless something is done about the haunting spectre of insecurity, the restoration of faith in values that are lasting and durable stands little chance.

The Way We Act

13

Does love need reason?

Love fears reason; reason fears love. Each tries hard to do without the other. But whenever they do, trouble is in store. This is, in its briefest rendition possible, the quandary of love. And of reason.

Their separation spells disaster. But negotiations, if they happen, seldom produce a tolerable *modus vivendi*. Reason and love speak different languages which do not easily translate; verbal exchanges produce more mutual incomprehension and suspicion than true understanding and sympathy. Reason and love do not really converse – more often than not they shout each other down.

Reason is a better talker than love, and so love finds it excruciatingly difficult, nay impossible, to redeem itself in discourse. Verbal duels end as a rule with reason triumphant and love wounded. Argument is not love's forte. Called on to make a case which reason would recognize as valid, love would make sounds which reason would find incoherent; at best it would choose to stay silent. Jonathan Rutherford has composed a concise summary of the long record of love's lost skirmishes: 'Love teeters on the edge of the unknown beyond which it becomes almost impossible to speak. It moves us beyond words.' When pressed to speak of love, we 'fumble for words', but 'the words just buckle and fold and disappear.' 'While I may have everything to say, I say nothing or I say very little.'[1] We all know what love is – until we try to say it loud and clear. Love would not recognize itself in words: words seem to be reason's property and a foreign and hostile territory for love.

As a defendant at the tribunal of reason, love is bound to lose its case. The case was lost before the trial started. Like the hero of Kafka's *Trial*, love is guilty of being accused; and if one may acquit oneself of the crimes one has been accused of committing, there is no defence against the charge of standing accused. This kind of guilt does not derive from 'the facts of the matter', but depends on who is in charge of the courts, who has the right to pass judgment and who must surrender to the verdicts. When reason sits in judgment, writes the rules of the judicial procedure and appoints the judges, love is guilty even before the prosecutor has risen to make his case.

And yet, as Blaise Pascal famously observed, 'le coeur a ses raisons.' The emphasis in this phrase, as Max Scheler pointed out, falls on two words: 'ses' and 'raisons'. 'The heart has *its* reasons, "its", of which the understanding knows nothing and can never know anything; and it has *reasons* – that is, objective and evident insights into matters to which every understanding is blind – as "blind" as a blind man is to colour or a deaf man is to tone.'[2] I see someone as 'blind' if he does not see what *I* see so clearly. And the charge of blindness works both ways. The heart, Scheler insists, has nothing to be ashamed of and nothing to apologize for. It can easily measure up to the standards which reason declares itself proud of. Though reason would not recognize them for what they are, there is an *ordre du coeur*, a *logique du coeur*, even a *mathématique du coeur* – every bit as coherent and elegant as those that reason lists proudly as its title to superiority. The point is, though, that the orders, the logics, the mathematics of, respectively, heart and understanding, or of love and reason, do not address the same aspects of experience and do not pursue the same objectives. This is why reason and love would not listen to each other and if they did they would hardly grasp meaning in the voice. The articulate speech of one sounds like incoherent jabber to the other.

I would suggest that there are at least three converging reasons why their communication will fail.

To start with, love is about value, while reason is about use. The world as seen by love is a collection of values; the world as seen by reason is a collection of useful objects. The two qualities – of 'value' and of 'use' – are notorious for being confounded and confused: is not a thing valuable *because* it is useful? This is, to be sure, reason speaking – and it has been speaking this way since its ancient awakening in Plato's dialogues. Since then reason has tried hard, and goes on trying, to annex 'value' and dump anything left over that resists annexation; to enlist 'value' in the service of 'use'; to make value into a handmaiden or a spin-off of use.

But value is the quality of a thing, while usefulness is an attribute of the thing's users. It is the incompleteness of the user, the dearth which makes the user suffer, the user's urge to fill the gap, which makes a thing useful. To 'use' means to improve the condition of the user, to repair a shortcoming; 'using' means to be concerned with the welfare of the user.

In Plato's *Symposium* Aristophanes links love to the desire for a completeness thus far missing: 'the desire for the whole and the pursuit of it is named Love,' he says. Socrates, as always, strives to lift mere description to the rank of the law of logic, to put 'necessary' for 'likely': 'isn't it necessary that the desiring desires what it lacks, or else does not desire if it does not lack?' So that no room be left for guessing and errors of judgement, Socrates sums up: everyone 'who desires, desires what is not in his possession and not there, what he has not, and what he is not himself and what he lacks.' This is, he insists, what we call 'desire'; this is what *desire must be*, unless it is something other than desire. But is this desire what we mean by 'love', as Aristophanes would imply? Socrates quotes at length the words he heard uttered by the wise woman Diotima of Mantinea (W. H. D. Rouse suggests that the English equivalent of that name would be 'Fearthelord from Prophetville'). Diotima points out that Love was conceived at Aphrodite's birthday party from the sexual union of Plenty and Poverty, and so Love was born neither rich nor poor, or rather poor but with 'designs upon beautiful and good'; Love was neither mortal nor immortal, or rather was a mortal with designs upon immortality. Love, in other words, 'is not in want and wealth'; love 'is not for the beautiful' – 'it is for begetting and birth in the beautiful', and this is so 'because begetting is, for the mortal, something everlasting and immortal'. 'It is necessary then from this argument that love is for immortality also.'[3]

What you desire, you want to use; more precisely, to 'use up', to strip from its otherness, make your possession or ingest – make it a part of your body, an extension of yourself. To use is to annihilate the other for the sake of the self. To love, on the contrary, means to value the other for its otherness, to wish to reinforce it in its otherness, to protect that otherness and make it bloom and thrive, and to be ready to sacrifice one's own comfort, including one's own mortal existence, if this is what is needed to fulfil that intention. 'Use' means a gain for the self; 'value' augurs its self-denial. To use is to take, to value is to give.

Use- and value-orientations set reason and love on separate and diverging tracks. But once on their proper tracks, reason and love also have radically different horizons. Those of love are infinite, never to be reached, constantly receding as the love progresses. Love is no more immortal than the lovers and may stop well short of infinity, but it is not love if it does not take infinity of time and boundlessness of space as its only acceptable limits. The one who loves would agree with Lucan, Seneca's nephew: 'I have a wife, I have sons: all of them hostages given to fate'; accept that the fate is forever open-ended and knows no limits, and concede that to love is to consent that this must be so. The intention of reason is, however, exactly the opposite: not to open the gate into infinity, but to shut it down, and securely. The act of use is an event in time, and an event which fulfils and exhausts itself in a limited time: things tend to lose their usefulness during the act of their use. Use may achieve duration only through repetition, not self-fulfilment; fulfilment would lead to its demise (it is in this sense that we may say of the kind of desire for 'useful objects' which tends to be beefed up by our consumer society that it desires to desire, not to be satisfied).

Let me quote Max Scheler again: 'Love loves and in loving always looks beyond what it has in hand and possesses. The *Triebimpuls* which arouses it may tire out; love itself does not tire.' Love, Scheler insists, is by its essence infinite; it 'demands for its satisfaction an *infinite* good'.[4] Taking a finite good or a finite state for the fulfilment of the love drive signals *infatuation*, a grave though common 'destruction and confusion' of *ordo amoris*. Love worthy of its name never stops and is never satisfied; one may recognize true love by the lover's suspicion that it has not yet reached the heights it should climb – not by his confidence that it has gone far enough, and even less by his complaint that it has gone too far.

What is the glory of love is also its misfortune. The *infinite* is also *indefinite*. It can't be pinned down, circumscribed, measured.

It resists definitions, explodes frames and trespasses on borders. Being its own self-transgression, love is constantly ahead of any, even the most instantaneous of snapshots; love may be told only as history, and that history is outdated the moment the story is told. From the point of view of reason, fond as it is of faithful copies and legible diagrams, love is burdened with the original sin of form-lessness. And since reason wants to arrest or channel the unruly flows, tame the wild and domesticate the elemental, love stands also accused on account of its evasiveness, waywardness and intractability. Reason, that pursuit of the useful, cuts infinity to the measure of the finite self. Love, being the pursuit of value, expands the finite self towards infinity. Understanding cannot venture that far and so it leaves the track in mid-run. Its inability to catch up and the abandoning of the chase that follows is mistaken for the proof of love's and value's vagueness, 'subjectivity', wrong-headedness, lack of sense and imprudence; and so, altogether, of its uselessness.

Finally, there is a third opposition which sets reason and love apart. Reason, one may say, prompts loyalty to the *self*. Love, on the other hand, calls for solidarity with the *Other*, and so implies subordination of the self to something endowed with greater importance and value.

In the advertising copy of reason, freedom figures most prominently, and what is promised in that copy is freedom to pursue and attain ends, whatever the ends deemed to be worthy of pursuit may be now or in the future; such freedom casts the 'outside' of the self, things and persons alike, as a collection of potential obstacles to action and of vehicles of action, or rather of obstacles that need to be remade into vehicles. It is the self's objectives which lend meaning to the elements of the 'outside'. No other grounds for meaning allocation can be acknowledged if reason is to stay true to itself and deliver on its promise. Any sign of autonomy and self-determination in the things or persons can be perceived and articulated only as a mark of their extant 'resistance power'. If that power is too great to be overcome, it needs to be 'reckoned with', and negotiation and compromise may then be a more prudent choice than outright assault – but, again, this will be in the name of the 'well-understood interest' of the self. If reason wishes to advise the actors in their capacity as moral selves, it can use no other language but that of the calculation of gains and losses, costs and effects – as it did through the 'categorical imperative' of Immanuel Kant.

By this reckoning, love is guilty of being deaf to reason's promptings. In the act of love, Max Scheler points out, a being 'abandons itself, in order to share and participate in another being as *ens intentionale*'. In and through the act of love a being 'joins the other object in affirming its tendency toward its proper perfection that he is active in assisting it, promoting it, blessing it'.[5] Reason offers the self the skill to convert the self's own intentions into the objectives guiding the conduct of others; love, on the contrary, inspires the self to accept the intentions of the other as its own objective. Reason at its ethical best agrees magnanimously to be tolerant of the Other. Love would not stoop to mere tolerance; it wants solidarity instead – and solidarity may mean self-denial and self-abnegation, the sort of attitude which reason would be hard put to justify.

But there is more to love than the unconditional acceptance of the otherness of the other and of the other's right to its otherness; more even than the consent to serve – to assist, promote, bless – the cause of that otherness. Love means signing a blank cheque: in as far as the other's right to otherness has been fully and truly agreed to, there is no knowing what that otherness might consist of now, let alone later. Emmanuel Levinas compares the Other of the Eros with the future – on account of the future's refusal 'to be grasped in any way', of its habit of 'falling upon us and taking hold of us' instead. 'I do not define the Other by the future,' explains Levinas, 'but the future by the Other'; 'the total alterity of the Other' is so complete and invincible that it may serve as the empirical reference needed to visualize the alterity of the future or of death... Love means entering into a relation with a mystery and acceding to its unsolvability. Love does not mean, nor does it lead to, 'grasping', 'possessing', 'getting to know', let alone getting mastery over the object of love or getting it under control. Love means *consent to a mystery of the other* which is akin to the mystery of the future: to something 'which in the world where everything is, never is'; something 'which can not be there while everything is'.[6] Future is always elsewhere, and so is the Other of love.

You may have noted that we have not made any reference to the feelings and passions normally associated with 'being in love' or 'falling in love'. If 'l'amour a ses raisons', as Pascal wanted, or has its laws, logic and mathematics, as Scheler suggested, if it is at all amenable to description in interpersonally valid language, it is only as a specific 'casting' of the self and of the Other, as a specific modality of the Other's presence and so also of the constitution of the Self. This having been noted, we can conceive of love as a mould for the ethical self and moral relationship. While reason bewares of stepping over the boundary of the ontological, love points towards the domain of the ethical. Ethics, we may say, is made in the likeness of love. Whatever has been said here of love applies in equal measure to ethics.

Before he is an *ens cogitans* or an *ens volens*, man is an *ens amans*, says Scheler, and adds: it can't be otherwise, since it is in the net woven of love and hate that humans catch the world which they later subject – as Schopenhauer would have said – to will and representation. Take love and hate away, and there would be no net and so no catch either. Levinas would concur with Scheler's assertion of the priority of ethics, though not necessarily with the argument advanced in support of its veridicality. As I understand it, Levinas's famous dictum 'ethics is before ontology', unlike Scheler's assertion, claims no empirical/ontological status. It conveys instead two propositions, one phenomenological, the other ethical. First: to grasp the meaning of the ethical, all previous knowledge of the ontological needs to be suspended on the ground of its irrelevance. Second: it is not the ethics which needs to justify itself in terms of being – but the other way round: *onus probandi* lies on the being, it is the being that must demonstrate its agreement with ethics. In other words, you cannot derive the 'ought' from the 'is'; but then you should not be worried by that, since it is the 'is' which should worry about its connection with the 'ought'. The assertion 'ethics is *before* ontology' needs to be read in ethical terms: what it says is that 'ethics is *better* than ontology.'

'The face of a neighbour', writes Levinas, 'signifies for me an exceptional responsibility, preceding every free consent, every pact, every contract.'[7] I was responsible before I entered any commitment which society knows how to petrify into a rule or legal obligation. But because no rule had yet been written down, while responsibility had already acquired force with the first sighting of the Other, that responsibility is *empty of content*: it says nothing about what is to be done – it only says that from now on all that is done will feel right or wrong depending on what its effects are on the Other. A remarkable thing about Levinas, a deeply religious thinker and keen Talmudic scholar, is that while using the concept of commandments profusely he spells out but one of them: 'thou shalt not kill.' That commandment suffices to ground the whole edifice of morality, since it requires assent to the perpetual company of the Other, to living together – with all its, unknown and unpredictable, consequences. It commands that we share lives, interact and talk; all the rest remains unspecified – a blank cheque yet to be filled in by our actions. And it is this unspecificity which ushers us into the land of the ethical.

Another great religious thinker and ethical philosopher of our century, Knud Løgstrup, is even more specific about the vexing yet blessed unspecificity of ethical demand: 'The demand gives no directions whatever about how the life of the person thus delivered [to our care] is to be taken care of. It specifies nothing in this respect but leaves it entirely to the individual. To be sure, the other person is to be served by word and action, but precisely which word and which action we must ourselves decide in each situation.'[8] Knowing that we are under command but not knowing what the command commands us to do means being sentenced to lifelong uncertainty. But, says Løgstrup, this is precisely what 'to be moral' means: certainty breeds irresponsibility, and absolute certainty is the same as absolute irresponsibility. Were we told exactly what to do, 'the wisdom, insight, and love with which we are to act' would 'no longer be our own'; the command would not be a call to humanity, imagination and insight – but to obedience; Christian ethics, in particular, would be 'ossified into ideology', and so we would all surrender to the temptation to 'absolutize the standpoints which presently prevail in contemporary laws, morality, and convention'.[9]

What exactly the status is of Levinas's 'unconditional responsibility' and Løgstrup's 'unspoken command' is a notoriously moot question. Answers steer uneasily between the two polarized standpoints taken in ethical philosophy: between the belief in Divine, prerational origins of ethics, and the conception of ethics as the codified 'will of society', a product of convention sedimented from human historical experience and arrived at through trial and error, even if guided on its way by rational consideration of the prerequisites of human cohabitation. Levinas and Løgstrup strive to reconcile the extremes and to show that, far from contradicting each other, the prerational presence of ethical demand, and *human* responsibility for making the *unspoken* word flesh, condition and propel each other. In Levinas's and Løgstrup's visions of ethics, there is room for both – and the presence of both is, moreover, indispensable.

But the combined message of the two great thinkers does not stop at the attempt to resolve the most vexing antinomy of ethical philosophy. The most important part of the message is the refutation of the outspoken or tacit assumption of all, or almost all, ethical thinking to date: that the cause of ethics suffers under conditions of uncertainty and gains from the self-confidence offered by the unambiguous letter of law – and so that 'to be moral' means, in the last instance, to conform to the ethical code. Against the common conception of morality cut in the likeness of law, Levinas and Løgstrup offer a view of morality as a challenge; as a matter of responsibility *for* the weakness of the Other, rather than of responsibility *to* a superior power. And against the idea that the resolution of ethical quandary is an essentially *finite* endeavour, bound to finish once the fully rational and non-contradictory code of ethics has been composed and its uncontested dominion has been decreed, Levinas and Løgstrup posit responsibility as the *never ending, eternal human condition*. What follows from the idea of unconditional responsibility and unspoken demand is that one can only recognize moral beings by their perpetual anxiety and self-reprobation: by the gnawing suspicion that they were not *moral enough* – that not everything has been done that could be done, and that the demand called for more than they heard when it called.

We are now ready to offer a tentative answer to the question in the title. And that answer is: yes, love needs reason; but it needs it as an instrument, not as an excuse, justification or hide-out.

To love, just as to be moral, means to be and to remain in a state of perpetual uncertainty. The lover, just like the moral person, sails between the tolerance which more often than not runs aground on the shallows of indifference, and the possessive impulse which all too easily and abruptly founders on the rock of coercion; and the lover and the moral self have no other waters to navigate. They need all the help they can get, and reason's promise of assistance sounds attractive. They need, after all, to ponder alternative courses of action and to count their risks and chances, gains and losses; they need to try the best they can to anticipate the effects of their actions on the well-being of the objects of their love or concern; they need to compare and evaluate the gravity of demands which cannot be met simultaneously due to the scarcity of their resources, and they need to calculate the best or the least harmful way to distribute the resources at their disposal. In all such and suchlike tasks, reason is second to none; no other human faculties will do the job better. But it is the craftsperson, not the tools, who is, and rightly, blamed for the defects of the product and expected to repent and recompense the damage. Deploying the powers of rational reasoning does not relieve the lover or the moral person from their responsibility for the consequences. That responsibility can only be renounced together with love and morality.

But this is not enough to spare the lover and the moral person their suffering. Uncertainty is at most times an unpleasant condition, and prospectless, incurable uncertainty is altogether nasty and repulsive. Those cast into such a condition may be excused for desperately seeking relief. Relief may come only in the form of an authority powerful enough to vouch for the propriety of certain steps and the inappropriateness of all the rest. Trust which the seekers of certainty invest in such an authority promises liberation from the burden of responsibility. The authority is now the one to take the blame should something go wrong.

Authorities come in many shapes and colours. There are merciless and cruel totalitarian rulers who threaten severe punishment for disobedience. There are milder versions of rule-by-command, in the form of bureaucratic hierarchies, which without throwing the stick away keep a constant supply of fresh carrots. And there are authorities without office and mailing address, anonymous authorities: the authority of numbers, armed with the threat of social ostracism, is most prominent among them. When brought to account for their actions, the blunderers can always point out, depending on the authority chosen to be trusted, that they 'only fulfilled orders', or that they simply 'followed the rules', or that 'all sensible people do the same.'

In our modern society these authorities have one thing in common: they all, explicitly or implicitly, claim to be speaking in the name of reason (it is awfully difficult in modern society to speak with authority without claiming a direct telephone line to reason).

When they say something is to be done, it not just 'must be done', but it 'stands to reason'. Whoever shows disobedience is not only a lawbreaker or a rule-breaker, but also an unreasonable person; the antagonist the culprits are up against is nothing less than sanity and rationality. This habit of rulers may create the impression that reason stands on the side of the power-holders – an illusion to which not just court poets but many sober and critical philosophers have fallen victim. One would, however, be well advised to set apart ideological uses of a thing from the thing itself. I propose that it is not through services rendered to the order-givers (or not by them primarily) that reason offers to help the shelter-from-responsibility-seekers.

That help comes through absolution from ethical worries. Certain choices – and particularly the most nerve-wracking and painful among them – are exempt from moral significance. The choosers are reassured that their pangs of conscience are neither here nor there: what you do needs to be measured, praised or condemned by other criteria, clearer and much less ambivalent than things as elusive and difficult to pinpoint as the welfare or misery of others and your responsibility for them. Love, evidently, is not good for thinking, and so it is no good for that *understanding* which is supposed to tell you *how to go on*; and morality shares that defect with love. If reason could offer a sensible argument against following moral impulses and in favour of disregarding them by pointing out that the actions in question are 'morally indifferent', the offer would find many zealous bidders. An example can show what is meant here.

One of the arguments most often heard in favour of dismantling the welfare state is: 'we cannot afford it.' There are just too many people without work and income, too many single mothers with no way to feed their children, too many ageing people relying on old age pensions; well, come to think of it, there are too many people altogether, young and old, male or female, white or black or yellow. We would gladly help them all, but that cannot be done without sharing our wealth, without higher taxes, and this would be harmful and foolish, since it would 'send the wrong signals' and discourage people from making money and more money yet, and so a depression would follow with no chance of 'consumer-led recovery'; 'we will all be worse off.' And so if you really care, don't be 'unwisely' generous. It may be sad and depressing not to be able to follow your heart, but love needs reason to save it from its folly. This may be circular reasoning, but welcome reasoning it undoubtedly is. Not only does it serve to absolve from a guilty conscience, but in addition it presents the refusal to share as ultimately a moral act.

This is what I mean by reason used to excuse love for its failing and as a hide-out from the unspokenness of ethical demand and the unconditionality of moral responsibility. These, I suggest, are wrong uses of reason. They offer an escape from a moral predicament, not the chance to cope and deal with its genuine dilemmas.

14

Private morality, immoral world

All great thinkers create powerful concepts and/or images of their own – but as a rule together with a complete universe to accommodate them and infuse them with sense: a whole world made to their measure, the world which is their home. For Levinas, such a world was 'the moral party of two', self-consciously a utopia in both of its inseparable senses (of 'no place', and of 'good place'). That moral party of two was for Levinas 'the primal scene' of morality, the test-tube in which moral selves germinate and sprout; it was also the only stage on which such selves can play themselves as they are, that is, *moral* beings, instead of playing scripted roles and reciting someone else's lines. The 'primal scene' of morality is the realm of 'face to face', of the tremendous encounter with the Other as a *Face*.

Morality (in Levinas's terms: being *for* the Other) has notoriously an awesome potential for love and hatred, for self-sacrifice and domination, care and cruelty; ambivalence is its prime mover; and yet inside the moral party of two it is, so to speak, capable of sustaining the universe on its own. Morality does not need codes or rules, reason or knowledge, argument or conviction. It would not understand them anyway; morality is 'before' all that (one cannot even say that the moral impulse is 'ineffable' or 'mute' – ineffability and dumbness come *after* language, but moral impulse triggered by the Face *precedes* speech). It sets its standards as it goes. It does not know of guilt or innocence – it is pure in the only true sense of purity: the purity of naivety. As Vladimir Jankélévitch pointed out,[1] one cannot be *pure* except under the condition of not *having* purity, that is to say, of not possessing it knowingly.

The moral party of two, postulated by Levinas as the birth-place and homeland of morality, *is* naive; it does not know (has not been told) that it is a party, let alone a moral one. Only when gazed upon from outside does the 'moral party' congeal into a 'couple', a 'pair', a 'they out there' (and by the law of reciprocation which rules outside, the 'they' is expected to be translated by those inside the 'couple' into 'we': with no loss or even change of meaning!). It is the outside gaze that 'objectifies' the moral party and thus makes it into a unit, a *thing* that can be *described* as it is, '*handled*', *compared* with others 'like it', *assessed, evaluated, ruled on*. But from the point of view of me as a moral self there is no 'we', no 'couple', no supra-individual entity with its 'needs' and 'rights'.

'Inside' the moral party there is just me, with my responsibility, with my care, with the command which commands me and me alone – and the Face, the catalyst and the midwife of all that. My togetherness with the Other won't survive the disappearance or the opting out of myself or the Other. There would be nothing left to 'survive' that disappearance.

The 'togetherness' of the 'moral party' is vulnerable, weak, fragile, living precariously with the shadow of death never far away – and all this *because* neither I nor the Other in this party is *replaceable*. It is precisely this *non-replaceability* which makes our togetherness *moral*. There is no one else to do what I haven't done, and so there is no excuse for me on account of others doing it instead, or of none of them doing a similar thing. Besides, because *each of us* is irreplaceable, thinking of actions in terms of 'interests' makes no sense: there is no way in which actions of either one of us could be classified as 'egoistic' or 'altruistic'. Good can be seen only in its opposition to evil – but inside a 'society' in which (in a jarring opposition to the 'genuine' society) *no one* is replaceable, how can one say that what is good for one partner may be bad for another? It is inside such a 'moral society', the 'moral party of two', that my responsibility cannot be fathomed and 'fulfilled', and feels unlimited, becomes a 'whole life' respons-ibility; and it is under this condition that the command needs no argument to gain authority, nor the support of a threat of sanctions, to be a command; it has felt like a command, and an unconditional command at that, all along.

But all this changes with the appearance of the *Third*. Now, true society appears, and the naive, unruled and unruly moral impulse – simultaneously the necessary and the sufficient condition of the 'moral party' – does not suffice any more.

The moral party broken into

Here, in society – unlike in the universe of two – Levinas's postulate of putting ethics 'before ontology' sounds odd: here, priority means 'being before', not 'being better'. The pristine, naive togetherness of I and the Other is neither pristine nor naive. There are now a lot of questions which can be, and are, asked about that togetherness and a lot of tests that togetherness may be asked to pass. Love now has self-love to reckon with, *Fürsein* has the *Mitsein* – sometimes as a competitor, always as a judge. Responsibility desperately seeks its limits, the 'command' is flatly denied as being 'unconditional'. Baffled, moral impulse pauses and awaits instructions.

Now I live in a world populated, as Agnes Heller wittily put it,[2] by 'All, Some, Many and their companions. Similarly, there is Difference, Number, Knowledge, Now, Limit, Time, Space, also Freedom, Justice and Injustice, and, certainly, Truth and Falsity.' These are the main characters in the play called Society, and all of them stay far beyond the reach of my moral (now *'merely* intuitive') wisdom, apparently immune to whatever I may do, powerful against my powerlessness, immortal against my mortality; secure against my blunders, so that my blunders harm only me, not Them. *They* are the characters who act now: as Agnes Heller puts it, 'Reason reasons, Imagination imagines, Will wills, and Language speaks (*die Sprache Spricht*). This is how characters become actors in their own right. They come into existence. They live independently from their creators...' And all this was made possible, nay inescapable, by the entry of the Third – that is, due to the 'moral party' outgrowing its 'natural' size and turning into society.

The Third is also an Other, but not the Other we encountered at the 'primal scene' staged by Levinas – where the moral play, not aware of being a moral play, was scripted and directed by my responsibility alone. The 'otherness' of the Third is of an entirely different order. The two 'others' reside in different worlds. They are two planets each with its own orbit which does not cross with the orbit of the other Other. Neither of the two would survive the swapping of orbits. The two Others do not converse with each other; when one speaks, the other one does not listen; if the other one did listen, she would not understand what she heard. Each one can feel at home only if the other one steps aside, or better still stays outside. The Other who is a Third can be met with only if we have already left the realm of Levinas's morality, and entered another world, the realm of *Social Order*, ruled by *Justice*. As Levinas puts it,

> this is the domain of the State, of justice, of politics. Justice differs from charity in that it allows some form of equality and measure to intervene, a set of social rules established according to the judgement of the State, and thus also of politics. The relationship between me and the other must this time leave room for the third, a sovereign judge who decides between two equals.[3]

What makes the Third so unlike the Other we met in the prime and pristine moral encounter? In his assessment of the sociological meaning and role of the third element, Georg Simmel brought the unique and seminal role of the Third down to the fact that in any triad 'the third element is at such a distance from the other two that there exist no properly sociological interactions which concern all three elements alike.'[4] That mutual distance when void of encounters congeals into 'objectivity' (read: disinterestedness, noncommitment). From the vantage point of the Third, what used to be a 'moral party' becomes a *group*, an entity endowed with a life of its own, a totality which is 'greater than the sum of its parts'. Thus the selves can be set and seen against the 'totality', their motives against the 'interest of the whole'. The selves turn into individuals, who are comparable, measurable, judged by extrapersonal, 'statistically average' or 'normative' standards – and the Third is firmly placed in the position of the potential jury, the umpire, the-one-who-passes-the-verdict. Against the moral selves' hopelessly subjective and so non-rational propulsions, the Third may now set the objective criteria of rational interests. Asymmetry of the moral relationship is all but gone, the partners are now equal, and exchangeable, and replaceable. Actors have now to explain what they do, lay down and stand up to the arguments, justify themselves by reference to standards which are not of their own making. The site is cleared for norms, laws, ethical rules and courts of justice.

And that site must be built upon, and urgently. Objectivity – that Trojan horse of the Third, has delivered a mortal, or at least potentially terminal, blow to the affection which moved the moral partners. 'A third mediating element deprives conflicting claims of their affective qualities,' says Simmel; but it also deprives affection of its authority as the life-guide. Reason – that enemy of passion – *must* step in, lest disorientation and chaos rule. Reason is what we call the *ex post facto* accounts of actions from which the passion of the naive past has been drained. Reason is what we hope will tell us what to do when passions have been tamed or extinguished and no longer propel us. We cannot live without reason once the survival of the 'group' is something else than the life of the Other sustained by my responsibility; once the unique Other has dissolved in the otherness of the Many. It is now a matter between my life and life of the many. Survival of the many and my own survival being two different survivals, I might have become an 'individual' but the Other has most certainly forfeited her individuality, now dissolved in a categorial stereo-type. My being-for has been thereby split into potentially conflict-ing tasks: of self-preservation and the preservation of the group.

When the Other dissolves in the Many, the first thing to be washed away is the Face. The Other(s) is (are) now faceless. They are *persons* ('persona' means the mask, and masks hide not disclose faces). I am dealing now with masks (classes, stereotypes, to which the masks/uniforms direct me) not faces. It is the mask which determines whom I am dealing with and what my responses ought to be. I have to learn the meaning of each *kind* of mask and memorize the responses each one calls for. But even then I cannot be totally secure. Masks may be put on and off, they hide more than they reveal. The innocent confidence of moral drive has been replaced by the unquenchable anxiety of uncertainty. With the advent of the Third, fraud crawls in – yet more horrifying in its premonition than in its confirmed presence, more paralysing still for being a non-exorcizable spectre. In society, one has to live with this anxiety. Whether I like it or not, I *must* trust the masks – not that I *can* trust them. Trust is the way to live with uncertainty, taking the risks, gambling – not the way to dispose of anxiety.

The 'moral party of two' is a *vast* space for morality. It is large enough to accommodate the ethical self in full flight. It scales the highest peaks of saintliness and reaches down to the underwater reefs of moral life – the traps that must be avoided by the self before (as much as after) it takes responsibility for its responsibility. But that party is too cramped a space for the human-being-in-the-world. It has no room for more than two actors. It leaves out most of the things that fill the daily bustle of every human being: pursuit of survival and self-aggrandizement, rational consideration of ends and means, calculation of gains and losses, search for pleasure, for deference or power, politics and economics... To be in the moral space, one needs now to *re-enter* it, and this can be done only by taking time off from daily business, bracketing off for a time its mundane rules and conventions. In order to come *back* to the moral party of two (can one really make a comeback? The party one *arrives at* is so starkly different from the one set by Levinas 'before ontology'), I and the Other must disrobe/be disrobed of all social trappings, stripped of status, social distinctions, handicaps, positions or roles; we must once more be neither rich nor poor, high nor lowly, mighty nor disempowered. We must now be *reduced* to the bare essentiality of our common humanity which in Levinas's moral universe was given to us at birth.

Can morality survive the break-in?

In the presence of the Third, says Levinas (in conversation with François Poirié),

> we leave what I call the order of ethics, or the order of saintliness or the order of mercy, or the order of love, or the order of charity – where the other human concerns me regardless of the place he occupies in the multitude of humans, and even regardless of our shared quality as individuals of the human species; he concerns me as the one close to me, as the first to come. He is unique.[5]

Beyond this order stretches the realm of choice, proportion, judgement – and comparison. Comparison already entails the first act of
violence: defiance of uniqueness. This violence cannot be avoided,
since among the multiplicity of others certain divisions (assignment to classes, to categories) are necessary – they are 'justified
divisions'. Ethics demands, one may say, a certain self-limitation;
for the ethical demand to be fulfilled, certain sacred axioms of
ethics must be sacrificed.

The liberal state, says Levinas – the state grounded on the
principle of human rights – is the implementation, and conspicuous manifestation, of that contradiction. Its function is nothing
less than to 'limit the original mercy from which justice origin-
ated'. But 'the internal contradiction' of the liberal state finds its
expression in perceiving 'beyond and above all justice already
incorporated in the regime, a justice more just...' 'Justice in the
liberal state is never definitive.' 'Justice is awoken by charity – such
charity as is before justice but also after it.' 'Concern with human
rights is not the function of the State. It is a non-state institution
inside the State – an appeal to humanity which the State has not
accomplished yet.' Concern with human rights is an appeal to the
'surplus of charity'. One may say: to something larger than any
letter of the law, than anything that the state has done so far. State-
administered justice is born of charity gestated and groomed
within the primary ethical situation. And yet justice may be administered only if it never stops being prompted by its original *spiritus
movens*; if it knows of itself as of a never-ending chase of a forever
elusive goal – the re-creation among individuals/citizens of that
uniqueness which is the birth-sign of the Other as Face; if it knows
that it *cannot* 'match the kindness which gave it birth and keeps it
alive' (*L'Autre, Utopie et Justice*, 1988) – but if it knows as well
that it can never *stop trying* to do just that.

Just what can one learn from Levinas's exploration of the 'world
of the Third', the 'world of the multiplicity of others' – the social
world?

One can learn, to start with, that this world of the social is
simultaneously the legitimate offspring and a distortion of the
moral world. The idea of justice is conceived at the moment of
encounter between the experience of uniqueness (as given in the
moral responsibility for the Other) and the experience of the
multiplicity of others (as given in social life). It cannot be

conceived under any other circumstances, it needs both parents
and to both it is genetically related, even if the genes, though being
complementary, also contain contradictory genetic messages.
Thus, paradoxically, morality is the school of justice – even if the
category of justice is alien to it and within the moral relationship
redundant (justice comes into its own together with comparison,
but there is nothing to compare when the Other is encountered as
unique). The 'primal scene' of ethics is thereby also the primal,
ancestral scene of social justice.

One learns also that justice becomes necessary when moral
impulse, quite self-sufficient inside the moral party of two, is
found to be a poor guide once it ventures beyond the boundaries
of that party. The infinity of the moral responsibility, the unlim-
itedness (even the silence!) of moral demand simply cannot be
sustained when 'the Other' appears in the plural (one may say
that there is an inverse ratio between the infinity of 'being for' and
the infinity of the others). But it is that moral impulse which makes
justice necessary: it resorts to justice in the name of self-preservation, though while doing so it risks being cut down, trimmed,
maimed or watered down...

In the *Dialogue sur le penser-à-l'Autre* (1987) the interviewer
asked Levinas:

> As far as I am an ethical subject, I am responsible for everything in
> everybody; my responsibility is infinite. Is it not so that such a
> situation is unlivable for me, and for the other, whom I risk terror-
> izing with my ethical voluntarism? Does not it follow that ethics is
> impotent in its will to do good?

To which Levinas gave the following answer:

> I do not know whether such a situation is unlivable. Certainly, such
> a situation is not what one would call agreeable, pleasant to live
> with, but it is good. What is extremely important – and I can assert
> this without being myself a saint, and without pretending to be a
> saint – is to be able to say that a human truly deserving that name,
> in its European sense, derived from the Greeks and the Bible, is a
> human being who considers saintliness the ultimate value, an unas-
> sailable value.

This value is not surrendered once the uncompromising ethical
requirement of 'being-for' is replaced by the somewhat diluted and

less stressful code of justice. It remains what it was – the ultimate value, reserving to itself the right to invigilate, monitor and censure all deals entered into in the name of justice. Constant tension and never-to-be-calmed suspicion rule in the relationship between ethics and the just state, its never eager enough or sufficiently reliable agent, its never industrious enough plenipotentiary. Ethics is not a derivative of the state; the ethical authority does not derive from the state powers to legislate and to enforce the law. It precedes the state, it is the sole source of the state's legitimacy and the ultimate judge of that legitimacy. The state, one may say, is justifiable only as a vehicle or instrument of ethics.

This is much – but far too little to account for the complex social/political processes which mediate between individual moral impulses and the overall ethical effects of political actions. Levinas's view of the ethical origins of justice and the state itself as an instrument of justice (and, obliquely, of ethics itself) is not, nor does it pretend to be, a sociological statement. It is in its intention and its final shape a phenomenological insight into the meaning of justice; or it can perhaps be interpreted as an 'etiological myth', displaying the case for the subordination of the state to ethical principles and its subjection to ethical criteria of evaluation. It can hardly be seen, though, as an insight into the process through which ethical responsibility for the other comes (or does not come, as the case may be) to be implemented on a generalized scale through the works of the state and its institutions. It certainly goes a long way towards explaining concerns with the plight of the 'generalized other' – the faraway Other, the Other distant in space and time; but it says little about the ways and means through which that concern may bring practical effects, and even less about the reasons for such effects falling so saliently short of needs and expectations, or not being visible at all.

Levinas's writings offer rich inspiration for the analysis of the endemic aporia of moral responsibility. They offer nothing comparable, though, for the scrutiny of the aporetic nature of justice. They do not confront the possibility that – just as in the case of assuming moral responsibility for the Other – the work of the institutions which Levinas wishes to be dedicated to the promotion of justice may fall short of moral ideals or even have consequences detrimental to moral values. Neither do they allow for the possibility that such detrimental consequences may be more than just a side-effect of mistakes and neglect, being rooted instead in the very way such institutions can – must – operate to remain viable.

Quite a few insights into the latter issue can be found in the work of Hans Jonas.[6] Unlike Levinas, Jonas puts our present moral quandary in historical perspective, representing it as an *event in time*, rather than an extemporal, metaphysical predicament. According to Jonas, for the greater part of human history the gap between 'micro' and 'macro' ethics did not present a problem; the short reach of the moral drive was not fraught with terminal dangers for the simple reason that the consequences of human deeds (given the technologically determined scale of human action) were equally limited. In recent times, however, the magnitude of immediate and oblique consequences of human action has grown exponentially and their growth has not been matched by a similar expansion of human moral capacity. What we are now able to do may have profound and radical effects on distant lands and distant generations we can neither explore nor imagine. Yet the same development that put in the hands of humankind powers, tools and weapons of unprecedented magnitude, requiring close normative regulation, 'eroded the foundations from which norms could be derived; it has destroyed the very idea of norm as such.' Both departures are the work of science, which brooks no limits to what humans can do, and is unlikely to accept that not all that *could* be done *should* be done: the ability to do something is, for science and for technology, science's executive arm, all the reason ever needed for doing it. And so – Jonas points out – while new powers need new ethics, and need it badly, they simultaneously undermine the very possibility of satisfying that need, by denying ethical considerations the right to interfere with, let alone to arrest, their own infinite, self-propelling growth.

This blind tendency must be reversed, Jonas demands. But how? By working out a new ethics, made to the measure of new human powers. This is a Kantian answer: what we need to pull ourselves out of the present quandary and stave off even greater catastrophes are, in Jonas's view, certain rules so apodeictically true that every sane person would have to accept them. We need, in other words, a sort of a categorical imperative mark two – like, for instance, 'Act so that the effects of your action are compatible with the permanence of genuine human life.'

Working out a categorical imperative for our present predicament is a daunting task, though, and for several reasons. First, negation of any of the candidates for 'imperative mark two' status, unlike the original Kantian imperative, does *not* entail logical contradiction. Secondly, it is notoriously difficult, nay impossible, to know for sure which actions inspired by the progress of technoscience are and which are not 'compatible with the permanence of genuine human life' – at least not before the damage, often irreparable, has been done. Even in the unlikely case of the new categorical imperative having been awarded unchallenged normative authority, the vexing question of its application would still remain open: how to argue convincingly that a controversial development should be stopped, if its effects cannot be measured in advance with that degree of precision, with that near algorithmic certainty, that would satisfy what scientific reason would be inclined to respect? If a truly algorithmic calculation of the looming dangers is not on the cards, Jonas suggests, we should settle for its second-best substitute, the '*heuristics* of fear': try our best to visualize the most awesome and the most durable among the consequences of a given technological action. Above all, we need to apply the 'principle of uncertainty': 'The prophecy of doom is to be given greater heed than the prophecy of bliss.' We need, Jonas implies, a kind of 'systematic pessimism ethics' – so that we may err, if at all, solely on the side of caution.

Kant's trust in the grip of ethical law rested on the conviction that there are arguments of reason which every reasonable person, being a reasonable person, must accept; the passage from ethical law to moral action led through rational thought – and to smooth the passage one needed only to take care of the non-contradictory rationality of the law, counting for the rest on the endemic rational faculties of moral actors. In this respect, Jonas stays faithful to Kant – though he is the first to admit that nothing as uncontroversial as Kant's categorical imperative (that is, no principle which cannot be violated without violating simultaneously the logical law of contradiction) can be articulated in relation to the new challenge to human ethical faculties. For Jonas, as for Kant, the crux of the matter is the capacity of legislative reason; and the promotion, as well as the eventual universality, of ethical conduct is ultimately a philosophical problem and the task of philosophers. For Jonas, as for Kant, the fate of ethics is fully and truly in the hands of Reason and its spokespeople, the philosophers. In this scheme of things there is no room left for the possibility that reason may, in some other of its incarnations, militate against what is, in its name, promoted by ethical philosophers.

In other words, there is no room left for the logic of human interests, and the logic of social institutions – those organized interests whose function is, in practice if not by design, to do exactly the opposite to what Kantian ethical philosophy would expect them to do: namely, to make the bypassing of ethical restrictions feasible and ethical considerations irrelevant to the action. Neither is there room left for the otherwise trivial sociological observation that for the arguments to be accepted they need to accord with interests, in addition to (or instead of) being rationally flawless. There is no room either for another equally trivial phenomenon, the 'unanticipated consequences' of human action – of deeds which bring results left out of account, or unthought of at the time the action was undertaken. Nor is there room for the relatively simple guess that when interests are many and at odds with each other, any hope that a certain set of principles will eventually prevail and will be universally obeyed must seek support in a sober analysis of social and political forces capable of securing that victory.

I suggest that a mixture of all those factors – overlooked or ignored and left out of account in Jonas's search for the new ethics – can be blamed for the curious paradox of our times, in which the *growing awareness of the dangers ahead goes hand in hand with a growing impotence to prevent them or alleviate the gravity of their impact.* Not that we disagree on values – on things we would like to see done and things that we wouldn't. Agreeing on shared purposes is almost childishly easy: no one wants war, pollution, the impoverishment of a growing part of the globe. More importantly yet, we seem to know better and better that if catastrophe is to be averted, the presently unruly forces must be kept in check and controlled by factors other than the endemically diffuse and dispersed, as well as short-sighted, interests. In practice, however, things we do not desire or that we downright resent take the place of things we wish to happen, while the consequences of human actions rebound with a blind, elemental force more reminiscent of earthquakes, floods and tornados than of a model of rational and self-monitored behaviour.

As Danièle Sallenave has reminded us,[7] Jean-Paul Sartre could aver a few decades ago that 'there are no such things as natural disasters'; but today natural disasters have turned into the prototype and model of all the miseries that afflict the world, and one could just as well reverse Sartre's statement and say that 'there are no other than natural catastrophes.' It is not just the dramatic changes in the degree of livability of our natural habitat (pollution of air and water, global warming, holes in the ozone, acid rain, salination or desiccation of the soil, etc.), but also the thoroughly human aspects of global conditions (wars, demographic explosions, mass migrations and displacements, flare-ups of ethnic hostilities, the growing gap between rich and poor, the social exclusion of large categories of the population) that come unannounced, catch us unawares and seem utterly oblivious to the anguished cries for help and to the most frantic efforts to design, let alone to provide, the remedy.

Ethics under siege

Obviously, these are not the result of Jonas's ethical strategy being followed. The dearth of ethical knowledge and understanding can hardly be blamed for what is happening. No one except lunatic fringes certified as lunatic fringes would seriously aver that it is good and beneficial to pollute the atmosphere, to pierce the ozone layer, or for that matter to wage wars, to overpopulate the land, to deprive people of their livelihood or to make them into homeless vagabonds. Yet all this happens despite its consensual, well-nigh universal and vociferous condemnation. Some other factors than ethical ignorance, or for that matter the philosophers' inability to agree on principles, must be at work if the grinding, systemic consistency of global damage more than matches the cohesion of ethical indignation. One may sensibly surmise that those other factors are entrenched in such aspects of social reality as are either left unaffected by ethical philosophy, or are able to successfully withstand or bypass its pressures; or better still, render ethical demands inaudible or – if audible – ineffective.

Among such factors, the increasingly deregulated market forces, exempt from all effective political control and guided solely by the pressures of competitiveness, must be awarded pride of place. Thanks to technical advances aided and abetted by the progressive dismantling of political constraints, capital is now free to move whenever and wherever it desires. The potential promoters and guardians of social justice have been thereby deprived of the economic muscle without which no enforcement of ethical principles could be contemplated. Political institutions stay local – while the real powers which decide the shape of things as they are and those yet to come have acquired a genuine *exterritoriality*; as Manuel Castells puts it in his monumental three-volume study of *The Information Age*,[8] power in the form of capital, and particularly financial capital, *flows* – while politics remains tied to the ground, bearing all the constraints imposed by its local character. Power has been, we may say, 'emancipated from politics'. But once this happens, that state in which Levinas invested his hopes for the promotion of morally inspired justice becomes all but a wishful thought's abstraction; and it is increasingly difficult to locate an agency capable of undertaking, let alone carrying through, the task of implementing the new categorical imperative Hans Jonas sought – were such imperative to be found, spelled out and universally agreed. We may say: the problem with the application of Levinas's ethics to the troubles of the contemporary world is first and foremost the question of an *agency gap*.

In the present-day world, mobility has become the most powerful and most coveted stratifying factor; the stuff from which the new, increasingly worldwide social, political, economic and cultural hierarchies are daily built and rebuilt. The mobility acquired by the owners and managers of capital means a new, indeed unprecedented in its radical unconditionality, disengagement of power from obligations: from duties towards employees, but also duties towards the younger and weaker, or yet unborn generations and towards the self-reproduction of the living conditions of all; in short, freedom from the duty to contribute to daily life and the perpetuation of the community. There is a new asymmetry emerging between the exterritorial nature of power and the continuing territoriality of the 'whole life' – which the now unanchored powers, able to move at short notice or without warning, are free to exploit and abandon to the consequences of that exploitation. Shedding responsibility for consequences is the most coveted and cherished gain that the new mobility brings to free-floating, locally unbound capital. The costs of coping with consequences need not now be counted in the calculation of the 'effectiveness' of investment.

The new freedom of capital brings to mind the absentee land-lords of yore, notorious for their much resented neglect of the needs of the populations which fed them. Creaming off the 'sur-plus product' was the sole interest the absentee landlords had in the existence of the land they owned. There is certainly some similarity here – but the comparison does not do full justice to the kind of freedom from worry and responsibility that the mobile capital of the late twentieth century acquired but the absentee landlords could never do so much as dream of.

In contradistinction to the absentee landlords of early modern times, the late modern capitalists and land-brokers (thanks to the new mobility of their by now liquid resources) do not encounter limits to their power sufficiently real – solid, tough, resistant – to enforce compliance. The sole limits that could make themselves felt and respected would be such as were administratively imposed on the free movement of capital and money. Such limits are, however, few and far between, while the handful that remain are under tremendous pressure, liable to be effaced, or just washed away through neglect. The moment that those on the receiving end – the targeted or the accidental victims of the profit-making drive – tried to flex their muscles and make their strength felt, capital would have little difficulty in packing its tents and finding a more hospitable – that is, unresisting, malleable, soft – environment. Capital has no need to engage if avoidance will do.

To put it in a nutshell: *rather than levelling up human condi-tions, the technological and political annulment of temporal/spa-tial distances tends to polarize them.* It emancipates certain humans from territorial constraints and renders certain commun-ity-generating meanings exterritorial – while denuding the territ-ory, to which other people continue to be confined, of its meaning and its identity-endowing capacity. For some people it augurs an unprecedented freedom from physical obstacles and an unheard-of ability to move and act over distance. For others, it portends the impossibility of appropriating and domesticating the locality from which they have little chance of cutting themselves free in order to move elsewhere. With distances no longer meaning anything, or at any rate not much, localities, separated by distances, also lose much of their meaning. This, however, augurs freedom of meaning creation for some, but portends ascription to meaninglessness for others. Some can now move out of the locality – any locality – at will. Others watch helplessly the sole locality they may inhabit moving away from under their feet.

Not only the capital, but information too now floats independently of its carriers; shifting of bodies and rearrangement of bodies in physical space is less than ever necessary in reordering meanings and relationships. For some people – for the mobile elite, the elite of mobility – that means, literally, 'dephysicalization', a new weightlessness of power. Elites travel in space, and travel faster than ever before – but the spread and density of the power web they weave is not dependent on that travel. Thanks to the new 'bodylessness' of power in its mainly financial form, the power-holders become truly exterritorial, even if, bodily, they happen to stay 'in place'. Their power is, fully and truly, not 'out of *this* world' – not of the physical world in which they build their heavily guarded homes and offices, themselves exterritorial, free from intrusion by unwelcome neighbours, cut off from whatever may be called a *local* community, inaccessible to whoever is, unlike them, confined to it.

And so another gap yawns – alongside that of agency. This gap grows and widens between the meaning-making elites and all the rest. Just as today's power-holders remind us of premodern absentee landlords, so the learned, cultivated and culturally creative elites show a striking similarity to the similarly extra-territorial, Latin-speaking and writing scholastic elites of medieval Europe. It seems that the modern nation-building episode was a sole exception to a much more permanent rule. The excruciatingly difficult task of reforging the mish-mash of languages, cults, lores, customs and ways of life into homogeneous nations under homogeneous rule brought the learned elites for a time into direct engagement with 'the people' (both 'intellectuals' and the 'people', as well as the idea of a link between knowledge and power, are *modern* inventions). That episode being now by and large over, at least in the affluent part of the globe, the home of the most influential section of the cultural elite – there seems to be no obvious ('objective') need for the continuation of that engagement. Cyberspace, securely anchored in websites on the internet, is the contemporary equivalent of medieval Latin – the space which the learned elite of today inhabit; and there is little the residents of that space could talk about with those still hopelessly mired in all-too-real physical space. Even less could they gain from that dialogue. No wonder that the word 'people' is fast falling out of philosophical fashion; it reappears in public discourse, if at all, during electoral campaigns.

The new states, just like the longer-living ones in their present condition, are no longer expected to perform most of the functions once seen as the *raison d'être* of nation-state bureaucracies. The function most conspicuous for having been dropped, or torn from the hands of the orthodox state, is the maintenance (as Cornelius Castoriadis put it)[9] of a dynamic equilibrium between the rhythms of the growth of consumption and the rise in productivity – a task which led sovereign states at various times to impose intermittently import or export bans, custom barriers, or state-managed, Keynes-style stimulation of internal demand. Any control of such a dynamic equilibrium is now beyond the means, and also in fact beyond the ambitions, of almost all the otherwise sovereign (in a strictly order-policing sense) states. The very distinction between the internal and the global market, or more generally between the 'inside' and the 'outside' of the state, is exceedingly difficult to maintain in any but the most narrow, 'territory-and-population policing' sense.

All three legs of the sovereignty tripod – economic, military, cultural – have now been shattered. No longer capable on their own of balancing the books, guarding their territory or promoting distinctive identities, contemporary states turn more and more into executors and plenipotentiaries of forces which they have no hope of controlling politically. In the incisive verdict of a radical Latino-American political analyst,[10] thanks to the new 'porousness' of all allegedly 'national' economies, and to the ephemerality, elusiveness and non-territoriality of the space in which they themselves operate, global financial markets impose their laws and precepts on the planet. ' "Globalization" is nothing more than a totalitarian extension of their logic to all aspects of life.' States have not enough resources or enough freedom of manoeuvre to withstand the pressure – for the simple reason that 'a few minutes is enough for enterprises and the states themselves to collapse' (as witnessed quite recently, we may add, in the cases of Mexico, Malaysia and South Korea).

In the cabaret of globalization, the state goes through a striptease and by the end of the performance it is left with only the bare necessities: its powers of repression. With its material basis destroyed, its sovereignty and independence annulled, its political class effaced, the nation-state becomes a simple security service for the megacompanies ... The new masters of the world have no need to govern directly. National governments are charged with the task of administering the affairs on their behalf.

The overall result of all this is that the 'economy' is being progressively exempted from political control; indeed, the prime meaning conveyed nowadays by the term 'economy' is that of 'the area of the non-political'. Whatever is left of politics is expected to be dealt with, as in the good old days, by the state – but anything to do with economic life the state is not allowed to touch except at its own, and its subjects', peril: any attempt in this direction would be met with prompt and furious punitive action from banks, stock exchanges and financial markets. The economic impotence of the state would once more be blatantly displayed, to the horror of its current governing team. According to the calculations of René Passet,[11] purely speculative intercurrency financial transactions reach a total volume of 1,300 billion dollars a day – fifty times greater than the volume of commercial exchanges and almost equal to the total of 1,500 billion dollars that is the sum of all the reserves of all the 'national banks' of the world. 'No state therefore', Passet comments, 'can resist for more than a few days the speculative pressures of the "markets".' The sole economic task which the state is allowed and expected to handle is to secure the equilibrated budget by policing and keeping in check local pressures for more vigorous state intervention in the running of businesses and for the defence of the population from the more sinister consequences of market anarchy.

As Jean-Paul Fitoussi has recently pointed out,

Such a programme, though, cannot be implemented unless in one way or another the economy is taken out of the field of politics. A ministry of finance certainly remains a necessary evil, but ideally one would dispense with a ministry of economic affairs (that is, of the governing of the economy). In other words, the government should be deprived of its responsibility for macroeconomic policy.[12]

For their liberty of movement and for their unconstrained freedom to pursue their ends, global finance, trade and the information industry depend on the political fragmentation, the *morcellement* of the world scene. They have all, one may say, developed vested interests in 'weak states' – that is, in such states as are *weak* but nevertheless remain *states*. Deliberately or subconsciously, such interstate, supralocal institutions as have been brought into being and are allowed to act with the consent of global capital exert coordinated pressures on all member or dependent states to systematically destroy anything which could stem or slow down the free movement of capital and limit market liberty. Throwing wide open the gates and abandoning any thought of an autonomous economic policy is the preliminary, and meekly complied with, condition of eligibility for financial assistance from world banks and monetary funds. Weak states are precisely what the New World Order, all too often looking suspiciously like a new world *disorder*, needs to sustain and reproduce itself. Weak quasi-states can be easily reduced to the (useful) role of local police precincts, securing the modicum of order required for the conduct of business, but need not be feared as effective brakes on the global companies' freedom.

The separation of the economy from politics and the exemption of the first from the regulatory intervention of the second, resulting in the disempowerment of politics as an effective agency, augurs much more than just a shift in the distribution of social power. As Claus Offe points out,[13] political agency as such – 'the capacity to make collectively binding choices and to carry them out' – has become problematic. 'Instead of asking what is to be done, we might more fruitfully explore whether there is anybody capable of doing whatever needs to be done.' Since 'borders have become penetrable' (highly selectively, to be sure), 'sovereignties have become nominal, power anonymous, and its locus empty.' We have not yet reached the ultimate destination; the process goes on, and seemingly unstoppably. 'The dominant pattern might be described as "releasing the brakes": deregulation, liberalization, flexibility, increasing fluidity, and facilitating the transactions on the financial real estate and labour markets, easing the tax burden, etc.' The more consistently this pattern is applied, the less power remains in the hands of the agency which promotes it; and the less the increasingly resourceless agency can retreat from following that pattern, if it is wished or pressed to do so.

One of the most seminal consequences of the new global freedom of movement is that it becomes increasingly difficult, perhaps altogether impossible, to reforge social issues into effective collective action. And, further, that the sections of societies traditionally charged with that task of reforging increasingly look the other way; nothing in their own position and socially framed vocations prompts them to take up once more the role which dropped, or was torn, from their hands. These two seminal departures taken together make the present-day world ever less hospitable to Levinas's ethics, while the clarion calls of Hans Jonas bear an uncanny resemblance to crying in the wilderness.

The two departures have been, with a mixture of amazement and relish, advertised as 'the end of history', or 'end of the age of ideology'. Having no programme and no vision of the good society, no model of social justice – indeed, no model of moral politics, or ethically oriented politics except that of politicians wary of using their powers to solicit bribes or sexual favours (through the noise aroused by Clinton's sexual levity, the crashing of the welfare state's foundations was all but inaudible) – has been, in a curious reversal of values, proclaimed to be a title to pride of the learned elites; insisting (except during electoral campaigns) that equity, justice, the public good, the good society or effective citizenship are still meaningful concepts and tasks worth pursuing can be done only at the risk of ridicule or indignation.

Can the intellectuals be the saviours?

Cornelius Castoriadis asserted in one of his last interviews that the trouble with our civilization is that it stopped questioning itself. Indeed – we may say that the proclamation of the demise of 'grand narratives' (or, in the case of Richard Rorty, of the retreat from 'movement politics', a kind that used to evaluate every step in terms of shortening the distance to an ideal state of affairs, in favour of the resolution of problems at hand, which is the principle of one-issue-at-a-time 'campaign politics') announces the disengagement of the knowledge classes, the grand refusal of the modern intellectual vocation.

There are two apparently sharply opposed, but in fact converging, ways in which the knowledge classes tend to wash their hands of that questioning of society which was once their defining trait.

The 'positive concept' of ideology is one of them. If all knowledge is ideological, if one can confront ideology only from the perspective of another ideology, if *il n'y a pas hors d'idéologie*, no outside standards with which to measure and compare the validity of different ideologies – then there is no 'problem of ideology' left, nothing the students of ideology need or ought to do apart from describing them *sine ira et studio*. Above all, no taking of a stand is required. Since there is no way in which one could establish a superiority of one world perception over another, the sole remaining strategy is to take them as they come, and go along with the brute fact of their vast and irreducible variety. If no critique of ideology is allowed, then the task of social reflection ends once it has been pointed out that ideology is everywhere and everything is ideological. The idea of an active engagement with society loses its justification and urgency.

Ironically, the ostensibly opposite view leads to the same practical conclusions. That other view, never quite absent from modern discourse and now gaining in force, is that the presence of ideology is the sign of a not-yet-fully modernized society; ideology is a backward, as well as harmful, variety of knowledge. If it persists, it can only be due to ignorance or an insidious conspiracy of self-appointed reformers of reality. On the occasion of his admission to the French Academy, Jean-François Revel defined ideology as an '*a priori* construction, elaborated in spite of, and with contempt for the facts and the laws; it is the opposite of, simultaneously, science and philosophy, religion and morality.'[14] How science, philosophy, religion and morality found themselves standing shoulder to shoulder as defenders of facts and laws, we can only guess. But a credible supposition is that the role of the commander has been assigned in that army to science – which, as Revel points out, tests its assertions against reality (unlike ideology, which – as Revel does not say – tests reality against its assertions). Revel hopes that science will eventually replace ideology. When it happens, Castoriadis's premonition will finally come true: society will stop questioning itself.

The announcement of the 'end of ideology' is a declaration of intent on the part of social commentators more than it is a description of things as they are: no more criticism of the way things are being done, no more judging or censoring the world through confronting its present state with an alternative of a better society. All critical theory and practice is from now on to be as fragmented, deregulated, self-referential, singular and episodic as postmodern life itself.

A case is often made, however, that the market/neoliberal apotheosis of economic results, productivity and competitiveness, with its cult of the winner and its promotion of ethical cynicism, is the present-day equivalent of the great ideologies of yore; an ideology, moreover, which comes closer to uncontested hegemony than any of its predecessors. On the face of it, much seems to speak in favour of this view. The point of similarity between the neoliberal worldview and a typical 'classic' ideology is that both serve as *a priori* frames for all future discourse, setting what is seen apart from what goes unnoticed, awarding or denying relevance, determining the logic of reasoning and the evaluation of results. And yet what makes the neoliberal worldview sharply different from other ideologies, indeed a phenomenon of a separate category altogether, is precisely the absence of questioning and any critical edge; its surrender to what is seen as the implacable and irreversible logic of social reality. The difference between the neoliberal discourse and classic ideologies of modernity is, one may say, the difference between the mentality of plankton and that of the swimmers or sailors.

Pierre Bourdieu has compared the apparent invincibility of the neoliberal worldview to that of the 'strong discourse' of Erving Goffman's asylum:[15] this kind of discourse is notoriously difficult to resist and repel because it has on its side all the most powerful, indomitable earthly forces which have already preselected the 'real' from the 'unrealistic' and made the world as it is. The neoliberal apotheosis of the market confuses *les choses de la logique avec la logique des choses*, while the great ideologies of modern times, with all their controversies, agreed on one point: that the logic of things as they are defies and contradicts what the logic of reason dictates. Ideology used to set reason *against nature*, the neoliberal discourse disempowers reason through *naturalizing* it.

Antonio Gramsci coined the term 'organic intellectuals' to account for those members of the knowledge class who took it upon themselves to elucidate the genuine, putative or postulated tasks and prospects of large sections of the population, thereby assisting in the elevation of one or another *klasse an sich* into the *klasse für sich*. That elucidation, 'putting the plight of a class into historical perspective', was the work of ideology; intellectuals turned 'organic' through engaging in ideological praxis. Let me remark that the adding of the qualifier 'organic' to the concept of the 'intellectual' renders the resulting combination pleonasmic; it is precisely the fact of being 'organic' in the Gramscian sense that makes the mere 'men and women of knowledge' into intellectuals.

When developing the *notion of ideology* as a device to change the world, as a lever lifting the classes of class society to the rank of self-conscious historical agents, or more generally as a contraption to reshape and condense heteronomous and heterogeneous populations into autonomous and homogeneous cultural units, intellectuals did act in an 'organic' role; in that case, however, they acted as 'organic intellectuals' *of themselves*, lifting the knowledge class not just to the *klasse-für-sich* status, but to the rank of a very special class of people with a peculiar missionary vocation, of a metaclass of sorts, the 'class-producing class'. Any notion of ideology allocates a crucial, historic agency to the men and women of knowledge, proclaiming them responsible for spelling out the values and purposes fit, adequate and proper to classes, ethnic groups, genders or nations, and for making their discoveries historically effective. This crucial underlying assumption of the concept of ideology casts the intellectuals in the role of culture creators, teachers as well as the guardians of values (notably *ethical* values); it demands direct engagement with the model of the just society and so the engagement with society itself or its selected sections, and, indeed, gives sense to the very idea of 'intellectuals' as women or men of knowledge *with a mission* to perform and a virtue to promote – as well as underpinning the collective bid of the knowledge class to a position of authority corresponding to that collective vocation.

The question is whether the currently widespread, perhaps dominant, gospel of the 'end of ideology' or the 'demise of grand narratives' (and, overarching them all, of the 'end of history') is an act of surrender on the part of the knowledge class and of withdrawal of the collective bid; or, on the contrary, whether it can be seen as another, updated version of the 'self-organic' strategy and, accordingly, of that ideology which supplies its justification and *raison d'être*.

It seems that if the knowledge class of the late modern or postmodern era does assume the role of organic intellectuals at all, it is only the role of organic intellectuals of themselves. What most conspicuously marks off the present-day thought of knowledge classes is its self-referentiality, its acute preoccupation with the conditions of its own professional activity and an increasingly non-committal stance taken towards other sectors of society; indeed, its almost total abandonment of the traditional 'synthesizing' role – an unwillingness to see in the rest of society anything more than an aggregate of individuals, coupled with the proclivity to theorize them as solitary, rather than collective, agents. The 'privatization' of the notion of agency in present-day social thought is a case in point – one of many.

It would be naive to blame the current seminal departure on another stage productions of the 'clerks' betrayal', and seek redress in the orthodox invocation of commitment as duty. The retreat from a public agenda to professional shelters can hardly be explained away by a (equally inexplicable, as it were) sudden change of heart or a spell of selfish mood. In all probability, the causes reach deeper, into the profound transformations in the way power and the ability to act and to act effectively which goes with power are in postmodern society distributed and exercised, and in the way the conditions of social life, including that of the knowledge classes, are reproduced.

Analysing the causes of the rapid weakening of links between the concerns and preoccupations of the knowledge classes and the public agenda, Geoff Sharp has recently pinpointed 'the insulation of the social theoretical "discourse" from the language of everyday life' as paramount among them.[16] Again, this insulation is not just an outcome of contingent choice nor is it a matter of character fault. It comes in the wake of a radical redeployment of intellectual resources and a change in the way in which intellectual work is conducted. In the terms I suggested using, we may say that the insulation in question may well be the only form which the self-referential ideology of the intellectuals might take if they were to remain under postmodern conditions, as throughout modern times, the 'organic intellectuals' of themselves; though, simultaneously, this form demands that the knowledge classes cease to be 'organic intellectuals' of anybody else.

The more general point, says Sharp,

> is that intellectual practice as such is radically dependent upon technological mediation for its distinctive way of constituting a form of life. Mediated action is its hallmark...It holds as well for the mediate manner in which the technosciences take hold of and constitute their objects; that is, by way of an intervening apparatus which allows that object to be re-represented and understood in ways which are unavailable to more directly sensate knowledge. Finally mediation allows all expressions of intellectual practice to constitute their objects more abstractly: which is to say, constitute them in different and typically more inclusive categories than is characteristic of the relations of mutual presence.

Let me add that with all their flaunted inclusivity and typicality the categories in question are not inclusive of the total human beings as they emerge and act in their everyday life. On the contrary: generalizing abstracted aspects of human agents, *pars pro toto*, the categories in question split and divide rather than 'make whole' and stand in the way of human life ever acquiring the totality it strives for. Whatever the case may be, though, let us note, after Sharp, 'the unprecedented way in which intellectually related practices are reconstituting the world of postmodernity in their own image: mediately, abstractly and via the textual archive'.

The world wide web which the knowledge classes inhabit, which they process and by which they are processed, leaves the *Lebenswelt* – the lived world – outside; it admits bits and parts of that world only when properly fragmented and so ready for processing, and returns them to the world outside in duly recycled, abstracted form. Cyberspace, the site of postmodern intellectual practice, feeds on fragmentation and promotes fragmentation, being simultaneously its product and its major *causa efficiens*.

The ascendance of ideology in the heyday of modernity was, notoriously, a mixed blessing. But so is its demise. Wise after the event, we know now the human costs of casting society into ideological straitjackets, of falling into the temptation of marrying ideological blueprints to the fervour of executive powers – and we are inclined to count them carefully before any new commitment is entered into. But we have yet to learn the costs of living without alternative signposts and yardsticks, of 'letting things go' and declaring the consequences to be as inevitable as they are unanticipated. Ulrich Beck's vision of the *Risikogesellschaft*, the risk society, is a glimpse of such living: living from one crisis to another, attempting to cope with one known problem only to provoke an unknown quantity of unknown problems, focusing on the management of local orders while losing sight of their contribution to global chaos. It is too early to celebrate the end of 'grand narratives', just as it is uncanny, perhaps also unethical, in the light of modern experience, to bewail their passing.

15

Democracy on two battlefronts

We've learned from Aristotle to tell the *oikos* (this familiar and cosy, though sometimes noisy and stormy private territory, where we meet some familiar others daily and face to face, talk and negotiate the ways of sharing our lives) from the *ecclesia* (that distant domain which we seldom visit in person but where public issues, the matters which affect the lives of each of us, are settled). There is a third area, though, stretching between the other two: the *agora*, a realm neither truly private nor fully public, a little bit of both. It is in the *agora* that 'the public' and 'the private' meet, are introduced to each other, get acquainted and learn by trial and error the difficult art of peaceful (and useful) cohabitation.

The *agora* is the homeground of democracy. By the frequency with which it is visited, by the number of people who visit it and the length of their stay, the pulse of democracy is measured. It is during those visits that the work of *translation* between *oikos* and *ecclesia* is performed. Democracy is, indeed, the practice of continuous translation between the public and the private; of reforging private problems into public issues and recasting public well-being into private projects and tasks. Like all translation, it is hardly ever perfect and always remains open to correction. And like all translation, it lays bare new layers of possibilities on both sides of the translating action. Friedrich Schleiermacher taught us that interpretation consists in a forever rotating 'hermeneutic circle'. One may think of translation in the same way. Democracy is a 'circle of translation'. When translation stops, democracy ends. Democracy cannot, without betraying its nature, recognize any translation as final and no longer open to negotiation. You can tell a democratic society by its never fully quelled suspicion that its job is unfinished: that it is not yet democratic enough.

Cornelius Castoriadis suggests that no formula has captured better the essence of democracy than *edoxe te boule kai to demo* ('it is deemed good by the council and the people') – used by the Athenians as a routine preambula to the laws they enacted and wished to be obeyed. 'It is *deemed* good' – not 'it *is* good'. What is deemed to be good today may not be so tomorrow, when the council and the people meet again in the *agora*. Laws which follow the meeting could only be obeyed as standing invitations to further meetings. The conversation between *ecclesia* and *oikos* can never grind to a halt.

The possibility and the practicality of translation depend on the same condition: on the autonomy of, simultaneously, the society and its members. The citizens have to be autonomous – free to form their own opinions and to cooperate in order to make words flesh. And the society has to be autonomous – free to set its laws and knowing that there is no other warrant of the goodness of the law than the earnest and diligent exercise of that freedom. The two autonomies complement each other, but only on condition that their territories overlap and that the overlapping realms comprise all the things needed for the shared life to be good. What makes the ongoing conversation between the council and the people meaningful, and their regular meetings worth the time and the effort they require, is the expectation that 'what is deemed good' by both sides will indeed become the law which both sides would obey and by which they will be ruled. To see sense in exercising their autonomy, citizens must know and believe that the society which calls on their thought and labour is also autonomous.

If this is what democracy is about, then it is nowadays exposed to a twofold threat. One threat comes from the growing impotence of the *ecclesia*, the public powers, to enact 'what is deemed to be good' and to implement what has been enacted. Another (not unrelated to the first) comes from the fading of the art of translation between *ecclesia* and *oikos*: public issues and private problems. The fate of democracy's survival is currently decided on the two battlelines where the twin threats are confronted.

To start with the first threat: power is increasingly detached from politics. Power, as Manuel Castells puts it, flows; while all the political institutions invented and entrenched in a two-hundred-year-long history of modern democracy stay, as before, tied to the ground. Power is these days global and exterritorial; politics is territorial and local. Power moves freely and with the speed of electronic signals, ignoring the limitations of space (Paul Virilio has suggested that while the obituaries of history are grossly premature, we are certainly witnessing the end of geography: distances do not matter any more). Politics, however, has no other agency except the state, the sovereignty of which is, as before, defined (and confined) in spatial terms. Power tends to be measured by the ability to avoid engagement or to disengage and escape at short notice or without notice, while the symptom of powerlessness is the inability to arrest or even to slow down the moves. Keeping the option of the 'vanishing act' open is fast becoming the global powers' principal strategy, while 'hit and run' becomes its most favoured tactic.

There is a widening gap between the outer limits of institutionalized political control and the space where the issues most relevant to human life are, by design or by default, settled. That space is beyond the reach of the sovereign state – so far the only totality which has come to embody and institutionalize the democratic procedure. Whenever any attempts were undertaken (half-heartedly, to be sure) by the assembly of sovereign states to fill the void collectively, they have failed abominably, as the toothless Uruguay resolutions – or the utter impossibility of arriving at a united stand on questions as essential as genetic engineering or cloning – have repeatedly demonstrated. The war in the former Yugoslavia has signalled many weighty departures – but it was also a nail in the coffin of that state sovereignty which underlay the world order and the practice of democracy during most of modern history, and a declaration of the irrelevance of the United Nations, that response to globalization which took the principle of state sovereignty as its starting point. There is no such thing in sight as global democracy.

Anthony Giddens has used the metaphor of the juggernaut to visualize the way in which modern life spread (the image of the 'juggernaut', a giant vehicle under which the faithful, gripped by religious ecstasy, allegedly jumped to be joyfully crushed and ground into pulp, was imported from India by its British rulers and replaced the image of the biblical Moloch in British imagery). However apt the metaphor may be in grasping the dynamics of modernity, it certainly captures unerringly the logic of globalization.

Religious ecstasy, to be sure, is these days confined to the court poets of the up-and-coming powers, or their preachers like Francis Fukuyama or Thomas Friedman. For the sober *Staatsmänner* of our profane times an updated version of *Staatsräson* will do; the mark of stately prudence is, increasingly, the TINA principle (an abbreviation proposed by Pierre Bourdieu for the 'There Is No Alternative' creed of the devotees of global free markets): there is nothing we can do to stop the game – and if you can't beat them, join them. One way or another, the outcome is much the same. Political wisdom boils down to throwing the gates wide open to the free movement of financial and trade capital and to make the country enticingly hospitable and seductive to the potent nomads by minimizing the rules and maximizing the flexibility of labour and financial markets. The *ecclesia*, in other words, uses its power to surrender its power. Governments vie with each other to tempt the juggernaut to ride their way.

Claus Offe observed a few years ago that our complex social reality has become so rigid that any critical reflection on its mechanism seems futile and of no practical consequence. But the 'toughness' of a beefsteak is itself a reflection of the sharpness of your knife and teeth. With knives no longer on the table and the teeth, healthy or ailing, pulled out one by one, there is nothing to bite the steak with...

This is why the most haunting of political mysteries is nowadays not so much '*what* to do', as '*who* would do it, if we knew'. Practicality of action being measured by the potency of the tools, not much action is expected by most reasonable people from their local *ecclesiae*, since they are only too well aware of how limited their freedom of manoeuvre has become. To anyone concerned with the welfare of the *oikos*, meetings in the *agora* to negotiate joint interests and the ways of promoting and protecting them seem increasingly to be a waste of time and effort. As for the professionals of the *ecclesia*, there seems to be no more reason for them either to visit the *agora*. After all, they can add little to the debate except further exhortations to take things as they come and bite them on their own, with private knives and dentures supplied by the shops.

The *agora* has been deserted. It has not stayed empty for long, though. It has been filled once more – this time by the sounds reverberating from the *oikos*. As Peter Ustinov, the witty British raconteur, observed – 'This is a free country, madam. We have the right to share your privacy in a public space.' Alain Ehrenberg, a French sociologist, picks one Wednesday evening in October 1983 as a turning point in French cultural (and not just cultural) history: on that evening a certain Vivianne, in front of millions of TV viewers, announced that her husband, Michel, suffers from premature ejaculation and that, not unexpectedly, she has never experienced any pleasure from their sex. Since that seminal event innumerable talk-shows and chat-shows have become the principal window opened by TV stations all over the globe on to the human world. What the viewers see through that window are people confessing the intimate *Erlebnisse* never before vented in public, and the major lesson they hear reiterated *ad nauseam* is that each one of us has to struggle with the same worries and that each one of us has to struggle with them alone, using their own wits and stamina and helped only by the clever gadgets expertly spied out in the department stores.

The 'private' has invaded the meant-to-be-public scene, but not to interact with the 'public'. Even while it is being thrashed out in public view, the 'private' does not acquire a new quality; if anything, the 'private' is reinforced in its privacy. The televised chats of 'ordinary people' like Vivianne and Michel, and the newspapers' 'exclusive' gossip about the private lives of show-business stars, politicians and other celebrities, are public lessons in the vacuity of public life and in the vanity of hopes invested in anything less private than private troubles and private cures. Lonely individuals nowadays enter the *agora* only to find the company of other lonely individuals like themselves. They return home reassured and reinforced in their loneliness.

This is the Gordian knot which binds the future of democracy hand and foot: the growing practical impotence of public institutions strips interest in common issues and common stands of its attraction, whereas the fading ability and vanishing will to translate private sufferings into public issues facilitates the job of the global forces which prompt that impotence while feeding on its result. It will take the insight and courage of an Alexander of Macedonia to cut the knot.

16

Violence, old and new

In the United States of America the fight against terrorism, at home and abroad, has been for many years now a major preoccupation of the federal government and the reason for feeding ever larger chunks of national income into the budgets of the police and armed forces. 'Terrorism' has become the generic name brought out each time that the marines or bomber pilots are sent on another mission, that another round of smart missiles is launched, or that new and tougher restrictions are imposed on the residents of inner cities. The concept of 'terrorism' comes in particularly handy when someone, somewhere, decides to resist the oppression gun-in-hand, especially if what they resist are the governments which long ago ceased to resist the American 'globalizing programme' of free trade and open borders. According to the San Diego professor Herbert I. Schiller, in the last decade alone the Iranians, the Libyans, the Palestinians and the Kurds have been denounced (notably by the Secretary of State, Madeleine Albright) as terrorists. Before that, during the last fifty years, the American army and its allies have burnt with napalm and otherwise massacred the terrorists in Korea, the Dominican Republic, Vietnam, Nicaragua, Iraq and quite a few other places.[1]

There is no doubt that terrorism is brutal and bloody, and that the people called 'terrorists' are ready and eager to murder as many mortals as needed to ensure the birth or survival of their cause. The point is, though, that whether the people who shoot, bomb and burn other people are labelled 'terrorist' or not depends not so much on the nature of their deeds as on the sympathy or antipathy of those who print the labels and paste them with glue strong enough to make them stick. Were it not for the labels, one could often confuse the terrorists and their victims – like that unnamed British soldier in Kosovo who shared his doubts with the *Guardian* correspondent Chris Bird: 'I think we were fed a bad line about the Kosovo Liberation Army. They are terrorists and we won their war for them. It's not only Serbs but the ethnic Albanians as well that are scared of them.'[2]

Terrorists do violence; more correctly, we call violence what the terrorists do. This reversible definition shows how tremendously difficult it is to define violence while referring solely to the attributes of the deed. Yes, it is the feature of violence to make people do things which otherwise they would not do and which they do not feel like doing; yes, violence means frightening people into acting against their will and thereby depriving them of their right to choose; and yes, for the sake of such effects harm is done to the human body, pain is inflicted, horror is spread by the spectacle of churned flesh and pools of blood or by rumours that the men and women bold or arrogant enough to resist had their flesh burned and their blood spilt. This is truth; but not the whole truth. Not all cruel, gory, no-holds-barred bending and twisting of human freedom and bodily integrity comes under the rubric of 'violence'. In order for such action to be dubbed 'violence' and condemned accordingly, some other conditions must be met which are not related to the nature of the actions, but to the persons of their perpetrators and the purposes which have been ascribed to them or self-declared. As to the victims of their actions, they would hardly spot the difference: they would be covered with blood, chased away from their homes, deprived of their property or their lives, and these things tend to feel alike whether their motive is genuine or putative. Pain feels exactly the same whether it has been classified as 'collateral damage' or a result of intention. More importantly yet, the victims have only the words of their tormentors to rely on when it comes to deciding what the intentions truly were and how much 'collateral damage' those intentions could absorb while remaining the noble intentions they are said to have been.

In short: violence is an essentially contested concept. The contest in which that concept is a stake concerns legitimacy. Violence is illegitimate coercion; more precisely, coercion which has been denied legitimacy. Calling an act of coercion, of forcing people to act against their will or taking away from them the chance to act ever again willingly or unwillingly, an 'act of violence' adds no new information to the description of the act, but conveys the decision of the speaker to question the actors' right to exercise coercion; and also to deny them the right to determine which words will be used to describe their actions. In the power struggle, violence is simultaneously a means and the stake. This dual role derives from the principal objective of that struggle, which is the legitimacy of coercion.

In his insightful analysis of the 'literary field' Pierre Bourdieu ridiculed the 'positivist' literary studies that attempt an inventory of immanent and 'objective' qualities of literature which, in their view, would allow it to be established equally 'objectively' what is and what is not a 'literary work' or who is and who is not a 'writer'. Against such hopes and intentions, Bourdieu points out that 'one of the major stakes in the struggles conducted inside the literary or artistic field is the definition of the field's boundaries' – that is, of the aggregate of people 'with the legitimate right to participate in the struggle'. The stake in question is the 'definition of legitimate practice' – and ultimately the right to articulate the 'authoritative', that is *binding*, definitions.[3] I suggest that this analysis, though dealing with literary or artistic struggles, has direct relevance to our topic: everything that has been said here by Bourdieu about the dynamics of the literary field concerns the attributes it possesses as a specimen of a wider class of 'social fields'. *All* social fields, however distinct and specific and whatever their tools and products, are sedimentations of past power struggles and are 'kept in shape' by ongoing power struggles. The essence of all power is the right to *define with authority*, and the major stake of the power struggle is the appropriation or retaining of the right to define and, no less importantly, of the right to invalidate and ignore the definitions coming from the adversary camp.

As Edward W. Said noted in the aftermath of the eruption of violence in Kosovo:

The International Tribunal which designated Milosevic a war criminal loses its credibility if, following the same criteria, it refrains from the inculpation of Clinton and Blair, Madeleine Albright, Sandy Berger, General Clark and all those who violated, simultaneously, all forms of decency and the laws of war. In comparison with what Clinton has done to Iraq, Milosevic is almost an amateur.[4]

We can safely assume that the naivety of these remarks was deliberate. Surely Edward Said, a most perceptive analyst of the fads and foibles of our civilization, must have known that the criteria followed by the International Tribunal were not those of the degree of cruelty and the volume of human suffering which that cruelty caused (let alone criteria as ethereal and elusive as 'decency'), but those of the *right to be cruel*; and that, consequently, the criteria applied by the tribunal to Milosevic and Clinton were, indeed, the same. It is by these criteria that the first could be declared a criminal and the other allowed to bask in the glory of bringing him to his knees. It is conceivable that some years ago, when the principle of state territorial sovereignty had not yet crumbled under the unremitting pressure of globalization, 'the same' criteria would have prompted the acquittal of Milosevic and a charge of aggression – the eponymically illegitimate violence – to be raised against NATO forces

In all order-building and order-maintenance endeavours legitimacy is, by necessity, the prime stake of the game and the most hotly contested concept. The fight is conducted around the borderline dividing proper (that is, unpunishable) from improper (that is, punishable) coercion and enforcement. The 'war against violence' is waged in the name of the monopoly of coercion. The 'elimination of violence', the declared objective of such a war, is visualized as the state in which that monopoly is no longer contested. The 'non-violence' presented as the attribute of civilized life does not mean the absence of coercion, but only the absence of *unauthorized* coercion. These are the prime reasons why the war against violence is unwinnable, and a 'non-violent' social order is very nearly a contradiction in terms.

Our modern civilization had enlisted the 'elimination of violence' as one of the principal items of the order-building agenda. Taking the project of modernity at its word and oblivious to the agenda which the choice of words was meant to hide or make more palatable, numerous scholars have theorized modern civilization as bent on the 'softening' of the human condition and the steady elimination of coercive methods of promoting order. So far, they have been sorely disappointed in their attempts to document convincing progress, though with each change of the setting and the rules of the ongoing power game they have celebrated in advance the breakthrough bound to come. The trouble with the game a-changing is that, while continuously refreshing the fading promises of better chances for the future, it cannot but repeatedly re-evaluate the past: what was recorded in its time as a triumph of civilized order tends to be rewritten some time later as a history of spine-chillingly cruel violence – as has been the fate of the 'pacification' of the 'violent tribesmen' of India, or of the taming of Indian savages in America and the aboriginal savages in Australia. Just how vulnerable and transient the borders are between violence and 'civilizing progress' is vividly shown by the notorious troubles of American history textbooks – successively denounced, censured, vilified and withdrawn one by one from circulation as 'politically incorrect', that is, jarring with somebody's idea of the legitimacy of gun-wielding by respective adversaries.

Two important conclusions follow.

First: it is impossible to say with any degree of objectivity whether modern history is a story of rising, or receding violence – as it is quite impossible to find a way of measuring 'objectively' the overall volume of violence.

To start with, there is Ludwig Wittgenstein's timely reminder that 'no cry of torment can be greater than the cry of one man... Or again, *no* torment can be greater than what a single human being may suffer... The whole planet can suffer no greater torment than a *single* soul'[5] – but even if one imprudently pushed aside this warning against the common yet misleading tendency to reduce the issue of pain infliction to the question of the pain sufferers' numbers, the problem would remain that the treatment of acts of coercion as 'violent acts' is much too inconstant and erratic to allow serious treatment of stochastic series, however diligently and laboriously they have been researched and collated. All estimates of historical tendencies to violence have thus far had a short life expectancy; they are bound to be as contentious and contested as the legitimacy of coercion and the classification of coercion as violence that depends on such legitimacy.

Second: contrary to the declarations of intent which accompany the promotion and entrenchment of a 'civilized order', a consistent and determined stand against violence is unlikely to be taken. Censure of violence could be cohesive only if it extended to coercion as such; but this is simply not on the cards. Order builders and order guardians are and cannot but be in a double frame of mind when it comes to the question of the usefulness of and the need for coercion. The idea of order-building would not occur to them in the first place were it not for the presence of 'obstacles to order' or 'enemies of order' needing to be suppressed, *coerced* into submission, so that order might triumph. A radically tolerant and all-permitting order is a *contradiction in terms*. Order building and order protection consist, principally, in the exemption of a large assortment of coercive measures from the opprobrium reserved for violence; its object being the redistribution of legitimacy, the guardianship of order is as much a struggle to eliminate violence, that is *illegitimate* coercion, as it is an effort to *legitimize* 'useful and necessary' coercion. Condemnation of force and compulsion can only be selective – and, more often than not, disputed.

The perception of endemic, 'ordinary' and 'normal' coercion as 'violence' varies together with the degree of legitimacy of the social order. If the order's claim to legitimacy is shaky and poorly grounded, much of the force deployed in the service of order will be conceived as violence; and conversely, challenge to the order's legitimacy will consist in the questioning and condemnation of its enforcement as violence. To deny the right to use force equals the refusal to grant legitimacy to the extant powers – refusal associated as a rule with a competitive power bid. In times of transition, much of the coercion endemic in the daily 'orderly' life of society surfaces in public consciousness as violence.

Ours are times of transition – and a transition no less profound and comprehensive than that which went down in history as the birth of modern society. No wonder that the impression of 'living in violent times' and the conviction that the volume and cruelty of violence are rising are so widespread. When the old institutional scaffoldings of daily routine are falling apart, few if any 'musts' once taken to be a 'part of life', unpleasant and irritating yet bound to be lived with and suffered in silence, stay as obvious and look as inevitable as before.

When securely institutionalized, coercion melts into the background of daily life, out of focus. The eyes rarely notice it and so it is 'invisible'; and the more routine, repetitive and monotonous the coercion is, the less its chance of drawing attention. It is only when the routine is broken or comes under pressure that the coercion which used to sustain it comes into view. This is also the moment when in the eyes of its targets coercion acquires all the trappings of violence: of an unwarranted, unjustified and inexcusable use of force, a wicked assault against personal integrity and sovereignty.

This is, however, but one part of the story. The rising frequency with which people nowadays resort to a use of force which, in the absence of institutionalized frameworks, can only be classified as violence cannot be dismissed as a *trompe-l'oeil* and blamed on the cognitive confusion natural at times of transition.

Ours are times of transition in as far as the old structures are falling apart or have been dismantled, while no alternative structures with an equal institutional hold are about to be put in their place. It is as if the moulds into which human relationships were poured to acquire shape have now themselves been thrown into a melting pot. Deprived of such moulds, all patterns of relationships become as suspicious as they are uncertain and vulnerable, amenable to challenge and open to negotiation. It is not just that the actual human relations, like all human attributes in the era of modernity, call for an effort to fit them into a pattern; the present-day problem is that the patterns themselves are no longer 'given'. The patterns themselves have now turned into tasks, and these tasks are to be performed under conditions which are marked by the absence of 'normative regulation' and of clear-cut criteria as to successful accomplishment. A curious game, whose rules and purposes are themselves its major stakes.

Since the pattern-making has no pre-established finishing line and there are no ready-made designs by which one can check the direction of the escapade, let alone measure its progress, the work can proceed only through a series of trials and errors. Pattern-making consists nowadays in a process of continuous experimentation. Any initial supposition which the experiments are meant to be testing tends to be vague or altogether absent; the purpose of experimentation is itself the topic of experiment.

The trial and error process of pattern-making takes, as a rule, the form of 'reconnaissance through battle'. In military practice the term refers to engaging the adversary in a skirmish in the hope of revealing the resources of the other side, its defensive or offensive capacities, and so what sort of response to one's own gambits one could expect or, conversely, how secure one can reasonably presume one's own position to be. Attempts to reconnoitre all these things through a brief yet intense military engagement are sometimes undertaken when the strategic plan has been completed and signed and what remains is to test just how realistic are the prospects of its success. But it happens as well that 'reconnaissance through battle' is initiated in order to find out how wide the range is of feasible options. With no plans worked out as yet, the setting of targets for action will depend instead on the results of the preliminary engagement and the conclusions one may derive concerning the strength and resolve of the resistance one is likely to encounter.

The currently rising volume of 'family' and 'neighbourhood' violence calls for a two-stage explanation. First, due to the perceived weakness of once all-powerful, self-evident and unquestioned patterns of relationships, much of the coercion entailed in their daily reproduction has been stripped of its past legitimacy and so tends nowadays to be reclassified as violence. Second, the new fluidity and flexibility of relationships released from patterned constraints prompt widespread use of 'reconnaissance by battle' stratagems: the strength, resourcefulness and resilience of the sides are put to a daily 'trial of force', in order to find out by how much one's own territory could be expanded, how far one may go without fear of counterattack, or how much nagging and pushing the other side is likely to bear with before it 'gets its act together' and responds in kind. This is use-of-force-in-search-of-legitimacy; and for the time being, as long as the sought-after legitimacy has not been won and securely fenced, the 'trial by force' is by definition an act of violence. If new patterns do not emerge and the armistice terms need to be reinforced or renegotiated daily, the coercion which always underlies 'peaceful cohabitation' may parade in the garb of violence for a long time to come.

The newly named varieties of family and neighbourhood violence – such as marital rape, child abuse, sexual harassment at work, stalking, prowling – illustrate the 'reclassification' processes. The phenomena which all these outrage-and-panic-generating catchwords try to grasp are not new. They have been around for a very long time, but either they were treated as 'natural' and suffered in silence like other unwelcome yet unavoidable nuisances of life, or they stayed unnoticed, like other features of 'normality'. Quite often, under the names of marital loyalty, parent–children intimacy or the arts of courtship, they were praised and keenly cultivated alongside other similarly indispensable conditions of the world order (so-called 'socialization' consists, after all, in inducing individuals to do willingly what according to the rules of their society they must do). The new names refer not so much to the phenomena they denote as to the refusal to put up with them as placidly as before. The new names, we may say, are the question marks replacing full stops. The phenomena they name are now questioned, their legitimacy is refuted, their institutional foundations are shaky and they no longer exude an air of solidity and permanence – and illegitimate coercion, as we remember, is violence.

Since old patterns no longer seem obligatory and their holding power feels less than overwhelming and awe-and-obedience-inspiring, while no new patterns are in sight that bid for universal consent and permanent institutional entrenchment, let alone that are likely to obtain either of them – more and more situations are experienced as fluid, underdefined and contentious, and so calling for constant vigilance and battle fatigue. Ours is increasingly an embattled society – one in which violence, accusations of violence and expectations of violence turn into major vehicles for individual and group self-assertion. The old principle *si vis pacem, para bellum* (if you would have peace, be ready for war) seems topical as never before – from the top to the bottom of the social system, whether at the global, local or domestic level.

The suspicion of violence is itself an ample source of anxiety: as the problem of legitimacy stays permanently unsolved and debatable, no demand likely to arise from the circumstances of sharing space, home or life is free from the charge of overt or hidden violence. No wonder there is an ambient fear of violence which prompts the strategy of disengagement: of territorial separation made safe by the modern equivalents of moats and drawbridges, like neighbourhood watch, gated condominiums, closed TV circuits and security or vigilante patrols, but also of the replacement of a 'till death us do part' type of commitment with 'trial marriages' and flexible households whose fragility and uncommitted character is protected by the cancellation-on-demand clause.

The institutionalized patterns crumble and disintegrate at all levels of social organization with similar consequences: at all levels ever more types of interaction are reclassified into the category of violence, while acts of violence of the 'reconnaissance by battle' kind become a permanent feature of the continuous deconstruction and reconstruction of power hierarchies. Two levels deserve particularly close attention: one, occupied until recently by state and nation merged into one; and another, heretofore poorly institutionalized, until recently virtually a 'no man's land' but keenly colonized now by the emerging 'global' – or in Alberto Melucci's vocabulary 'planetary' – system.

The construction of modern nation-states was a story of violence perpetrated by the relatively few resourceful and successful ethnicities upon the multitude of inchoate, lesser and hapless ones – the 'would be' but 'never to be' nations. Histories are written by victors, and so the suppression and physical or cultural extermination of defeated minorities never given the chance to write their own histories came to be recorded and retold as an edifying and uplifting story of progress or of a civilizing process: of a gradual yet relentless pacification of daily life and purification of human interaction from violence. When surveyed with the benefit of hindsight, that purification looks rather like the successful elimination of *unauthorized* coercion and the institutionalization ('naturalization') of *authoritative* coercion embroidered into the tissue of human bonds. Later repainting of the picture notwithstanding, the matter of violence was for many decades confined to the problem of anti-social, criminal margins. With the stormy beginnings of the nation-states conveniently forgotten, a clear and no longer disputed line could be drawn between coercion dressed as 'defence of law and order' and 'naked' and 'savage', but scattered and dispersed violence, easy to locate and isolate.

This is no longer the case, though. With the sovereignty of nation-states continually eroded by globalizing pressures and the threshold requirements for bids for self-determination radically lowered, the power-assisted, compulsory assimilation and incorporation of ethnic minorities and the annihilation of their separate identities (the updated version of Claude Lévi-Strauss's ethnological category of the *anthropophagic* strategy – the prime technique of order-building deployed by nation-states in the past) is no longer available; the sporadic attempts to deploy it now tend to be

spectacularly ineffective. Accordingly, the deployment of the alternative strategy (a present-day rendition of Lévi-Strauss's *anthro-
poemic* strategy) – that of disengagement, mutual separation,
eviction and deportation – is a temptation difficult to resist. That
other who is no longer assimilable needs to be destroyed or
deported beyond the boundary of a community which can only
rely upon the uniform similarity of its members when it comes to
the imposition and defence of patterns of cohabitation. For the
newly emerging states, a policy of compulsory assimilation and the
suppression of local traditions, memories, customs and dialects is
no longer a feasible or viable option. We've entered the period of
ethnic cleansing as the principal expedient of nation-building
strategy.

The emergent nations bidding for their nation-states have no
benefit of already-enforced-and-entrenched, authoritative institutions to back their fragile and hotly contested, more postulated
than real, identity. They have yet to crystallize themselves out from
the medley of cultures, languages and beliefs in which they have
been dissolved; they still need to distil their separate identity by
distinguishing and isolating the hopelessly mixed ingredients of the
solution. Since they cannot resort to 'legitimate coercion', whatever they do to attain this objective may only be classified as
violence.

And violent it must be: for the aspiring nations, a killing frenzy
is a matter not so much of life or death, as of birth or miscarriage.
There are few if any substitutes for the 'original crime' as a foolproof adhesive to hold together scattered individuals for a long
time to come and to cement them into a compact and closely-knit
national community. Only the future 'sovereign nation' will be
willing and able to absolve the accomplices by rejecting the
charge of violence and effectively protect them from punishment
as well as from haunting memories of guilt. The most awesome
enemies of the up-and-coming nation are therefore the turncoats,
the infidels, the lukewarm and the indifferent; the dirtier everyone's hands, the more common and more universally felt will be
the need to have those hands washed, and only the 'sovereign
nation' will be potent enough to declare them clean. Violence
is needed, first and foremost, to force the unwilling patriots-by-
appointment to partake in the violent acts. The official and
publicly declared enemies, the objects of 'ethnic cleansing', are

by this reckoning the ill-starred victims of 'collateral damage' done in the course of the efforts at 'closing the ranks' by the state/nation struggling to be born.

The new outburst of violence at the local level, once pacified under the administration of the sovereign nation-states, would not occur were it not for the steady erosion of that sovereignty by the pressures generated at the level of the 'planetary system'. Resorts to violence at these two levels are closely related and interdependent; but each level presents problems of its own and tends to generate a different kind of violence.

At the level of nations-in-search-of-a-state, territory is the stake of inter-ethnic warfare. Whoever stays in the field after the battle wins the war. Whatever tactic has been chosen therefore requires direct engagement with the adversary. This need for engagement is magnified by the previously discussed solidarity-in-crime factor: the experience of cruelty committed must be personal and direct and so impossible to argue away, and its memory must stay vivid and ineradicable. In this respect the 'birth of national community' kind of violence differs radically from the order-building or order-maintenance coercive operations, including genocides, carried out by established nation-states. The latter were obliged to resort to bureaucratic anonymity, 'floating responsibility' and depersonalization of individual action, and to the sheltering of the perpetrators from the gory results of their actions; but the mass murder that accompanies the birth of a new nation must be committed in full view to be effective. The bloodstains on the hands of the murderers must be visible, and best of all unwashable.

This requirement does not, however, bind the violent acts perpetrated in the course of the brand-new 'global wars', of which the Gulf War and the NATO Kosovo campaign have supplied the most seminal examples. Territorial gains were not among the aims of these wars; quite the contrary, the eventuality of invading and bringing the territory under the administration and management of the attackers was shunned and most meticulously avoided; preventing this was the major, perhaps the decisive factor in strategic calculation. The war aim was to force the enemy – reluctant to throw its territory open to 'global forces' – into submission, but oblige it to bear responsibility for the day-to-day running of local affairs, leaving it with the amount of resources necessary to keep the territory hospitable and comfortable for global trade and finance, but not enough for it to try once more to make the country into a fortress.

The aim of the new type of 'global war' is not territorial aggrandizement, but throwing any remaining closed doors wide open for the free flow of global capital. To paraphrase Clausewitz, we may say that this war is primarily the 'promotion of free global trade by other means'. For this reason, the aims of such a war could hardly be served by such old-fashioned measures as confrontation, engagement and combat, which inevitably imply entering commitments and bearing the consequences. Ideally one would leave the selection of targets entirely to computers and smart, self-guiding missiles. Short of that ideal, the war planners tried to reduce the tasks of the army professionals to running the software programs and monitoring the computer screens. The new, global era wars are wars at a distance, hit-and-run wars: the bombers leave the scene before the enemy can manage any response and before the carnage can be seen.

Richard Falk has compared this new war with torture: like the torturer, the attacker is fully in charge and free to select any violent methods of pain infliction which he deems effective and so 'rational'. Such a comparison is not fully correct: torture, unlike the new war of the globalization era, made an encounter and, indeed, interaction between the torturer and the victim both unavoidable and 'productive'. The new global wars, unthinkable without the electronic technology which renders time instantaneous and annihilates the resistance of space, are won by the avoidance of encounter and by denying the adversary any chance of responding. This difference, to be sure, only magnifies the privileges which the attackers in a hit-and-run global war share with the torturer. Their freedom of manoeuvre is nearly absolute and so is their impunity. Casualties are counted only 'down there' on the ground – but the attackers will never touch the ground if they are lucky; and all the odds are that luck will be on their side.

In this, I suggest, lies the most sinister potential of wars which the military arm of the globalizing forces is able and willing to launch. The prospect of utter impunity, coupled with the redundancy of time-consuming, costly and risk-fraught ideological mobilization and the irrelevance of 'patriotic capital', as well as with freedom from the need to clean up the mess and devastation caused by the assault, combine into a temptation which may be not just difficult to resist but all too easy (indeed, 'rational') to surrender to. All those who pursue the politics of global free trade and global capital flow find that this particular 'other means' has a lot to recommend it, and there is very little to advise them against taking this option, let alone to prevent them from taking it once that is what they have resolved to do.

A century likely to go down in history as one of violence perpetrated by nation-states on its subjects has come to a close. Another violent century – this time a century of violence prompted by the progressive disablement of the nation-states by free-flowing global powers – is likely to succeed it.

17

On postmodern uses of sex

In his beautiful book-long essay *La llama doble – Amor y erotismo*,[1] published in 1993, the great Mexican thinker Octavio Paz explores the complex interaction between sex, eroticism and love – three close relatives, yet so unlike each other that each needs a separate language to account for its own existence. The central metaphor of the book, most fittingly, is one of fire: above the primordial fire of sex, lit by nature long before the first stirrings of humanity, rises the red flame of eroticism, above which quivers and shivers the delicate blue flame of love. There would be no flame without fire; yet there is more, much more, to the red and blue flames, and to each one of them, than there is in the fire from which they arise.

Sex, eroticism and love are linked yet separate. They can hardly exist without each other, and yet their existence is spent in an ongoing war of independence. The boundaries between them are hotly contested – alternatively, but often simultaneously, the sites of defensive battles and of invasions. Sometimes the logic of war demands that the cross-border dependencies are denied or suppressed; sometimes the invading armies cross the boundary in force with the intention of overpowering and colonizing the territory behind. Torn between such contradictory impulses, the three areas are notorious for the unclarity of their frontiers, and the three discourses that serve (or perhaps produce) them are known to be confused and inhospitable to pedantry and precision.

Sex, so Octavio Paz reminds us, is the least human of the three. Indeed, sex is natural, and not a cultural product: we share it with a large part of the non-human species. In its natural form, untainted by culture, sex is always the same; as Theodore Zeldin has observed,[2] 'there has been more progress in cooking than in sex.' It is but the erotic sublimation of sex, fantasy and sex substitutes that are infinitely variable. All '*history* of sex' is therefore the history of the *cultural manipulation* of sex. It began with the birth of eroticism – through the cultural trick of separating sexual *experience* (in the sense of *Erlebnis*, not *Erfahrung*), and especially the *pleasure* associated with that experience, from reproduction, that primary function of sex and its *raison d'être*. Nature, we may say, is taking no chances and for that reason it cannot but be wasteful; it showers its targets with bullets so that at least one bullet will hit the bull's eye. Sex is no exception; sexually reproducing species are as a rule supplied with quantities of sexual energy and the capacity for sexual encounters far in excess of what reproduction proper would require. And so eroticism is not just a purely cultural feat and in no way an act of violence committed on nature, an 'unnatural' act; nature virtually tempted human wits into the invention, lavish as nature is in turning out huge, redundant and untapped volumes of sexual energy and desire. That surplus is a standing invitation to cultural inventiveness. The uses to which that reproductively redundant and wasted excess may be put are a cultural creation.

Eroticism is about recycling that waste. It depends on filling the sexual act with a surplus value – over and above its reproductive function. Human beings would not be erotic creatures were they not first sexual beings; sexuality is the only soil in which the cultural seeds of eroticism may be sown and grow – but this soil has limited fertility. Eroticism starts from reproduction, but it transcends it from the beginning; reproduction, its life-giving force, soon turns into a constraint. To freely manipulate, to process at will the surplus capacity for sexuality, eroticism must be 'replanted' into other soils of greater potency and additional nutritional power; culture must emancipate sexual delight from reproduction, its primary utilitarian application. Hence the reproductive function of sex is simultaneously the indispensable condition and a thorn in the flesh of eroticism; there is an unbreakable link, but also a constant tension between the two – that tension being as incurable as the link is unbreakable.

Theoretically speaking, there are several tension-management strategies. They have all been tried, and the 'history of sex' may be told in terms of the focus shifting from one strategy to another, different strategies gaining temporary cultural dominance in various historical eras. The choice, however, is limited. By and large it is confined to the redeployment of cultural forces either on the sex/eroticism or the eroticism/love frontier, and certain combinations between the troop movements in both territories.

With great simplification we may say that throughout the modern era two cultural strategies have vied with each other for domination. One – officially promoted and supported by the legislative powers of the state and the ideological powers of the church and the school – was the strategy of reinforcing the limits imposed by the reproductive functions of sex upon the freedom of erotic imagination, relegating the unmanageable surplus of sexual energy to the culturally suppressed and socially degraded spheres of pornography, prostitution and illicit – extramarital – liaisons. The other – always carrying a tinge of dissent and rebelliousness – was the romantic strategy of cutting the ties linking eroticism to sex and tying it instead to love.

In the first strategy, eroticism had to justify itself in terms of its sexual (reproductive) utility, with the third element – love – being a welcome, yet supernumerary, embellishment. Sex was 'culturally silent' – it had no language of its own, no language recognized as public vernacular and a means of public communication. Mid nineteenth-century intercourse, as Stephen Kern has noted,[3] was by comparison with twentieth-century sex 'deadly serious' and 'abruptly over'; it was 'abruptly over' since 'the post-coital interlude was particularly embarrassing, because eyes opened, lights came on, and couples were obliged to look at one another or else away and begin to speak or else endure a nerve-wracking silence.' In the second strategy, love was accorded the sole legitimizing power, and eroticism was cast in the image of a handmaiden of love, while its link with sexuality was either frowned upon or reduced to the role of a non-essential, even if pleasurable, attribute. In both strategies, eroticism sought anchorage in something other than itself – either in sex or in love; both strategies were variants of the policy of alliance, and the potential allies were sought beyond the borders of eroticism. Both strategies assumed that the cultural manipulation and redeployment of surplus sexual energy needed a functional justification, not being able to stand on its own and be 'its own purpose' or a value in its own right. Both strategies stemmed as well from the tacit assumption that, left to itself, human erotic inventiveness would easily run out of control, playing havoc with the delicate tissue of human relations; it needed, therefore, outside, authoritative and resourceful powers to contain it within acceptable limits and stave off its potentially destructive potential.

Seen against that background, the late modern or postmodern rendition of eroticism appears unprecedented – a genuine breakthrough and novelty. It does not enter an alliance with either sexual reproduction or love, claiming independence from both neighbours and flatly refusing all responsibility for the impact it may make on their fate; it proudly and boldly proclaims itself to be its only, and sufficient, reason and purpose. As Mark C. Taylor and Esa Saarinen put it, with a wonderful epigrammatic precision,[4] 'desire does not desire satisfaction. To the contrary, desire desires desire.' When (seldom, and in whispers) voiced before, such claims were classified as the heresy of libertinism and exiled to the Devil's Island of sexual disorder and perversion. Now the self-sufficiency of eroticism, the freedom to seek sexual delights for their own sake, has risen to the level of a cultural norm, changing places with its critics, now assigned to the *Kunstkammer* of cultural oddities and relics of extinct species. Nowadays eroticism has acquired a substance it was never before able to carry on its own shoulders, but also an unheard-of lightness and volatility. Being an eroticism 'with no strings attached', untied, unbridled, let loose – postmodern eroticism is free to enter and leave any association of convenience, but is also an easy prey to forces eager to exploit its seductive powers.

It has become the folklore of social science to lay the responsibility for the 'erotic revolution' at the door of 'market forces' (an address all the more convenient for the mystery surrounding its notoriously elusive resident). Eager to fill the void left by Divine Providence and by the laws of progress, the scientifically oriented study of changing human behaviour lights on 'market forces' – no worse, and in many respects better, than other candidates for the vacant position of the 'main determinant'. I for one am not particularly worried by the void staying empty and the position remaining unfilled. 'Market forces' can be blamed, at the utmost, for exploiting without scruples the resources already at hand, and for exploiting them while being guided solely by their commercial potential and being oblivious to all other, including the culturally devastating or morally iniquitous, aspects of the matter. Charging them with the power to conjure up the resources themselves would be like accepting the alchemist's authorship of the gold found in the test-tube: an exercise in magical rather than scientific reasoning (though, frankly, the difference between the two within social studies is far from unambiguous). It takes more than the greed of profit, free competition and the refinement of the advertising media to accomplish a cultural revolution of a scale and depth equal to that of the emancipation of eroticism from sexual reproduction and love. To be redeployed as an economic factor, eroticism must first have been culturally processed and given a form fit for a would-be commodity.

So let me leave aside the 'commercial' uses of eroticism, not really surprising in a society in which the care for whatever is seen as a human need is increasingly mediated by the commodity market – and concentrate instead on somewhat less obvious, and certainly less fully described and far too little discussed, links between the erotic revolution and other aspects of the emergent postmodern culture. Among such aspects, two in particular seem to be directly relevant to our topic.

The first is the collapse of the 'panoptic' model of securing and perpetuating social order. That model, as you know, has been described in detail by Michel Foucault, in reference to Jeremy Bentham's idea of the universal solution to all tasks requiring the instilling of discipline and so the obtaining of the desirable sort of conduct from a great number of people. That solution, according to Bentham, was *seeing without being seen*, a surreptitious surveillance with its objects being made aware that they might be closely scrutinized at every moment, yet having no way of knowing when they are indeed under observation. Foucault used Bentham's idea as a paradigm of the order-making activity of modern powers. Factories, workhouses, prisons, schools, hospitals, asylums or barracks, whatever their manifest functions, were also throughout the modern era manufacturers of order; in this lay their latent, yet arguably the paramount social function. Among all the panoptical institutions two were decisive for the performance of that latter function due to their vast catchment area. The two panoptical institutions in question were industrial factories and conscript armies. Most male members of society could be reasonably expected to pass through their disciplining treadmills and acquire the habits that would guarantee their obedience to the order-constituting rules (and later to enforce those habits on the female members in their capacity as the 'heads of the families'). Yet in order to perform their role, such panoptical institutions needed men capable of undertaking industrial work and army duties – able to endure the hardships of industrial work and army life. Industrial invalidity and disqualification from army service meant exclusion from panoptical control and drill. Ability to work and to fight became therefore the measure of the 'norm', while inability was tantamount to social abnormality, deviation from the norm, alternatively subjected to medical or penal treatment. Modern medicine gave that norm the name of 'health'. A 'healthy man' was a person capable of a certain amount of physical exertion, that required by productive work and/or military exploits; the norm guiding the assessment of the state of health and the infinite variety of possible abnormalities was therefore 'objectively measurable'. It could be easily set as a target; hitting or missing the target could be defined with considerable precision.

Contemporary society needs neither mass industrial labour nor mass (conscript) armies. The era when factories and troops were the decisive order-sustaining institution is (at least in our part of the world) over. But so as well is panoptical power as the main vehicle of social integration, and normative regulation as the major strategy of order maintenance. The great majority of people – men as well as women – are today integrated through seduction rather than policing, advertising rather than indoctrinating, need creation rather than normative regulation. Most of us are socially and culturally trained and shaped as sensation seekers and gatherers, rather than as producers and soldiers. Constant openness to new sensations and the greed for ever new experience, always stronger and deeper than before, are conditions *sine qua non* of being amenable to seduction. It is not 'health', with its connotation of a steady state, of an immobile target on which all properly trained bodies converge, but 'fitness' – implying being always on the move or ready to move, a capacity for imbibing and digesting ever greater volumes of stimuli, a flexibility and resistance to all closure – that grasps the quality expected from the experience collector, the quality she or he must indeed possess to seek and absorb sensations. And if the mark of 'disease' was incapacity for factory or army life, the mark of 'unfitness' is a lack of *élan vital*, an inability to feel strongly, *ennui, acidia*, a lack of energy, of stamina, of interest in what the colourful life has to offer, a lack of desire and desire to desire....

'Fitness' as a definition of the desirable bodily state presents, however, problems from which the norm of 'health' was free.

First – 'health' is a norm, and norms are clearly delineated from above and below alike. 'Fitness' has perhaps its lower, though rather blurred and murky threshold, but cannot, by definition, have an upper limit; 'fitness' is, after all, about the constant ability to move further on, to rise to ever higher levels of experience. Hence 'fitness' will never acquire the comforting exactitude and precision of a norm. 'Fitness' is a never-to-be-reached horizon looming forever in the future, a spur to unstoppable efforts, none of which can be seen as fully satisfactory, let alone the ultimate. Pursuit of fitness, its little triumphs notwithstanding, is shot through with incurable anxiety and is an inexhaustible source of self-reproach and self-indignation.

Second – since it is solely about the *Erlebnis*, subjectively lived-through sensations, fitness cannot be intersubjectively compared nor objectively measured; it can hardly even be reported in inter-personally meaningful terms and so confronted with other sub-jects' experiences. Much as counsel is needed to make up for that immanent ungraspability of evidence, there is possibly an ultimate limit to the counsellor's intervention; name-giving and quotations of statistical averages will stop short of breaking open the lone-liness of the sensation-seeker. As we know from Ludwig Wittgen-stein, there is no such thing as private language, but one would need nothing less than a private language to express sensations – the most thoroughly and uncompromisingly private ingredient of the *Lebenswelt*. Indeed, a Catch-22 – demanding no less than the squaring of a circle.

One way or another, since certainty can only be an interper-sonal, social achievement, the fitness-seekers can never be sure how far they got and how far they still need to go. Third – in the game called fitness the player is simultaneously the fiddle and the fiddler. It is bodily pleasurable, exciting or thrilling sensations which a fit person seeks – but the sensations collector *is that body* and, at the same time, that body's owner, guardian, *trainer and director.* The two roles are inherently incompatible. The first requires total immersion and self-abandonment, the second calls for a distance and sober judgement. Reconciliation of the two demands is a tall order – if at all attainable, which is doubtful. Added to the two troubles previously signalled, this additional worry makes the plight of the fitness-seeker an agony of which their health-conscious ancestors had no inkling. All three troubles daily generate a lot of anxiety; what is more, however, that anxiety – a specifically *postmodern* affliction – is unlikely ever to be cured and ended. It is also diffuse, as Jean Baudrillard pointed out; and diffuse, unfocused anxieties admit of no specific remedies...

Sexual delight is arguably the summit of pleasurable sensations; indeed, a pattern by which all other pleasures tend to be measured and of which they are, by common consent, but pale reflections at best, inferior or counterfeit imitations at worst. Whatever has been said above about the sensation-gathering life strategy in general applies in a magnified measure to the specifically postmodern rendition of eroticism, that 'cultural processing' of sex. All the contradictions inherent in the life of a sensation collector in general affect sexual life with a concentrated impact – but there is an extra difficulty arising from the inborn monotony and inflexibility of sex (sex, let us remember, being a phenomenon of nature and not of culture, leaves little room for the inventiveness typical of culture). In its postmodern rendition, sexual activity is focused narrowly on its orgasmic effect; for all practical intents and purposes, postmodern sex *is about orgasm.* Its paramount task is to supply ever stronger, infinitely variable, preferably novel and unprecedented *Erlebnisse*; little can be done, however, in this field and so the ultimate sexual experience remains forever a task ahead and no actual sexual experience is truly satisfying, none makes further training, instruction, counsel, recipe, drug or gadget unnecessary.

There is another aspect of the relation between the present-day erotic revolution and the wider postmodern cultural transformations which I wish now to bring to your attention.

Sex, as we know, is nature's evolutionary solution to the issue of continuity, the durability of life forms; it sets the mortality of every individual living organism against the immortality of the species. Only humans know that this is the case; only humans know that they are bound to die, and only humans may imagine the perpetuity of the human kind; only for them the transient existence of the body runs its course in the shadow of the perpetuity of humanity as a whole. Such knowledge has tremendous consequences; it is by no means fanciful to suppose that it lies behind the notorious dynamics of human cultural inventions, which are all, as a rule, contraptions meant to render the duration of social forms immune to the transience and inborn perishability of individual human lives; or, rather, ingenious workshops where durability is continually produced out of the transient – where the fragile, timebound existence of human bodies is reforged into the solid perpetuity of humanity.

Sex lies at the heart of that alchemy. Sex is the material substratum of that cultural production of immortality and the pattern or supreme metaphor for the effort to transcend individual mortality and stretch human existence beyond the lifespan of individual humans. Sex is involved – centrally and inextricably – in the greatest feat and the most awe-inspiring of cultural miracles: that of conjuring up immortality out of mortality, the interminable out of the temporal, the imperishable out of the evanescent. The enigma of that logic-defying miracle, that mind-boggling puzzle of the most vulnerable and abstruse accomplishment of culture, saturates every sexual act: the communion of two mortal beings is lived through as the birth of immortality... With the advent of human awareness of mortality, sex irretrievably loses its innocence.

Located on the other side of eroticism, love is the emotional/intellectual superstructure that culture built upon the sexual differences and their sexual reunion, thereby investing sex with rich and infinitely expandable meanings which protect and reinforce its power to recast mortality into immortality. Love is a cultural replica or a refined likeness of that overcoming of the opposition between the transience of sexual bodies and the durability of their reproduction, which is matter of factly accomplished in the sexual act. Like sex itself, love is therefore burdened with ambiguity, residing as it does on the thin line dividing the natural from the supernatural, the familiar present and the enigmatic, impenetrable future. Love of another mortal person is one of the principal cultural ventures into immortality; it is, we may say, a spiritual mirror held to the sexually created biological eternity. Like sex, love is a source of incurable anxiety, though perhaps an anxiety deeper still for being soaked through with the premonition of failure. In love, the hope and the promise of 'eternal love' are invested in a body which is anything but eternal; the eternity of love and of the beloved is culture's saving lie, helping to assimilate what in fact defies comprehension. A mortal person is loved as if it were immortal, and it is loved by a mortal person in a way accessible only to eternal beings.

We have noted before that a most prominent mark of the postmodern erotic revolution is a cutting of the ties connecting eroticism on one side to sex (in its essential reproductive function) and on another to love. Precautions are taken in postmodern culture to secure the emancipation of erotically inspired activity from the constraints imposed biologically by the reproductive potential of sex and culturally by love's demands for eternal and strictly select-ive, in fact exclusive, loyalty. Eroticism has thereby been set free from both the links tying it to the production of immortality, physical or spiritual. But in this spectacular liberation it was not alone; it followed the much more universal trends affecting in equal measure the arts, politics, life strategies and virtually every other area of culture.

It is a general feature of the postmodern condition that it flattens time and condenses the perception of an infinitely expandable flow of time into the experience (*Erlebnis*) of *Jetztzeit*, or slices it into a series of self-sustained episodes, each to be lived through as an intense experience of the fleeting moment and cut away as thor-oughly as possible from both its past and its future consequences. The politics of movements is being replaced with the politics of campaigns, aimed at instant results and unconcerned with their long-term repercussions; concern with lasting (everlasting!) fame gives way to a desire for notoriety; historical duration is identified with instant (and in principle effaceable) recording; works of art, once meant to last 'beyond the grave', are replaced with deliber-ately short-lived happenings and one-off installations; identities of a kind meant to be diligently built and to last for a life's duration are exchanged for identity kits fit for immediate assembly and equally instant dismantling. The new postmodern version of immortality is meant to be lived instantly and enjoyed here and now; no longer is it a hostage to the merciless and uncontrollable flow of objective time.

The postmodern 'deconstruction of immortality' – the tendency to cut off the present from both past and future – is paralleled by tearing eroticism apart from both sexual reproduction and love. This offers to erotic imagination and practice, as to the rest of postmodern life politics, a freedom of experiment they never enjoyed before. Postmodern eroticism is free-floating; it can enter a chemical reaction with virtually any other substance, feed and draw juices from any other human emotion or activity. It has become an unattached signifier capable of being wedded semiotically to virtually unlimited numbers of signifieds, but also a signified ready to be represented by any of the available signifiers. Only in such a liberated and detached version may eroticism sail freely under the banner of pleasure-seeking, undaunted and undiverted from its pursuits by any other than aesthetic, that is *Erlebnis*-oriented, concerns. It is free now to establish and negotiate its own rules as it goes, but this freedom is a fate which eroticism can neither change nor ignore. The void created by the absence of external constraints, by the retreat or neutral lack of interest of legislating powers, must be filled or at least attempts made to fill it. The newly acquired underdetermination is the basis of an exhilaratingly vast freedom but also the cause of extreme uncertainty and anxiety. No authoritative solutions to go by, everything to be negotiated anew and ad hoc...

Eroticism, in other words, has become a sort of a Jack of all trades desperately seeking a secure abode and steady job yet fearing the prospect of finding them... This circumstance makes it available for new kinds of social uses, sharply different from the ones known from most of modern history. Two in particular need to be briefly discussed here.

The first is the deployment of eroticism in the postmodern construction of identity. The second is the role played by eroticism in servicing the network of interpersonal bonds on the one hand, and the separatist battles of individualization on the other.

Identity ceased to be a 'given', the product of the 'divine chain of being', and became instead a 'problem' and an individual task with the dawn of modern times. In this respect there is no difference between 'classic' modernity and its postmodern phase. What is new is the nature of the problem and the way the resulting tasks are tackled. In its classic modern form, the problem of identity for most men and women consisted in the need to *acquire* their social definitions, to build them using their own efforts and resources, from performances and appropriations, rather than inherited properties. The task was to be approached through setting a target – a model of the identity desired – and then, throughout one's life, doggedly sticking to the itinerary determined by the target set. At the sundown of the classic era of modernity Jean-Paul Sartre summed up that time-honoured experience in his concept of the 'life project' which not so much expresses as creates the 'essence' of the human individual. Identities of postmodern men and women remain, like the identities of their ancestors, human-made. But they no longer need to be meticulously designed, carefully built and rock solid. Their most coveted virtue is *flexibility*: all structures are to be light and mobile so that they can be rearranged at short notice, one-way streets are to be avoided, no commitment should be so strongly binding that it cramps free movement. Solidity is anathema, as is all permanence – now a sign of dangerous maladjustment to the rapidly and unpredictably changing world, to the surprise opportunities it holds and the speed with which it transforms yesterday's assets into today's liabilities.

Eroticism cut free from its reproductive and amorous constraints fits the bill very well; it is as if it were made to measure for the multiple, flexible, evanescent identities of postmodern men and women. Sex free from reproductive consequences and stubborn, lingering love attachments can be securely enclosed within the frame of an episode: it will engrave no deep grooves on the constantly regroomed face which is thus insured against limitations on the freedom to experiment further. Free-floating eroticism is therefore eminently suitable for the task of tending to the kind of identity which, like all other postmodern cultural products, is (in George Steiner's memorable words) calculated for 'maximal impact and instant obsolescence'.

Free-floating eroticism also stands behind what Anthony Giddens[5] has dubbed 'plastic sex'. A hundred years or so ago, when eroticism was tightly wrapped around sexual reproduction, given no right to independent existence and denied the claim to its own *telos*, men and women were culturally expected and pressed to live up to fairly precise standards of maleness and femininity, organized around their respective roles in reproductive sex, protected by the requirement of a lasting attachment of partners. That was the era of the norm, and the boundary between the normal and the abnormal was clearly drawn and closely guarded. The difference drawn between sex and its 'perversion' left little room for the imagination. This did not have to be the case, and is not now – when but a small parcel of the vast erotic territory is dedicated to the reproductive aspects of sex and the territory as a whole allows for free movement and has but a few long-lease residences. For males and females alike, the way sexuality is erotically exploited bears no direct relation to the reproductive role and there is no reason why it should be limited to the experience obtainable through the performance of that role. Much richer sensual fruits of sexuality can be harvested through also experimenting with other than straightforwardly heterosexual activities. As in so many other areas, so too in sexuality the realm once thought to be ruled by nature alone is invaded and colonized by cultural troops; the gender aspect of identity, like all other aspects, is not *given* once and for all – it has to be *chosen*, and may be discarded if deemed unsatisfactory or not satisfying enough. This aspect, like all other constituents of postmodern identity, is therefore permanently underdetermined, incomplete, open to change, and so a realm of uncertainty and an inexhaustible source of anxiety and soul-searching, as well as fear that some precious kinds of sensation have been missed and the pleasure-giving potential of the body has not been squeezed to the last drop.

Let me say now a few words about the role assigned to eroticism in the weaving and unstitching of the tissue of interpersonal relations.

In his *Introduction* to *The History of Sexuality*[6] Michel Foucault argued convincingly that in all its manifestations, whether those known since time immemorial or such as have been discovered or named for the first time, sex served the articulation of new – modern – mechanisms of power and social control. The medical and educational discourses of the nineteenth century construed, among other notions, the phenomenon of infantile sexuality, later to be turned by Freud, *ex post facto*, into the cornerstone of psychoanalysis. The central role in this articulation was played by the panic contrived around the child's proclivity to masturbate – perceived simultaneously as a natural inclination and a disease, a vice impossible to uproot and a danger with an incalculable damaging potential. It was the task of the parents and the teachers to defend children against this danger – but in order to make the protection effective, it was necessary to spy the affliction in every change of demeanour, every gesture and facial expression, strictly ordering the child's whole life to make the morbid practice impossible. Around the never-ending struggle against the threat of masturbation a whole system was constructed of parental, medical and pedagogical invigilation and surveillance. In Foucault's words, 'control of infantile sexuality hoped to reach it through a simultaneous propagation of its own power and of the object on which it was brought to bear.' The indomitable and merciless parental control needed to be justified in terms of the universality and resilience of the infantile vice, and so the vice was bound to be shown – by the universality and resilience of the controlling practices – to be itself universal and resilient.

> Wherever there was the chance [that the temptation] might appear, devices of surveillance were installed; traps were laid for compelling admissions; inexhaustible and corrective discourses were imposed; parents and teachers were alerted, and left with the suspicion that all children are guilty, and with the fear of being themselves at fault if their suspicions were not sufficiently strong; they were kept in readiness in the face of this recurrent danger; their conduct was prescribed and their pedagogy recodified; an entire medico-sexual regime took hold of the family milieu. The child 'vice' was not so much an enemy as a support...
>
> More than the old taboos, this form of power demanded constant, attentive, and curious presences for its exercise; it presupposed proximities; it proceeded through examination and insistent observation; it required an exchange of discourses, through questions that extorted admissions, and confidences that went beyond the questions that were asked. It implied a physical proximity and an interplay of intense sensations... The power which thus took charge of sexuality set about contacting bodies, caressing them with its eyes, intensifying areas, electrifying surfaces, dramatizing troubled moments. It wrapped the sexual body in its embrace.

The manifest or latent, awakened or dormant sexuality of the child used to be a powerful instrument in the articulation of modern family relationships. It provided the reason and the impetus for the comprehensive and obtrusive parental interference with children's lives; it called the parents to be constantly 'in touch', to keep children constantly within parental sight, to engage in intimate conversations, encourage confessions and require confidence and secrets sharing.

Today, on the contrary, the sexuality of children is becoming an equally powerful factor in loosening human bonds and thus liberating the individual's choice-power, and particularly in terms of parent–child separation and 'keeping one's distance'. Today's fears emanate from the sexual desire of the parents, not of the child; it is not in what children do following their own impulse, but in what they do or may do at the behest of their parents that we are inclined to suspect sexual undertones; it is what parents like to do with (and to) their children that frightens and calls for vigilance – only this is a kind of vigilance which advises caution, parental withdrawal and reticence. Children are now perceived mainly as sexual *objects* and potential victims of their parents as sexual *subjects*; and since parents are by nature stronger than their children and placed in a position of power, parental sexuality may easily lead to the abuse of that power in the service of the parents' sexual instincts. The spectre of sex also haunts, therefore, family homes. To exorcise it, one needs to keep children at a distance – and above all abstain from intimacy and overt, tangible manifestations of parental love...

Great Britain has been recently witnessing a virtual epidemic of 'sexual exploitation of children'. In a widely publicized campaign, social workers, in cooperation with doctors and teachers, charged dozens of parents (mainly fathers, but also a growing number of mothers) with incestuous assaults against their children; child victims were forcibly removed from parental homes, while readers of the popular press were treated to blood-curdling stories about the dens of debauchery into which family bedrooms and bathrooms had been turned. Newspapers brought news of sexual abuse of the juvenile wards in one care home or borstal after another.

Only a few of the publicly discussed cases were brought to trial. In some cases the accused parents managed to prove their innocence and get their children back. But what happened could not unhappen. Parental tenderness lost its innocence. It has been brought to public awareness that children are always and everywhere sexual objects, that there is a potentially explosive sexual underside to any act of parental love, that every caress has its erotic aspect and every loving gesture may hide a sexual advance.

As Suzanne Moore noted,[7] an NSPCC survey reported that 'one in six of us was a victim of "sexual interference" as a child', while according to a Barnardo's report, 'six out of 10 women and a quarter of men "experience some kind of sexual assault or interference before they are 18".' Suzanne Moore agrees that 'sexual abuse is far more widespread than we are prepared to accept', but she points out nevertheless that 'the word abuse is now so overused that almost any situation can be constructed as abusive.' In once unproblematic parental love and care an abyss of ambivalence has been revealed. Nothing is clear and obvious anymore, everything is shot through with ambiguity – and from things ambiguous one is advised to steer clear.

In one of the widely publicized cases, three-year-old Amy was found in school making plasticine sausage-like or snake-like objects (which the teacher identified as penises), and she talked of things that 'squirt white stuff'. The parents' explanation that the mysterious object squirting white stuff was the nasal spray against congestion, while the sausage-like things were images of Amy's favourite jelly sweets, did not help. Amy's name was placed on the list of 'children at risk', and her parents went into battle to clear their names. As Rosie Waterhouse comments on this and other cases,[8]

> Hugging, kissing, bathing, even sleeping with your children – are these natural patterns of parental behaviour or are they inappropriate, oversexualised acts of abuse?
>
> And what are normal childish pastimes? When children draw pictures of witches and snakes, does this mean they are symbols of frightening, abusive events? These are fundamental questions with which teachers, social workers and other professionals involved in caring for children frequently have to grapple.

Maureen Freely has recently vividly described the panic that haunts the postmodern family homes in the result:[9]

> If you're a man, you are likely to think twice about going over to a sobbing, lost child and offering your help. You'll be reluctant to grab a 13-year-old daughter's hand when crossing a dangerous intersection, and ... you will balk at taking film containing pictures of naked children of any age into Boots. If *Pretty Baby* came out today, it would most certainly be picketed. If *Lolita* were published for the first time in 1997, no one would dare call it classic.

Parent–child relationships are not the only ones that are presently undergoing a thorough check-up and are in the process of being reassessed and renegotiated in these times of the postmodern erotic revolution. All other kinds of human relations are – keenly, vigilantly, obsessively, sometimes in a panic-stricken fashion – purified of even the palest of sexual undertones that might stand the slightest chance of condensing those relations into permanence. Sexual undertones are suspected and sniffed out in every emotion reaching beyond the meagre inventory of feelings permitted in the framework of a mismeeting (or quasi-encounter, fleeting encounter, inconsequential encounter),[10] in every offer of friendship and every manifestation of a deeper-than-average interest in another person. A casual remark on the beauty or charm of a workmate is likely to be censured as sexual provocation, and an offer of a cup of coffee as sexual harassment. The spectre of sex now haunts company offices and college seminar rooms; there is a threat involved in every smile, gaze, form of address. The overall outcome is a rapid emaciation of human relations, stripping them of intimacy and emotionality, and a wilting of the desire to enter into them and keep them alive.

But not just companies and colleges are affected. In one country after another, the courts legalize the concept of 'marital rape'; sexual services are no longer marital rights and duties, and insisting on them can be classified as a punishable crime. Since it is notoriously difficult to interpret a partner's conduct 'objectively', unambiguously, as either consent or refusal (particularly if the partners share a bed nightly), and since to define the event as a rape rests on the decision of only one partner, virtually every sexual act can, with a modicum of good (or rather ill) will, be presented as an act of rape (which certain radical feminist writers were quick to proclaim as the 'truth of the male sex as such'). Sexual partners need to remember on every occasion, therefore, that discretion is the better part of valour. The ostensible obviousness and unproblematic character of marital rights, which was once meant to encourage the partners to prefer marital sex over sex outside marriage, allegedly a more risky affair, is now more and more often perceived as a trap; as a result, the reasons for associating the satisfaction of erotic desire with marriage become less and less evident or convincing – particularly when satisfaction without strings attached is so easy to obtain elsewhere.

A weakening of bonds is an important condition for the success-ful social production of sensation-gatherers who happen to be also fully fledged, effective consumers. If once upon a time, at the threshold of the modern era, the separation of business from household allowed the first to submit to the stern and unemotional demands of competition and remain deaf to all other, notably moral, norms and values – the present-day separation of eroticism from other interhuman relations allows it to be submitted without qualification to the aesthetic criteria of strong experience and sensual gratification. But there are huge costs to be paid for this gain. At a time of the re-evaluation of all values and the revision of historically shaped habits no norm of human conduct can be taken for granted, and none is likely to stay uncontested for long. All pursuit of delight is therefore shot through with fear; habitual social skills are looked upon with suspicion, while new ones, particularly ones that are commonly accepted, are in short supply and slow in coming. To make the plight of postmodern men and women still worse, the few rules of thumb which emerge from the confusion add more of their own because of their seemingly insol-uble contradictions. Postmodern culture eulogizes the delights of sex and encourages every nook and cranny of the *Lebenswelt* to be invested with erotic significance. It prompts the postmodern sensa-tion-seeker to develop in full the potential of the sexual subject. On the other hand, though, the same culture explicitly forbids treating another sensation-seeker as a sex object. The trouble is, however, that in every erotic encounter we are subjects as well as objects of desire and – as every lover knows only too well – no erotic encounter is conceivable without the partners assuming both roles, or better still merging them into one. Contradictory cultural signals covertly undermine what they overtly praise and encour-age. This is a situation pregnant with psychic neuroses all the more grave for the fact that it is no longer clear what the 'norm' is and therefore what kind of 'conformity to the norm' could heal them.

18

Is there life after immortality?

Life owes its value to death; or, as Hans Jonas put it, it is only because we are mortal that *we count days and the days count*. More exactly, life has value and the days have weight because we, humans, are aware of our mortality. We *know* that we must die and that our life, to quote Martin Heidegger, means *living towards death*.

The awareness that death is inevitable might easily have deprived life of value if knowledge of the fragility and finitude of life had not bestowed an outstanding value on durability and infinity. Eternity is what eludes us and what we cannot make our own, and even to try to grasp it could not be done without the expense of tremendous effort and exorbitant self-immolation. And as we know from Georg Simmel, all value derives from the sacrifice it demands; the value of any object is measured by the difficulty of its acquisition.

Directly, awareness of the transitoriness of life bestows value only on eternal duration. It validates life obliquely: in so far as we know that however brief our life may be, the stretch of time between birth and death is our only chance of transcendence, of getting a foothold in eternity. Like the moon's, life's shine is but a reflection of a sun: the Sun of immortality. No moment that may leave its trace in eternity can be allowed to pass intestate. Moments can be used sensibly, or wasted. We count days, and the days count.

For this reflected glory of life one more condition must be met. We need knowledge as to how to reforge transience into durability: how to build a bridge leading from finitude to infinity. Awareness of death comes uninvited, but that other knowledge, the knowledge of *transcendence*, must be painstakingly constructed. Neither common sense nor even reason will supply that knowledge matter-of-factly. If anything, they will deride its vanity and put mortals off the search.

It was in spite of reason and logic, rather than following their advice, that human culture undertook the task of bridge-building. We call 'culture' the kind of human activity which in the last account consists in making the volatile solid, linking the finite to the infinite, and otherwise building bridges connecting mortal life to values immune to the eroding impact of time. A moment of reflection would suffice to reveal that the pillars of the bridge stand in quicksands of absurdity. Leaving this worry to the melancholy of philosophers, let us note however that the cunning of culture allows pillars to be erected on the most friable of foundations which are resilient enough to carry bridge-spans sufficiently tough and solid to allow a sense of extemporality to flow into the all-too-temporary life.

Culture has managed to build many sorts of bridges. The vision of life after death has been one of the most commonly used. Contrary to its critics, that vision does not clash with common experience. We all know that thoughts have an existence somehow independent of those who think them; we know that they come from times when their thinkers were not yet around, and expect them to be rethought in such mysterious times when their present thinkers will be no more. And from this experience it is but one small step to the idea that the soul, the unfleshy substratum of thoughts, leads an existence different from that of its fleshy and temporal casing. To believe in the immortality of the body is a tall order; but it is equally difficult to doubt the longer-than-life existence of the soul. At least its mortality cannot be proved 'beyond reasonable doubt' – not in the tribunal of human imagination with human experience called to the witness stand. But if the duration of the soul is, by comparison with bodily life, eternal – its brief cohabitation with the body is but an overture to a life infinitely more lasting and so infinitely more precious and important. That overture acquires formidable importance: all the motifs, harmonies, counterpoints of the long, long opera to follow need to be drafted and encapsulated in its brief timespan. Cohabitation with the body may be laughably short by comparison with the longitude of the soul's later lonely existence, but it is during that living together that the quality of eternal life is decided: left alone, the soul won't be able to change anything in its fate. The mortal has power over the immortal: mortal life is the only time to collect credits for eternity. 'Later' means too late. And so mortal carriers of immortal souls count days, and their days count.

The Reformation, particularly in its Calvinist rendition, objected to that sinful manifestation of conceit. How dare human mortals imagine that what they do here on earth is potent enough to bind the verdicts of God? To question the omnipotence of God is itself a mortal sin, and at any rate it would not alter the sentence of *predestination*; well before the souls embarked on their brief trips to earth, it was already decided who were the damned and who were to be saved. In one go, the doctrine of predestination shattered the bridge Christianity had laboriously constructed. Shattering that bridge could – it should – strip earthly life of meaning and direction, spawn universal apathy, and in the end make life, with its absurdity unmasked, unlivable. Paradoxically, the opposite happened. Once more the cunning of culture defied and pushed aside logic.

As Max Weber explained, instead of breeding inaction Calvinist predestination released an unprecedented volume of human energy. If God-administered eternity is immune to human actions, there is no reason to measure human earthly life by its standards. The born-of-fear religiosity of the Reformation was from the beginning pregnant with humanist secularism – it set humans free to focus on things other than those kept in the secret compartments of divine offices; on things which we, humans, are able to comprehend and to direct to our advantage. Whether they did or did not believe in life after death, it was no longer the custom of reasonable people to think daily about the effects their deeds would have on eternal life according to the arithmetic put by God at the disposal of human creatures. There must be other ways to make the days count: other bridges into eternity, bridges which humans might design, build, map and use.

Indeed – brand new, modern bridges were soon thrown over the precipice separating the transient from the durable. Modern bridges differed from the ones that had now collapsed by putting human guards and guides on both ends. Not that they were built with the *intention* of evicting the sacred and the divine from human life; their description as the products of secularization is justified only in as far as they were secular *in their consequences*. There was little practical difference between disbelief in the existence of God and the belief in God's silence and inscrutability. Nietzsche's charge of God's murder meant merely that the life of humans in our modern times made the question of God's existence or non-existence irrelevant. We live *as if* we were alone in the universe. It has been a principle of modern thought that propositions which cannot be proved or disproved with the means available to humans are meaningless and thus unworthy of serious discourse. Of things you cannot talk about, Ludwig Wittgenstein warned, you should keep silent.

Two kinds of bridges are particularly 'modern', that is, made to the measure of the orphaned beings allowed only to rely on the limbs they have or the vehicles they invent. Bridges of the first kind are meant, so to speak, for the pedestrians: for the use of individual wanderers. Bridges of the second kind are built to accommodate public transport vehicles. The modernity of both lies not so much in their novelty (from time immemorial, there were gangplanks in place where these bridges have been built), but in the centrality of the role they play in modern times in the absence of alternative passages to immortality.

The bridges for individual use are the opportunities to stay alive in the memory of posterity: as a person, unique and irreplaceable, with a recognized face and one's own name. The body will disintegrate into inorganic matter – dust will join dust – but the 'person' (like the soul of yesteryear) will persist in its *individual* being. Humans are mortal; their glory may escape death. This bridge performs its function very well: indeed, it provides the needed *link* between transience and duration – the transience that is human fate and the duration as human achievement. Again, it is worth one's while to count days, and again the days count. It *does* matter how one lives one's life. One needs to *earn* the memory of posterity – currying their favours by enriching their not-yet-begotten lives, or forcing them to remember by leaving one's personal stamp on the shape of the world they will inhabit. Everyone will die, but some will stay in the world as long as there are people with memory, as the archival documents have not fallen apart and the museums have not been burned.

This sort of bridge has been built since the beginning of history (indeed, building such bridges started history off): first by the despots and the tyrants. Pharaohs and emperors ordered their remnants to be put in pyramids which would withstand time and which no passer-by would be able to overlook; the stories of their exploits were to be engraved in indestructible stone or sculpted on to columns and arches no one could bypass. The people who built the pyramids and chiselled the tablets remained anonymous and perished without trace – but their labours paved the way to immortality.

Modernity, having invented 'man-made', 'do-it-yourself' history, opened the road to immortality to all state rulers, legislators and army commanders – but also to 'spiritual rulers', discoverers and inventors, poets and dramatists, painters and sculptors; to all people whose presence in the world 'made a difference' and thereby *made history*. History textbooks are filled lavishly with their names and likenesses. There are many suggestions as to how to date the beginning of modernity, but the moment when painters put their signatures to their murals or canvases, and the names of composers started to be pronounced as frequently as (or more often than) the names of their high and mighty patrons serves the purpose better than most.

Individual bridges, as their name makes clear, are not fit for common, let alone mass, use. Moreover, they perform their function only in as far as they are not crowded. Not that the conditions of entry have been set too high to be met by anybody other than exceptional persons; it is rather that the criteria of admission have been set in such a way as to *make* those who pass them few and so exceptional. The essence of such bridges is to set the few apart from the grey and anonymous mass of the many – and this accomplishment depends on the mass being kept anonymous and grey. Those who use this bridge may stay in memory as individuals only because all the rest have been forgotten and their countenances washed away and dissolved.

Not all has been lost, though, as far as that faceless 'rest' is concerned. There are bridges of the second kind, meant for those who have been barred access to the first. If the passes for the first bridge are in short supply and offered only to exceptional persons in recognition of their exceptionality – access to the second, public bridge is on the contrary free to everyone who does not stand out but obeys the law and mundane routine. Contrary to the bridges of the first kind, the psychological effectiveness of public bridges as the links between mortal life and eternity grows together with the numbers of people who use them.

The bridges of the second kind offer a collective escape from individual mortality. Individual duration is not on offer, but every person, however small and insignificant, can 'make a difference' to the future by his or her contribution to the survival of something greater and more durable than any human being: of the nation, of the cause, of the party, of lineage or kin. Individual life is not inconsequential: individual mortality can be instrumental in the attainment of collective immortality. No one will remember faces and names – but those who once bore them will leave a lasting trace, if not in memory, then at least in the happy life of their successors. In central squares of all modern capitals you'll find the graves of 'unknown soldiers'; both words in that two-word expression are equally important.

Among the collectivities whose duration lent sense to individual transience, two stood out for their capacity to accommodate everyone or almost everyone among the living: nation and family.

Everyone belongs to a nation, but the nation is a community of its *loyal* sons and daughters. The perpetuity of nations depends on the devotion of its members – all of them together and every one of them separately. If the survival or security of the nation is in danger, all the better, since the link between what one does daily and the eternal existence of the nation becomes all the more salient and everything one does acquires gravity. A nation which stopped demanding sacrifice from its members would become useless as a vehicle of immortality. But for a large part of its modern history, Europe – that battlefield of nation-states and nations-in-search-of-state – knew only of nations (or nations-in-waiting) stern and harsh in their demands. No nation ever felt truly secure and so confident enough to lower the pitch of its battle-cries and to allow complacency or lapses of vigilance. It always mattered what the nation's sons and daughters did or what they neglected to do. The nation's tower-clocks ticked on loudly, and so everyone knew that the days were being counted and that for this reason they counted.

The family was another totality on which the collective solution to the drama of individual mortality focused: every single member of kin is mortal, but the family can be spared mortality. In the case of the family, it was not the grave of the unknown soldier or the cenotaph, but the family album – bursting with yellowing photos of long forgotten ancestors and reserving a few empty pages for the likeness of the yet unborn – that reminded of the inseparability of duration and transience. Browsing through the album made one think of one's duties but also of the value of the duty well performed. One was born into something much more durable than one's own vulnerable body, and by fulfilling one's calling – marrying, making children and enabling them to marry and make children of their own – one could make sure that this something would stay durable. Once more, one had to count days to make them count. As Henry David Thoreau put it: 'As if you could kill time without injuring eternity' . . .

Nation and the family were not, of course, the sole collective bridges to immortality put by modernity in place of the salvation-of-the-soul challenge to which there were no modern, instrumental-rational, solutions. There were many such bridges and many new ones go on being added daily – from political parties and movements to football clubs and celebrity-fan associations. None of those other bridges, however, could seriously compete with nations and the family when it came to the comprehensiveness and the 'democracy' of the solution: nations and the family have no equals as far as the matter crucial for all collective solutions – their accessibility, or 'carrying capacity' – is concerned. No wonder that the crisis currently afflicting both puts modern civilization in a profound and unprecedented quandary.

Nation and family have ceased nowadays to epitomize perpetual duration. Of all supra-individual entities known to human beings from their daily experience, nations and families came closest to the idea of eternity – of an existence whose beginnings dissolve in ancient history and whose prospects are infinite, and which dwarfs the vexingly brief duration of individual life. Nations and families used to be secure havens of perpetuity in which the brittle vessels of mortal life could be anchored; solid passageways into duration which, so long as they were kept in good repair, would outlast any of their users. But they can no longer boast either of those qualities.

Nations could serve as tangible embodiments of eternity as long as they remained securely entrenched in the awesome powers of the state. But the era of nation-states is today coming to an end.

No longer are nation-states protected by their once absolute economic, military, cultural and political sovereignty; all such sovereignties, one by one, have to surrender to the pressure of globalizing forces. Whatever a state may do on its own looks laughably inadequate when compared with the might of exterritorial and nomadic capital. On the other hand, the capacity for manifold sovereignty is no longer held as a test which a would-be nation must pass before it is awarded, like the nations *tout court*, the right to self-preservation; nationhood is no longer a rare privilege which needs defending and can be effectively defended against competing claims. As Eric Hobsbawm quipped, every speck on the map can today claim an office of presidency and a parliament building of its own. Granting national status, together with statehood, comes easy because of its harmlessness; the smaller and weaker the territorial political units become, the less constrained is the rule of exterritorial forces. Unfortified by the nation-state's indivisible rule, nations seem suddenly fragile and transient, and above all too weak, too insecure and not ancient enough to carry the burden of eternity. Since they are no longer fortresses, most of the nations are not *besieged* fortresses either; and since there are no visible threats to their continued existence, there is little, if anything, that the loyalty and efforts of the nation's sons and daughters could change in their future. Their days do not count, at least on this account.

Families brought their mortal members in touch with eternity as long as they offered what, from the point of view of the members, was a 'posthumous life'. Today the life expectation of families does not exceed that of their members, and few people can assert with confidence that the family they've just created will outlive them. Instead of serving as firm fixtures holding the continuous chain of kinship together, marriages become meeting points where chains are broken and identities of family lineages are blurred, diluted or dissolved. Marriages 'till death us do part' are replaced everywhere by Anthony Giddens's 'confluent love' partnerships, assumed to last as long (but no longer) than the blatantly transient satisfaction derived from the cohabitation by either of the partners.

To cut the long story short: the two principal mass-capacity bridges erected in modern times for the two-way traffic between individual mortality and eternal values are crumbling. The consequences for the human condition, for the stakes of life and for life strategies, are enormous: for the first time in history, counting days and making days count is devoid of reason and an institutional basis. There are no obvious, credible or believable, let alone trustworthy, connecting points between transience and duration, between whatever may be packed into the limited span of an individual life and whatever can be expected or hoped to survive beyond the limits of bodily mortality.

The inventory of consequences is long and far from recorded in full. I will confine myself to a quick survey of but a few items from a very long list.

First comes the unprecedented pressure exerted on the bridges built to hold only individual travellers: the roads to immortality once reserved for the chosen few are mobbed by crowds eager to gain entry. As we have seen before, these bridges are singularly unfit for mass traffic. Once the entry passes are distributed generously and at a cut price, the passage on offer changes its character; what is being sold is the 'experience' or sensation of immortality, rather than the thing itself (trade in 'experiences of...' is nowadays brisk and big business: this is the main attraction by which the visitors to theme parks, safari parks, holocaust museums or disneylands are tempted). True, the 'immortality' on offer relates to the prototype it imitates as a mass-production dress relates to a *haute couture* unique original; it is, though, commonly available at a price many can afford. One can hardly complain if it is made of a friable stuff which will not last longer than the current season.

Fame used to be the royal road to individual immortality. It has been replaced by *notoriety*, which is an object of consumption rather than *oeuvre* – something laboriously produced. Like all objects of consumption in a society of consumers, notoriety is designed to bring instantly obtainable and fast-exhausted satisfaction. A society of consumers is also a civilization of spare parts and disposables, in which the art of repair and preservation is redundant and has been all but forgotten. Notoriety is disposable as much as it is instant. So is the experience of immortality; and since the experience stands now for what was meant to be experienced, immortality which is neither instant nor disposable is well-nigh impossible to conceive of. Nor is it much in demand.

In the race for notoriety, the once-upon-a-time sole bidders for fame – the scientists, the artists, the inventors, the political leaders – have no advantage over pop stars and film stars, pulp-fiction writers, models, goal-scorers, serial killers or recidivist divorcees. All need to compete on the same terms and the success of each is measured by the same criteria of the number of copies sold or TV time and ratings. This rebounds on the fashion in which their activity is perceived and they themselves perceive it: in the allocation of scholarly or artistic prestige, momentary but frequent appearances on mass-rating TV shows count for more than years of unspectacular research or assiduous experimentation. All objects of consumption must pass George Steiner's test of maximal impact and instant obsolescence.

The breathtaking pace at which fashions change, celebrities are born and disappear (only to be 'recycled' in the next rehearsal of orchestrated nostalgia), belies all suspicion that the days count. Common experience teaches that time is running not in a straight line but in coils and twirls difficult to predict and quite impossible to design in advance: time is not irreversible, nothing is lost forever though nothing is obtained and possessed forever either, and what is happening at the moment does not bind the shape of tomorrows. Truly, days do not count and there is little point in counting them. The ancient slogan *carpe diem* has acquired an altogether different sense and carries a new message: collect your credits now – thinking of tomorrow is a waste of time. The culture of credit cards has replaced the culture of savings accounts. Credit cards were introduced into general use two decades ago under the slogan 'take the waiting out of wanting'.

Immortality has lost its most crucial and attractive attribute: the guarantee of irreversibility and irrevocability. The table has been turned round: it is now death, and death alone, which can be assigned the status of the ultimate. Death is no longer a passage to something else. It does not usher into eternity; death is the end of the *sensation of eternity* which can only be ecstatic and momentary and which has made the thing itself redundant and its characteristics of durable 'sameness' all but repulsive. In a sense, this bankruptcy of immortality lends a new attraction to mortal life. True, that life is no longer the only chance we have to earn a residential permit from eternity; but it is now our only chance to taste and enjoy immortality, albeit in its apparently debased form of endemically volatile notoriety.

The 'new and improved' significance of mortal life has also, however, its consequences, which make it a mixed blessing. At all times and places most people have wished their life to be longer and so have done what they could to postpone the moment of death. But hardly ever has the urge to fight death back played such a central role in shaping life strategies and life's purposes as it does today. A long life and a fit life – the kind of life which allows the consumption of all the pleasures life has to offer – is today the supreme value and the principal objective of life efforts. For this new hierarchy of values the technology of cloning comes in handy: in the age of spare parts it brandishes the prospect of making replaceable the most precious part of them all...

Bodily life being the only thing there is, it is impossible to conceive of an object more precious and more worthy of care. Our times are marked by an obsessive preoccupation with the body. The body is a fortress surrounded by shrewd and surreptitious enemies. The body must be defended daily, and since the traffic between the body and the hostile 'world out there' cannot be barred altogether (though people afflicted with anorexia, the disease made to the measure of our times, do earnestly try), all points of entry, the bodily orifices, must be closely and vigilantly guarded. Whatever we eat or drink or breathe in or let touch our skin may be unmasked tomorrow as poison, if its virulence has not been revealed already. The body is an instrument of enjoyment, and so it must be fed the attractions the world has in store; but the body is also the most precious of possessions, and so it must be at all costs defended against the world conspiring to weaken and in the end to destroy it. The irremediable contradiction between actions called for by these two obviously incompatible considerations is bound to be an inexhaustible source of anxiety; I suggest that it is the principal cause of the most common and typical neuroses of our time.

The history of culture is often written as the history of the fine arts. There is a good reason for that otherwise biased (and, as the writers of histories go, narcissistic) habit: at all times the arts, knowingly or unknowingly, mapped – and so made familiar and liveable – the new territories which the rest of the people were about to enter. We are entitled to seek in contemporary arts the prodromal symptoms of life still to come and thus far too inchoate to be noticed elsewhere.

Charles Baudelaire dreamt of painters who, when recording the fleeting moment, would reveal the grain of eternity it wraps. Hannah Arendt suggested that the sole criterion of the greatness of art is its eternal power to impress and arouse. The Gothic cathedrals build to outlast any other human constructions, the frescoes covering the walls of baroque churches, engraving the fragile beauty of mortal faces in un-ageing marble, the Impressionists' obsession with the ultimate truth of human vision – all met these demands and criteria.

At the centre of critics' attention and on the shortlists of the most prestigious and coveted artistic prizes today are works of art which build transience, contingency and friability into the very modality of their existence. The currently most notorious artworks manifest their derision for or indifference to immortality. Of the installations put together for the duration of the exhibition the spectators know that they will be dismantled – cease to exist – the day the exhibition closes. It is not just that the installations do not last: they claim access to the gallery space on the grounds of their brittleness and evident temporariness. It is the vanishing and passing away which is these days on display in the palaces of art.

A most popular way to capture the attention of the art world today, indeed a foolproof recipe for notoriety, is a happening. It happens only once: it won't ever be repeated in the same form and sequence. A happening is born with the stigma of death; the nearness of demise is its main attraction. It differs from theatrical performance which will hopefully stay on stage for weeks and months to come. In happenings neither the spectators nor the performers know how they are going to proceed, and the excitement of the event lies precisely in that ignorance – in the awareness that the succession of events has not been scripted in advance.

Even ancient and venerable masters such as Matisse or Picasso, Vermeer or Rubens, whom one would think to be solidly entrenched in eternity, need to force their way into the present through spectacle and hype; the crowds are pulled by the episodicity and brevity of the event and switch their attention to other equally episodic events once the excitement is over.

Contemporary art, from the highbrow and sublime to the popular and vulgar, is a continuous rehearsal of the brittleness of immortality and the revocability of death. Our civilization of spare parts is also one of endless recycling. No demise is ultimate and final, just as all eternity is until-further-notice.

Some time ago Michael Thompson published a profound study of the role of the durable and the transient in social history.[1] He demonstrated the close link between durability and social privilege, and between transience and social deprivation. The high and mighty of all epochs made a point of surrounding themselves with durable, possibly indestructible objects, leaving to the poor and the indolent breakable and friable objects soon to be turned into rubbish. Ours is probably the first era to reverse that relation. The new mobile and exterritorial elite promotes a lofty unconcern for possessions, a resolute rejection of attachment to objects, and a facility (as well as lack of regret) in abandoning objects once their novelty has worn off. Being surrounded with the leftovers of yesterday's fashion is a symptom of retardation or deprivation.

Ours is the first culture in history to put no premium on duration and to manage to slice the lifespan into a series of episodes lived through with the intention of staving off their lasting consequences and avoiding firm commitments which would make such consequences constraining. Eternity, unless it is served up for instant experience, does not matter. The 'long term' is but a package of short-term *Erlebnisse* amenable to endless reshuffling and with no privileged order of succession. Infinity has been reduced to a series of 'here and nows'; immortality, to the endless recycling of births and deaths.

I do not suggest that what we face today is a 'cultural crisis'. Crisis – the perpetual transgression and forgetting of the forms already created and experimentation with forms new and untried – is the natural condition of all human culture. What I do suggest is that at this stage of continuous transgression we have arrived at a territory which no humans have ever inhabited – a territory which human culture in the past considered uninhabitable. The long story of transcendence has brought us finally to the condition in which transcendence, that leap into eternity leading to permanent settlement, is neither coveted nor seems necessary for the liveability of life. For the first time, mortal humans manage to do without immortality, and do not seem to mind.

I repeat: we have not been here before. It remains to be seen what 'being here' is like and what its lasting consequences (sorry for using outmoded terms) will be.

Notes

Lives told and stories lived: an overture

1 Ernest Becker, *The Denial of Death* (New York: Free Press, 1997), pp. 26–7.
2 Ibid., p. 7.
3 Émile Durkheim, in *Sociologie et philosophie* and 'La science positive de la morale en Allemagne'; here quoted after Émile Durkheim, *Selected Writings*, trans. Anthony Giddens (Cambridge: Cambridge University Press, 1972), pp. 115, 94.
4 Ulrich Beck, *The Reinvention of Politics*, trans. Mark Ritter (Cambridge: Polity Press, 1997), p. 51.
5 Ulrich Beck and Elisabeth Beck-Gernsheim, *The Normal Chaos of Love*, trans. Mark Ritter and Jane Wiebel (Cambridge: Polity Press, 1995), p. 7.
6 Ulrich Beck, *Risk Society*, trans. Mark Ritter (London: Sage, 1992), p. 137.
7 Stuart Hall, 'New ethnicities', ICA Documents 7 (London, 1988), p. 27. Here quoted after Lawrence Grossberg, *We Gotta Get Out of This Place: Popular Conservatism and Postmodern Culture* (London: Routledge, 1992), p. 47.
8 Grossberg, *We Gotta Get Out of This Place*, p. 54.

1   The rise and fall of labour

1   See Paul Bairoch, *Mythes et paradoxes de l'histoire économique* (Paris: La Découverte, 1994). See, in English, Bairoch, *Economics and World History: Myths and Paradoxes* (London: Harvester-Wheatsheaf, 1993).
2   Daniel Cohen, *Richesse du monde, pauvretés des nations* (Paris: Flammarion, 1998), p. 31.
3   See Karl Polanyi, *The Great Transformation* (Boston: Beacon Press, 1957), esp. pp. 56–7 and ch. 6.
4   As reported in *Chicago Tribune*, 25 May 1916.
5   Richard Sennett, *The Corrosion of Character: The Personal Consequences of Work in the New Capitalism* (New York: Norton, 1998), pp. 42–3.
6   Geert van der Laan, 'Social work and social policy in the Netherlands', paper of a lecture delivered during the East–West dialogue on social work held in Dresden, 1998.
7   Sennett, *The Corrosion of Character*, p. 24.
8   See Robert Reich, *The Work of Nations* (New York: Vintage Books, 1991).
9   See Alain Peyrefitte, *La société de confiance. Essai sur les origines du développement* (Paris: Odile Jacob, 1998), pp. 514–16.
10 Nigel Thrift, 'The rise of soft capitalism', *Cultural Values* (Apr. 1997), p. 52.
11 See Pierre Bourdieu, *Contre-feux. Propos pour servir à la résistance contre l'invasion néo-liberale* (Paris: Liber-Raisons d'Agir, 1998), p. 97; in English as *Acts of Resistance*, trans. Richard Nice (Cambridge: Polity Press, 1998).
12 Jacques Attali, *Chemins de sagesse. Traité du labyrinthe* (Paris: Fayard, 1996), p. 84.

2   Local orders, global chaos

1   Richard Sennett, *The Corrosion of Character* (New York: Norton, 1998).

3   Freedom and security

This essay was previously published in a German version as 'Freiheit und Sicherheit: Die unvollendete Geschichte einer stürmischen Beziehung', in Elisabeth Anselm, Aurelius Freitag, Walter Marschnitz and Boris Marte (eds), *Die Neue Ordnung der Politischen: Die Herausforderungen der Demokratie am Beginn des 21 Jahrhunderts* (Frankfurt: Campus, 1999).

1 See Sigmund Freud, *Civilization and its Discontents*, ed. James Strachey, trans. Joan Riviere (London: Hogarth Press, 1973), pp. 52, 13, 14, 30, 33.
2 Ibid., p. 13.
3 Ibid., p. 61.
4 Ibid., pp. 23–4.
5 Alain Ehrenberg, *La fatigue d'être soi. Dépression et société* (Paris: Odile Jacob, 1998).
6 Norbert Elias, *The Society of Individuals*, ed. Michael Schröter, trans. Edmund Jephcott (Oxford: Blackwell, 1991).
7 Ulrich Beck, *Risk Society: Towards a New Modernity*, trans. Mark Ritter (London: Sage, 1992), originally *Risikogesellschaft: auf dem weg in eine andere Moderne* (Frankfurt: Suhrkamp, 1986).
8 Joël Roman, *La Démocratie des individus* (Paris: Calmann-Lévy, 1998).
9 Ulrich Beck, *Ecological Enlightenment: Essays on the Politics of Risk Society*, trans. Mark Ritter (Atlantic Highlands: Humanities, 1995), p. 40.
10 Pierre Bourdieu, 'La précarité est aujourd'hui partout', in *Contrefeux* (Paris: Liber-Raisons d'Agir, 1998), pp. 97, 96; in English as *Acts of Resistance*, trans. Richard Nice (Cambridge: Polity Press, 1998).
11 See Pierre Bourdieu, 'Le néo-liberalisme, utopie (en voie de réalisation) d'une exploitation sans limites', in ibid., p. 110.
12 See Manuel Castells, *The Information Age: Economy, Society and Culture* (3 vols, Oxford: Blackwell, 1998).
13 Cornelius Castoriadis, *La Montée de l'insignifiance* (Paris: Seuil, 1996), p. 99.
14 See Jacques Rancière, *Aux bords du politique* (Paris: La Fabrique, 1998).
15 See Claus Offe, Ulrich Mückenberger and Ilona Ostner, 'A basic income guaranteed by the state: a need of the moment in social policy', in Claus Offe, *Modernity and the State* (Cambridge: Polity Press, 1996).

4 Modernity and clarity

1 See *Scepticism from the Renaissance to the Enlightenment*, ed. Richard H. Popkin and Charles B. Schmitt (Wiesbaden: Otto Harrasowitz, 1987), p. 9.

2   M. F. Burneyot, 'The sceptic in his place and time', in ibid., p. 26.
3   Esequiel de Olaso, 'Leibniz and scepticism', in ibid., p. 156.
4   Emmet Kennedy, *Destutt de Tracy and the Origins of 'Ideology'* (Philadelphia: American Philosophical Society, 1978), p. 48.
5   F. J. Picavet, *Les Idéologues* (New York: Burt Franklin, 1971), p. 110.
6   Richard H. Popkin, *The History of Scepticism from Erasmus to Spinoza* (Berkeley: University of California Press, 1979), p. 244.
7   Eric Voegelin, *From Enlightenment to Revolution*, trans. John H. Hallowell (Durham, N.C.: Duke University Press, 1975), pp. 51, 61.
8   See Picavet, *Les Idéologues*, pp. 203–11.
9   Destutt de Tracy, *Éléments d'idéologie*, vol. 1 (Paris: J. Vrin, 1970), pp. 299–300.
10 See *Kant's Political Writings*, ed. Hans Reiss, trans. H. B. Nisbet (Cambridge: Cambridge University Press, 1970), pp. 186, 188.
11 Bronislaw Baczko, *Lumières de l'Utopie* (Paris: Payot, 1978); here quoted after the English translation, *Utopian Lights; The Evolution of the Idea of Social Progress*, trans. Judith L. Greenberg (New York: Paragon, 1989), esp. pp. 219–35.
12 No one explored the intricacies of the will better than Hannah Arendt, in her *The Life of the Mind*, vol. 2: *Willing* (New York: Harcourt Brace Jovanovich, 1978).
13 Sigmund Freud, *Civilization and its Discontents*, trans. Joan Riviere (London: Hogarth Press, 1973), pp. 30, 14.

5   Am I my brother's keeper?

This chapter was previously published in *European Journal of Social Work* 3.1 (March 2000).

1   Let me remark in passing that the term 'the third way' is likely to be used solely by those writers and politicians who have renounced the hope of taming the uncouth, often savage market forces, but are not ready fully to admit their capitulation; the spokespeople for the 'first', the dominant capitalist-market way, now free from the 'second', the socialist alternative, would hardly need to resort to the term, since they would not see much difference between what is being proposed under the 'third way' label and what they had been saying all along.

7   Critique – privatized and disarmed

This essay was previously published in *Zeitschrift für Kritische Theorie* 9 (1999).

9   Uses of poverty

1 As reported in *Le Monde* of 10 Sept. 1998.
2 See Jean-Paul Maréchal, 'Demain, l'économie solidaire', *Le Monde Diplomatique* (Apr. 1998), p. 19.
3 Zygmunt Bauman, *Globalization: The Human Consequences* (Cambridge: Polity Press, 1998).
4 See Alain Gresh, 'Les aléas de l'internationalisme', *Le Monde Diplomatique* (May 1998).

10   Education

This essay was previously published in Agnieszka Bron and Michael Schemmann (eds), *Language-Mobility-Identity: Contemporary Issues for Adult Education in Europe* (Münster: Litverlag, 2000).

1 Margaret Mead, *Continuities in Cultural Evolution* (New Haven: Yale University Press, 1964), p. 79.
2 Gregory Bateson, 'Social planning and the concept of deutero-learning', in *Steps to an Ecology of Mind* (Frogmore: Paladin, 1973), p. 140.
3 Gregory Bateson, 'The logical categories of learning and communication', in ibid., pp. 264–6.
4 'Le délabrement de l'Occident', an interview with Cornelius Castoriadis conducted in 1991 by Olivier Mongin, Joël Roman and Ramin Jahanbegloo; cf. Cornelius Castoriadis, *La montée de l'insignifiance* (Paris: Seuil, 1996), p. 73.
5 See Régis Debray, *Le pouvoir intellectuel en France* (Paris: Ramsay, 1979).
6 Much more than educational practice, which cannot but follow, in each of its concrete manifestations taken separately, the traditional urge to pattern and structure; the centre of gravity lies, after all, not in separate educational events, but in their variety and, indeed, in their lack of coordination...

11   Identity in the globalizing world

1 Stuart Hall, 'Who needs "identity"?', in Stuart Hall and Paul du Gay (eds), *Questions of Cultural Identity* (London: Sage, 1996), p. 1.
2 Arland Ussher, *Journey through Dread* (New York: Devin-Adair, 1955), p. 80.

3 See Vincent Vycinas, *Earth and Gods* (The Hague: Martinus Nijhoff, 1969), pp. 36–7.
4 See Alain Peyrefitte, *La société de confiance. Essai sur les origines du développement* (Paris: Odile Jacob, 1998), pp. 514–16.
5 See Stevie Davies, *Renaissance View of Man* (Manchester: Manchester University Press, 1978), pp. 62ff.
6 See Jean-Jacques Rousseau, *The First and Second Discourses*, first published in 1749 and 1754, trans. Victor Gourevitch (New York: Harper and Row, 1986), pp. 148ff.
7 Daniel Cohen, *Richesse du monde, pauvretés des nations* (Paris: Flammarion, 1997), p. 84.
8 Erik H. Erikson, *Identity: Youth and Crisis* (London: Faber and Faber, 1974), pp. 17–19.
9 Zbyszko Melosik and Tomasz Szkudlarek, *Kultura, Tozsamosc I Edukacja* (Kraków: Impuls, 1998), p. 89.
10 Christopher Lasch, *The Minimal Self: Psychic Survival in Troubled Times* (London: Pan Books, 1984), p. 38.
11 Pierre Bourdieu, 'La précarité est aujourd'hui partout', in *Contrefeux* (Paris: Liber-Raisons d'Agir, 1998), pp. 96–7. Translated as *Acts of Resistance* (Cambridge: Polity Press, 1998).
12 Christopher Lasch, *Culture of Narcissism* (New York: Warner Books, 1979), pp. 29–30.
13 Eric Hobsbawm, *The Age of Extremes* (London: Michael Joseph, 1994), p. 428.
14 Eric Hobsbawm, 'The cult of identity politics', *New Left Review* 217 (1996), p. 40.
15 Jock Young, *The Exclusive Society* (London: Sage, 1999), p. 164.
16 Jonathan Friedman, 'The hybridization of roots and the abhorrence of the bush', in Mike Featherstone and Scott Lash (eds), *Spaces of Culture* (London: Sage, 1999), p. 241.
17 'Who needs "identity"?', p. 3.

12   Faith and instant gratification

This essay was previously published in *Concilium* 4 (1999).

13   Does love need reason?

This essay was previously published in a German version under the title *Braucht die Liebe das Vernunft?* in *Rhein Reden* 1 (2000).

1 Jonathan Rutherford, *I Am No Longer Myself Without You: An Anatomy of Love* (London: Flamingo, 1999), p. 4.

2 Max Scheler, 'Ordo Amoris', in *Selected Philosophical Essays*, trans. David R. Lachterman (Evanston: Northwestern University Press, 1973), p. 117.

3 Plato's 'Symposium', in *Great Dialogues of Plato*, trans. W. H. D. Rouse (New York: Mentor Books, 1956), pp. 87, 95–6, 101–2.

4 'Ordo Amoris', pp. 113, 114.

5 Ibid., p. 110.

6 Emmanuel Levinas, *Le temps et l'autre* (Paris: PUF, 1979), pp. 64, 80ff.

7 See Emmanuel Levinas, *Autrement qu'être ou au-delà de l'essence* (The Hague: Nijhoff, 1974).

8 Knud Ejler Løgstrup, *The Ethical Demand*, trans. Theodor I. Jensen (Notre Dame: University of Notre Dame Press, 1997), p. 56.

9 See *The Ethical Demand*, pp. 110–13.

14 Private morality, immoral world

An abbreviated version of this essay was previously published as 'The world inhospitable to Levinas', *Philosophy Today* 43.2 (Summer 1999).

1 Vladimir Jankélévitch, *Traité des vertus* (Paris, 1968).

2 Agnes Heller, *A Philosophy of History in Fragments* (Oxford: Blackwell, 1993).

3 Interview with Emmanuel Levinas by Roger-Pol Driot in *Le Monde*, 2 June 1992.

4 Georg Simmel, *The Sociology of Georg Simmel* (Glencoe: Free Press, 1950).

5 Emmanuel Levinas, in conversation with François Poirié, *Qui êtes-vous?* (Lyon: Éditions la Manufacture, 1987).

6 Hans Jonas, *The Imperative of Responsibility* (Chicago: University of Chicago Press, 1984).

7 *Le Monde Diplomatique*, July 1995.

8 Manuel Castells, *The Information Age* (3 vols, Oxford: Blackwell, 1998).

9 Cornelius Castoriadis, *La Montée de l'insignifiance* (Paris: Seuil, 1996).

10 Reported in *Le Monde Diplomatique*, Aug. 1997.

11 *Le Monde Diplomatique*, July 1997.

12 *Le Monde*, 29 Aug. 1997.

13   Claus Offe, *Modernity and the State: East, West* (Cambridge: Polity Press, 1996).
14   Reported in *Le Monde*, 12 June 1998.
15   *Le Monde Diplomatique*, Mar. 1998.
16   In *Arena* 10 (1998).

15   Democracy on two battlefronts

This essay was previously published in a German version as 'Zerstreuung der Macht', *Die Zeit*, 18 November 1999.

16   Violence, old and new

This essay was previously published in a German version as 'Alte und neue Gewalt', *Journal für Konflikt- und Gewaltforschung* I (2000).

1   Herbert I. Schiller, 'Décervelage à l'américaine', *Le Monde Diplomatique*, Aug. 1999, p. 15.
2   Chris Bird, 'This is what will happen to all of us', *Guardian*, 29 July 1999, p. 2.
3   Pierre Bourdieu, 'Le champ intellectuel: un monde à part', in *Choses dites* (Paris: Minuit, 1987), p. 171.
4   Edward W. Said, 'La trahison des intellectuels', *Le Monde Diplomatique*, Aug. 1999, p. 7.
5   Recorded by the students of Wittgenstein in 1944; quoted after *German Essays on Religion*, ed. Edward T. Oakes (New York: Continuum, 1994), pp. 224–5.

17   Postmodern uses of sex

This essay was previously published in *Theory, Culture and Society* 15.3–4 (1999).

1   Here quoted after the Polish translation, *Podwójny Płomień* (Kraków: Wydawnictwo Literackie, 1996).
2   Theodore Zeldin, *An Intimate History of Humanity* (New York: HarperCollins, 1994), pp. 86ff.
3   Stephen Kern, *The Culture of Love: Victorians to Moderns* (Cambridge, Mass.: Harvard University Press, 1992).
4   Mark. C. Taylor and Esa Saarinen, *Imagologies: Media Philosophy* (London: Routledge, 1994).

5 Anthony Giddens, *The Transformation of Intimacy: Sexuality, Love and Eroticism in Modern Societies* (Cambridge: Polity Press, 1992).

6 Michel Foucault, *The History of Sexuality*, vol. 1: *An Introduction* (London: Penguin, 1990), pp. 40–4, 103–7.

7 Suzanne Moore, 'For the good of the kids – and us', *Guardian*, 15 June 1995.

8 Rosie Waterhouse, 'So what is child abuse?', *Independent on Sunday*, 23 July 1995.

9 Maureen Freely, 'Let girls be girls', *Independent on Sunday*, 2 Mar. 1997.

10 See my chapter on 'Forms of togetherness', in *Life in Fragments* (Oxford: Blackwell, 1995).

18   Is there life after immortality?

1 Michael Thompson, *Rubbish Theory: The Creation and Destruction of Value* (Oxford: Oxford University Press, 1979).